TENNYSON AND *THE PRINCESS*

Reflections of an Age

Tennyson and *The Princess*

Reflections of an Age

by

JOHN KILLHAM

UNIVERSITY OF LONDON

THE ATHLONE PRESS

1958

Published by
THE ATHLONE PRESS
UNIVERSITY OF LONDON
at 2 Gower Street, London wc1
Distributed by Constable & Co Ltd
12 Orange Street, London wc2

Canada
University of Toronto Press
Toronto 5

U.S.A
Essential Books Division
Oxford University Press Inc
New York

© *John Killham, 1958*

Printed in Great Britain by
WESTERN PRINTING SERVICES LTD
BRISTOL

In memory of

A. M. K.

. . . since the emotions of the poet, during composition, follow a regular law of association, it follows that to accompany their progress up to the harmonious prospect of the whole, and to perceive the proper dependence of every step on that which preceded, it is absolutely necessary *to start from the same point*, i.e. clearly to apprehend that leading sentiment of the poet's mind, by their conformity to which the host of suggestions are arranged.

A. H. HALLAM 'On Some of the Characteristics of Modern Poetry, and on the Lyrical Poems of Alfred Tennyson.' *Englishman's Magazine*, August 1831.

PREFACE

THE EARLY VICTORIAN AGE supplies many examples of *littérature engagée* and of criticism favouring it. To the reader who finds pleasure in imaginatively subduing himself (as far as he can) to the spirit of the past, some of the better specimens of 'sociological' poems and novels of that period are especially attractive, for their authors clearly met considerable difficulties in making art out of social criticism; consequently such a reader can learn much of great interest about the mind of an artist and the quality of an age. *The Princess* is a case in point. Tennyson wrote it when at the height of his powers, yet his genius did not really find its fullest release in treating contemporary problems. In one sense it is a perfect example of an encounter between a man of marked talents and a moment which was inimical to their expression. It is that encounter which is my theme. By tracing developments which took place in the two decades from his going up to Cambridge to the publication of the poem I shall try to suggest how it came about that *The Princess* took the strange form it did.

To sketch these developments I shall trespass in the fields of historians and others who possess seignorial rights in their subjects. If in so doing I wander from the true path, it will be from ignorance and not from evil intent. Poets do not very often address themselves to specific reforms, but Tennyson in *The Princess* departed from the rule, and I can only plead that

> syn I have bigonne
> Myn auctor shall I folwen if I konne.

To many writers on Tennyson and topics relating to his poem I am much indebted, and I acknowledge my obligations generally here and individually in footnotes throughout the text. I wish particularly to express my thanks for help received at various stages in the writing of this book to Professor Geoffrey Tillotson, Mrs. Kathleen Tillotson, Sir Charles Tennyson,

Preface

Professor T. J. B. Spencer, Professor E. F. Shannon Jnr., Mrs. Catharine Barham Johnson and Miss Mary Barham Johnson. I deeply appreciate their kindness in sparing time from their own busy days for advising and guiding me on subjects in which they themselves are long experienced.

I should like here to thank the Librarian and his staff at the University College of North Staffordshire for much help and invariable kindness. I am also indebted to the staff of the Reading Room of the British Museum and to the officers of the Athlone Press.

Unless otherwise indicated, all quotations from the poems of Tennyson are drawn from W. J. Rolfe's edition (1898) in the Cambridge Poets series. The changes Tennyson made in the successive editions of the poem have been regarded simply as stages in the composition of the work we read today.

University College of E.J.K.
North Staffordshire, Keele
April 1958

viii

CONTENTS

LIST OF ABBREVIATIONS

Browning: *The Letters of Elizabeth Barrett Browning*, ed. F. G. Kenyon (1897).

Donne: Catharine B. Johnson, *William Bodham Donne and his Friends* (1905).

Fitzgerald: *Letters and Literary Remains of Edward Fitzgerald*, ed. W. Aldis Wright (1902–3).

Materials: *Materials for a Life of Alfred Tennyson collected for my grandchildren*, privately printed by Hallam, Lord Tennyson (1895).

Memoir: Hallam, Lord Tennyson, *Alfred Tennyson; a Memoir by his son* (1897).

Mitford: *Letters of Mary Russell Mitford*, Second Series, ed. Henry Chorley (1872).

MLN: *Modern Language Notes*, Baltimore.

Motter: *The Writings of Arthur Hallam*, ed. T. H. Vail Motter (1943). The Modern Language Association of America General Series xv.

PMLA: *Proceedings and Transactions of the Modern Language Association of America*, Baltimore.

PQ: *Philological Quarterly*, Iowa.

Record: Frances Anne Kemble, *Record of a Girlhood* (1878).

Shannon: Edgar Finley Shannon Jnr., *Tennyson and the Reviewers* (1952).

SP: *Studies in Philology*, Chapel Hill.

Study: Samuel Edward Dawson, *A Study; with critical and explanatory notes, of Lord Tennyson's poem 'The Princess'* (second edn., 1884).

Trench: M. Trench, *Richard Chenevix Trench, Archbishop; Letters and Memorials* (1888).

Weill: Georges Weill, *L'École Saint-Simonienne—son histoire, son influence jusqu'à nos jours* (Paris, 1896).

Works: *The Works of Tennyson with notes by the author*, ed. with Memoir by Hallam, Lord Tennyson (1913).

CHAPTER I

Facts and Problems

IN the middle decades of the last century, there appeared a number of long poems treating of love and marriage in a new way. Not only were the points of view a departure from the traditional ones: the poets sought to communicate them by providing stories and characters, as if they were really writing little novels in verse: moreover, these verse-narratives were clearly intended to leave the reader to reflect upon a social question—the position of women in life. Now this topic, though profoundly important at all times, and particularly so at that time, is notoriously difficult to handle. It can very easily become prosaic, or sentimental, or worst of all, comic. The novel is perhaps the safest way of dealing with these difficulties, for the novel has a very long-standing tradition of combining realism with comic relief. Fielding's *Amelia* is an early essay in directing sympathy towards women by simply narrating the facts of a ruined life, and deftly hinting the point to be drawn—'. . . upon my soul, I believe that from the damned inconstancy of your sex to ours, proceed half the miseries of mankind.' 'O Mr. Booth, our sex is damned by the want of tenderness in yours.' But Fielding is careful to make us smile at Major Bath's tenderness towards his sister, so that he may exorcise the imp in us which might lead us to laugh in the wrong place.

But poems are not novels. The poet, who often seeks to go more directly to the central human concern, may have to forgo some of the novelist's artifices for keeping the theme in a place where only those who wish to can look at it, simply because it is the theme he is trying to make people aware of. He has to devise a method of his own, to experiment and adapt. In poems like *The Princess, Aurora Leigh, The Bothie of Tober-na-Vuolich* and *The Angel in the House,* we can see the ways in which four poets sought to treat the age-old theme of love and marriage by attempting to give to poetry some of the qualities of novels, or in other words, to tell stories and show character in action. These poems were all published between 1847 and 1862, so it looks as if there was some special stimulus at this period to cause some of the best poets of the day to select this subject and to write as if they had made some new discovery about it.

The boldest attempt was the first to appear—Tennyon's *The Princess*, published in 1847, but much revised in later editions. Always an experimenter—consequently inviting failure—Tennyson often achieves brilliant success. It is this which makes the study of his methods, even in works of less popularity nowadays, particularly worthwhile. Accordingly this book attempts to show what went into the making of that poem, not to prove that it is an overlooked masterpiece, but simply to show that the poem, properly understood is a great deal more valuable than some estimates have allowed.

It is quite mistaken to think that it is a melodious and over-wrought poetical recommendation of a reactionary and even silly solution of what was called the 'woman-question'. In fact, it is time that the still popular belief that Tennyson was a good poet for some things, but inclined to give in to a supposed demand for poetic 'narcotics'[1] was disposed of. Since some

---

[1] This opinion was fostered by Sir Harold Nicolson in his *Tennyson: Aspects of his Life, Character and Poetry* (1923), together with a number of other doctrines, which although formulated with the kindest of intentions—reviving enthusiasm for a part of Tennyson's poetry—have themselves impeded a re-assessment. One example is the view that Tennyson was possessed of 'a very unconvincing intelligence', an opinion unfortunately reinforced by W. H. Auden. But the most injurious of these attitudes is that upon which the whole thesis was constructed. This is that there were really two Tennysons, 'the prosperous Isle-of-Wight Victorian', and 'the black, unhappy mystic of the Lincolnshire wolds'. This supposed distinction was used by Sir Harold to justify his rejecting a good deal of Tennyson which did not conform with his critical standard of that time. This was related to the belief that the spirit of Poetry is 'a spirit in its essence winged for some divine excess'. This intensely Romantic view was not to be applied to Tennyson without some such insistence that the poet was not always true to his better self. The supposed reasons for this betrayal are the familiar ones, reminiscent of Arnold's view of Gray ('For had his lot fallen among other circumstances, or in a less cloying age . . .') and of Browning's condemnation of Wordsworth ('He

critics have thought it sufficient merely to point to *The Princess* to put this beyond doubt, I hope that my examination of the poem will do something to call this whole theory into question. The poem was really a serious attempt, artfully disguised, to change an outworn attitude to an important human problem. The way Tennyson chose involved him in an experiment of a particularly risky sort, since the poem sprang from contemporary thinking which was beyond the mass of readers of poetry whom he particularly sought to interest.

That he was intending to reach a wide public is shown by his careful omission of much of the scientific matter which in poems earlier in date of composition was allowed to appear, and also by his using for the narrative part of his poem a story of a very popular sort at the time. But his motive is not satisfactorily accounted for, in my view, by those cynical critics who regard a bid for a wide audience as no more than a wish for popular success and large profits. The charming medley of incidents by which he sought to attract this wide audience may admittedly have partially failed in its end, and the themes between which he (and others) at the middle of the century saw a connection have appeared increasingly bizarre. Today it has become the poetic counterpart of the problem-pictures we see at the Royal Academy; we see what it says, but are less certain what it means. But if we reconstruct the diverse elements of the medley, we can not only understand it, but are also presented with a remarkable insight into the poet's mind and that of his contemporaries. All poems relating to social questions lose a good deal of their interest when the reforms they present for public consideration are realized, but when a poet of Tennyson's calibre writes one, we are left with a bonus—a very valuable impression of a past age, an impression which only poetry can convey. Though the topicality has gone, *The Princess*, properly understood, is a vivid

chose the easier and more prosperous course: he became the Laureate of his age'). But Tennyson, artistically speaking, is remarkably true to himself, though his poetic personality is complex. While capable of composing Romantic lyrics, like Keats he often wrote controlled narrative poems which obviously aspire to communicate more than a single emotional impulse.

reflection of an age. This is far from saying that it is a sort of literary photograph. What we have is, I think, more rare; a glimpse of the aspirations of the age in the colours in which they presented themselves to a truly poetic imagination. Shelley said in the Preface to *The Revolt of Islam* that there must be

a resemblance which does not depend upon their own will between all the writers of any particular age. They cannot escape from subjection to a common influence which arises out of an infinite combination of circumstances belonging to the times in which they live; though each is in a degree the author of the very influence by which his being is thus pervaded.

This is certainly so. The best poets seem able to express the spirit of their age in the most permanent colours, and yet be original. It was Tennyson's seeking for a new form of expression, one capable of representing the singular diversity of his time, that led him to forgo conventional unity in preference for a 'medley'. We are doing him a great injustice if we assume that there was not design behind the composition. In other words, we must approach it with respect and a desire to understand.

We must, for instance, avoid regarding this poem about marriage as a failure because it does not comply at all points with the romantic concept of love. Tennyson did not look at marriage as Spenser, or Blake, or Shelley had done. Even within his lifetime, entirely new views on the subject had swum into ken, though now we can only trace their emergence into the light by examining books and articles which are forgotten, though in their day they represented feelings which created bitter controversy and passion. To some people, the 'woman question'—which is always a contemporary issue—is irresistibly amusing: and as I shall show, Tennyson himself was perhaps trying to get the laugh on his side when he began his poem. But the relationship of men and women in a complex and swiftly-altering society must change, and change will inevitably set up tensions in a relationship which must serve so many personal and social ends. In *The Princess*, Tennyson was attempting to sketch out the lines of a new type of relationship. We can be certain that he was aware of the Socialist

4

theories which were undermining conventional attitudes to marriage, and when we have all the facts, it is not possible to regard his attitude towards marriage in the poem as a piece of unthinking conservatism. He shows himself too bold a speculator for that. He was trying to show that even the most advanced of women should not reject legal marriage, as some were tempted to do, because there were reasons for its continuance hardly considered before; and he sought a wide audience because he believed his reasons deserved it. Other poets, as I have mentioned, were soon to respond to the promptings they felt to deal with the topic, and two of them also show an awareness of the Socialist theories which contributed to the genesis of *The Princess*. This fact should warn us against too light a dismissal of Tennyson's poem, for it suggests that marriage may not have been regarded by the Victorians merely 'as the ultimate solution, the ultimate "hushing-up" of what might or might not have been a self-indulgent youth'.[1] The poets, at any rate, were interested in something more than that.

I said earlier that I was not bent on showing that *The Princess* is a great success—indeed Tennyson himself in later years was not of that opinion. Frederick Locker-Lampson tells us that in 1869 he spoke to him about it 'with something of regret, of its fine blank verse, and the many good things in it: "but", said he, "though truly original, it is, after all, only a medley" '.[2] All the same, the poem achieved great success with the reading public for a surprisingly long time. In 1849, Edward Fitzgerald, though not as solitary as he supposed in not being pleased with it, reported that it seemed to be greatly admired in London coteries. No less than seventeen editions appeared in England in the thirty years after publication, and in 1882, Samuel Edward Dawson, then residing in Montreal, felt the need to 'explain' the poem, and published a modest study which had the good fortune to draw from the poet himself a letter containing valuable *obiter dicta* which Dawson quickly published in a second edition. Where Dawson had led, others followed. Editions with explanatory matter appeared in 1892, 1896, 1904 (two), 1905, 1908, 1910 (two), and more were

[1] ibid., p. 251. [2] *Memoir*, ii, p. 70.

published in the U.S.A. The poem was studied in schools and colleges on both sides of the Atlantic up to the beginning of the first world war, and even acting versions were devised and published, probably in support of the women's suffrage movement. For over sixty years, *The Princess* was a really popular poem, and its eclipse came only when the full force of the reaction against the Victorians was felt.

The poem is a poetic romance, not only improbable in itself, but overlaid with secondary improbabilities like having a tournament and a geological expedition in the same work; sometimes it is exotic, sometimes more or less realistic, as the fairy tale or the college occupies the limelight. Why should the poet have selected or devised so extraordinary a tale to illustrate the theme of marriage and women's higher education? The evidence suggests that he thought it would have a wide appeal in an age when such stories were extraordinarily popular; but that also he saw that an old romantic tale curiously pre-figured the contemporary real-life situation. Once the fantastic seemed to him to be coming unexpectedly into accord with the facts of mundane nineteenth-century existence, he was able to incorporate into the fantasy some of the other oddly-matched elements of this most bewildering of periods. The surprising contrasts all had a *raison d'être*, a hidden connection, to those who had the insight to perceive it. Unfortunately, the reconstruction and fitting together of the attisudes which provide the key to understanding the poem can today only afford an intellectual satisfaction; but to a contemporary reader, to whom they were a natural part of ordinary experience, they gave the pleasure of recognition—felt, not merely understood.

Something must be said about the point in Tennyson's career at which the poem was conceived, for on this much turns. Many of the new poems published in the 1842 volumes and *In Memoriam* were composed years before, and the seeds of a number of later works were sown in his mind while a young man. *The Princess* likewise was planned a long time before it was published. In a footnote to the chapter devoted to discussing the poem in the *Memoir*, Hallam Tennyson states: 'He talked over the plan of the poem with my mother

6

in 1839.'[1] In the notes to his edition of the *Works* he goes
further:

> The plan of *The Princess* may have suggested itself when the pro-
> ject of a Women's College was in my father's mind (1839), or it may
> have arisen in its mock-heroic form from a Cambridge joke, such as
> he commemorated in the lines 'The Doctor's Daughter'.[2]

This is obviously conjecture, and the only important fact is
that the poem was planned in 1839. But this is a very important fact, for to have fixed upon the plan the poet must have
had the basic story in mind. Now briefly this story is that of a
Princess who forbids all men to invade her privacy to woo her
by imposing a death penalty upon any suitor rash enough to
attempt it; she is first thwarted in this by the defection of one
of her trusted counsellors, but afterwards regains her liberty
as the result of a tournament, or trial by battle, in which the
offending Prince's party is defeated. Notwithstanding this,
she unexpectedly forgoes her proud independence, and marries
the defeated suitor after all. In this summary I have deliberately omitted all reference to the fact that the Princess's
motive for wanting to live a life free from men's intrusion was
that she was bent on presiding over a College for her own
oppressed sex. My reason for doing so is that this motive is so
obviously a graft upon a romantic tale—rather resembling the
plot of *Love's Labour's Lost* with the sexes reversed   that we
might well believe that it could have existed independently of
it. But upon this plan the poem must have been designed in
1839. Now what appears to be an early draft of the beginning
of *The Princess*, which Sir Charles Tennyson on other evidence
thinks must have been composed in the 1830's, clearly shows
that the story to be unfolded was to be on the same lines as

---

[1] ibid., i, p. 248. This footnote was not included in *Materials for a
Life of Alfred Tennyson collected for my children*, which he had privately
printed in 1895, and used as the basis of the published *Memoir*.

[2] *Works*, p. 928. The *Memoir* has the same words, save that 'in the air'
replaces 'in my father's mind'. 'The Doctor's Daughter' is a poem quoted
by Hallam Tennyson in the *Memoir* as one he had found in an old MS
book which he believed dated from the Cambridge days. But all Tennyson himself said was that it was an old song of his which at one time he
had intended to insert in *The Princess*.

that finally published in 1847.[1] So it seems likely that at least two years before the 1842 *Poems* were published, the story was sufficiently ordered in Tennyson's mind for him actually to attempt composition.

Bearing this in mind will save us from drawing a false conclusion from the poet's own admission that had it not been for Sterling's adverse criticism in the *Quarterly Review* of the 'Morte d'Arthur', one of the 1842 poems, he would have proceeded next with the composition of an Arthurian epic in twelve books.[2] From this confession it might be deduced that Tennyson, in turning to writing *The Princess* instead, *suddenly* showed signs of 'submitting' to the demand for literature relating to the problems of the age, a notion which can be made to sustain the opinion that the poet 'consented to incorporate in his poetry the current Victorian fallacies as to the relations of the sexes, and to preach a compromise which has little justification either in honesty or even in eugenics', and that 'what exasperates is that Tennyson had conceived Ida quite honestly, so that his subsequent repudiation of her can only be ascribed to cowardice'.[3] Both these views are in any case entirely mistaken. Leaving aside the circumstance that Tennyson shows very early a concern with the problems of his age, to remember that *The Princess* was planned before the 1842 volumes appeared disposes of the belief in any self-betrayal as the result of criticism directed at the latter. Of course it remains to be shown that the tale was not deliberately altered as composition proceeded, and this I shall do in a later chapter (Chapter X).

Although the poem was planned in 1839, and composition seemingly begun, nevertheless when we first hear of his being engaged upon the writing of the poem in 1845 we learn nothing of the earlier planning. Aubrey de Vere was seeing Tennyson in the spring of this year, and he noted down something of what passed in his journal. I propose giving rather full extracts,

---

[1] 'Tennyson Papers: IV. The making of "The Princess" ', *The Cornhill Magazine*, 153 (Jan.– June 1936), p. 673. Notebooks containing the bulk of the poem in MS, dating from about 1845 onwards, are also described in this article. See below, p. 204 n. 2.

[2] Shannon, p. 95 and p. 204, n. 6.

[3] Nicolson, op. cit., pp. 249, 250.

Facts and Problems

since they are revealing as to the poet's state of mind at the
time, and show that he could write in his most 'Victorian'
manner without necessarily having had even a foretaste of 'the
soft, sweet smell of the laburnum, and success', which Sir
Harold Nicolson blamed for the corrupting of the true Tennyson:

April 17 1845 *(London).*
I called on Alfred Tennyson, and found him at first much out of
spirits. He cheered up soon, and read me some beautiful Elegies,
complaining much of some writer in 'Fraser's Magazine' who had
spoken of the 'foolish facility' of Tennysonian poetry. I went to the
House of Commons . . . went back to Tennyson who 'crooned' out
his magnificent Elegies till one in the morning.[1]

April 18.
Sat with Alfred Tennyson who read MS poetry to Tom Taylor
and me. Walked with him to his lawyer's: came back and listened to
the 'University of Women'. Had talk with him on various subjects,
and walked with him to Moxon's. As I went away, he said he would
willingly bargain for the reputation of Suckling or Lovelace, and
alluded to 'the foolish facility of Tennysonian poetry'. Said he was
dreadfully cut up by all he had gone through.[2]

From this it can be seen that enough of the poem was written
in April 1845 to justify reading it aloud, and that it was called
the 'University of Women'—whereas the title of the MS fragment seemingly dating from a date nearer 1839 was 'The New
University'.

May 10.
I went to Alfred Tennyson, who read me part of his 'University
of Women', and discussed poetry, denouncing exotics, and saying
that a poem should reflect the time and place. . . .[3]

It is interesting to see that although some readers would judge
The Princess to be sufficiently exotic, Tennyson was during the
earliest period of its (continuous) composition taking the view
that poetry should reflect the time and place.

[1] Wilfrid Ward, *Aubrey de Vere, a Memoir* (1904), p. 71. The review
was of *Bon Gaultier's Book of Ballads, Fraser's Magazine,* xxxi (1845),
p. 420.
[2] ibid., pp. 71–2.   [3] ibid., p. 74.

Facts and Problems

July 14.

Went out to Hampstead with a copy of the 'Waldenses'. Called on Alfred Tennyson, who railed against the whole system of society, and said he was miserable.

July 16.

. . . On my way in, paid a visit to Tennyson, who seemed much out of spirits, and said he could no longer bear to be knocked about the world, and that he must marry and find love and peace or die. He was very angry about a very favourable review of him. Said that he could not stand the chattering and conceipt of clever men, or the worry of society, or the meanness of tuft-hunters, or the trouble of poverty, or the labour of a place, or the preying of the heart on itself . . . He complained much about growing old, and said he cared nothing for fame, and that his life was all thrown away for want of a competence and retirement. Said that no one had been so much harassed by anxiety and trouble as himself. I told him he wanted occupation, a wife, and orthodox principles, which he took very well.[1]

Edward Fitzgerald also mentioned *The Princess* this year. He reported on 12 June 1845 that Tennyson had got two hundred lines of a new poem in a butcher's book, and said also that he believed that the poet was at that time at Eastbourne.[2] Edmund Lushington, Tennyson's brother-in-law, also remembered that in the hottest part of the summer of that year he went down to see Tennyson for a few days while he was lodging at Eastbourne:

He had then completed many of the cantos in 'In Memoriam' and was engaged on 'The Princess', of which I had heard nothing before. He read or showed me the first part, beyond which it had then hardly advanced. He said to me, 'I have brought in your marriage at the end of "In Memoriam",' and then showed me those poems of 'In Memoriam' which were finished and which were a perfectly novel surprise to me.[3]

Later in the summer of this same year, 1845, Tennyson went to Llanberis, where he wrote a poem called 'The Golden Year'.

---

[1] ibid., p. 87. [2] Fitzgerald, i, p. 223.

[3] *Memoir*, i, p. 203. The marriage of Edmund Lushington to Cecilia Tennyson which is celebrated in the conclusion of *In Memoriam* took place on 14 October 1842, nearly three years before, a circumstance which I shall show later to be of some significance.

He included it in the fourth edition of his poems in 1846. In it, the 'speaker' describes how he and an old friend James, walking in Wales, met a poet, Leonard, at Llanberis. The speaker gently mocked Leonard:

> . . . I banter'd him and swore
> They said he lived shut up within himself,
> A tongue-tied poet in the feverous days . . .

Leonard replied, somewhat ruefully,

> 'They call me what they will,' he said:
> 'But I was born too late; the fair new forms,
> That float about the threshold of an age,
> Like truths of Science waiting to be caught—
> Catch me who can, and make the catcher crown'd—
> Are taken by the forelock. Let it be . . .'

He then recites a poem he has just made, a poem in the form of a blank verse lyric like those in *The Princess*. This poem looks forward to a millennium,

> When wealth no more shall rest in mounded heaps,

and the nations shall co-operate in universal peace, poverty having been banished—a vision reminiscent of that entertained by the speaker in 'Locksley Hall', published in 1842. James, however, denounces such sentiments; to him, it is as foolish to dream about the future as it is to look back to a Golden Age; only in present work can man solve his problems. It is obvious, I think, that Tennyson in this poem was discussing an issue with which he himself was faced, and the poem is by way of an apology. But what is abundantly clear is that he cannot accept the doctrine of Work. It is naturally uncongenial. He can only express a dream of the far future, a dream whose very expression contributes to the working out of men's destiny. I think *The Princess* was also intended not so much as a poem contributing to the work in hand, but rather as a blueprint for the far future, pointing the direction to the 'Golden Year', a phrase which actually occurs in it. Ida, the Princess, prophesies that the women of 'the golden year' will ever celebrate the memory of the men who defended their cause. For her, the emancipation of women is an essential contribution

11

Facts and Problems

to the coming of a better society. The poet Leonard's concept of what the better society was to be like is quite explicit:

> 'When wealth no more shall rest in mounded heaps,
> But smit with freer light shall slowly melt
> In many streams to fatten lower lands,
> And light shall spread, and man be liker man
> Thro' all the season of the golden year.
> 'Shall eagles not be eagles? wrens be wrens?
> If all the world were falcons, what of that?
> The wonder of the eagle were the less,
> But he not less the eagle. Happy days
> Roll onward, leading up the golden year.'

The vision has a curiously Socialist tinge.

By the beginning of the next year, Tennyson's dissatisfaction with life was converted into real illness. Elizabeth Barrett wrote to Robert Browning on 31 January 1846:

[Tennyson] is seriously ill with an internal complaint and confined to his bed, as George [her brother] heard from a common friend. Which does not prevent his writing a new poem—he has finished the second book of it—and it is in blank verse and a fairy-tale, and called the 'University', the university members being all females. If George has not diluted the scheme of it with some law from the Inner Temple, I don't know what to think—it makes me open my eyes. Now isn't the world too old and fond of steam, for blank verse poems, in ever so many books, to be written on the fairies?[1]

Very little progress in composition seems to have been made in six months, and we learn little more of the poem during the whole of 1846 save that Tennyson was well enough to go with Moxon to Switzerland and there write the superb lyric 'Come down, O maid', which, while retaining the flavour of the Theocritan idyll, is wonderfully pertinent to the poem in which it was to find a place. In 1847 he took the hydropathic cure at Umberslade, a fact which was reported in the press, together with the news that he was about to publish; he privately denied the latter, demanding what would be the use of that in a

---

[1] *The Letters of Robert Browning and Elizabeth Barrett, 1845–1846*, ed. Robert Browning (1899), i, p. 444.

general election. He was still at Umberslade on 22 May. While there, he corrected proofs of the poem, being uncertain whether to publish immediately or in the autumn,[1] and complaining at 'the publicities and gabblements of the 19th Century' which had betrayed his intentions. He conjured Moxon to show the proofs to no one. Mary Russell Mitford reveals that the poet was not equally careful: she wrote on 7 August to Mrs. Partridge (and later to Mrs. Ouvry in almost the same words) that:

> William Harness has been dining with the heroine of 'Locksley Hall' and her husband. His new poem is a 'Commonwealth of Women'.—A man gets in, and you can imagine the *dénouement*. It is said to be very beautiful, but not favourable to female intellect or character.[2]

She wrote again on 31 August 1847:

> Alfred Tennyson's poem is printing. It is long; and my friend Mr. Dyce (a man of consummate taste) says that it is beautiful, but that it gives a low idea of women. He is a great torment to Mr. Moxon, keeping proofs a fortnight to alter, and then sending for revises.[3]

She wrote, it would seem, in similar vein to Elizabeth Barrett Browning, who replied on 20 August 1847:

> Surely nobody was ever so happy before. I shall wake some morning with my hair all dripping out of the enchanted bucket, or if not we shall both claim the 'Flitch' next September, if you can find one for us in the land of Cockaigne, drying in expectancy of the revolution in Tennyson's 'Commonwealth'. . . . Do you hear, as we do, from Mr. Forster, that his new poem is his best work? . . . The subject seems almost identical with one of Chaucer's. Is it not so?[4]

Mrs. Browning was very curious indeed to know more of the poem, asking Miss Mitford on 1 October (postmark) and 8 December for details of it. They agreed that his other poems implied an underestimate of women. But Miss Mitford had not yet satisfied her curiosity by Christmas Day, 1847, according to another letter written then. It was only on that day that

---

[1] *Memoir*, i, pp. 236, 270, 241.   [2] Mitford, i, p. 235. See also ii, p. 88.
[3] ibid., i, p. 238.   [4] Browning, i, p. 339.

the volume was published; just too late for purchase as a gift book.[1] It had seemingly taken more than two and a half years in continuous composition, and perhaps as long as eight years in the gestation. Sales were slow at first, but we have seen how popular the book became. Tennyson was vexed at its first reception according to Miss Mitford's report to Mrs. Browning, who asked on 15 April 1848: 'Why did Mr. Harness and others who "never could understand" his former divine works praise this in manuscript till the poet's hope grew to the height of his ambition?'[2] With swelling demand, the poet was soon at work altering and modifying.

The reception the critics gave to the poem was by no means consistent, and inevitably the unusual form the poem took was a stumbling-block, causing many to believe Tennyson to be below his best:

What the poem contains is greater than the poem itself. Why should Mr. Tennyson have thrown all this into a medley? He had something serious to say—why graft it on burlesque? . . . Eminently, in the manliness of his thoughts, in the largeness of his view, and in his power of clothing the familiar in our human passions and affections 'with golden exhalations of the dawn', he is worthy to be the poet of our time. *Why does he not assume his mission?*

In these words, Forster, writing in *The Examiner* for 8 January 1848,[3] expressed what troubled the majority of contemporary reviewers. They expected Tennyson to treat contemporary problems with appropriate seriousness. They did not recognise that although he was portraying the age, he was portraying it by way of fantasy so that he could move into the realm that really mattered—that of the far future. This was why he chose so strange a treatment for his theme. But it has nevertheless to be recognised that critics in 1848 found the *form* of the poem curious, even disappointing. And by the time of Dawson's study of 1882 a new complication had arisen. Dawson acknowledged that the poem was not admired nearly as much as other works by the poet, earlier and later in date of publication. F. W. Robertson had explained Tennyson's popularity

[1] Mitford, ii, p. 19, and Shannon, p. 97.
[2] Browning, i, p. 361.   [3] Quoted by Shannon, p. 115.

in terms of his power to interpret his age: but, for his part, Dawson saw the poet to be doing something much more profound:

> A great poet is more than a seer of the things which are; he is a prophet of the things which are beginning to be. He is the exponent of the aspirations and the tendencies of his age. He reduces into coherent form, and clothes with beauty, the unuttered thoughts of which his age is dimly conscious . . . In this way, poets are true seers; in advance of their age, they utter its innermost and half-conscious thought.[1]

Then follows the claim that this poem was a *prophetic* utterance, and was undervalued because people had not yet come to see its full significance:

> Now this poem, 'The Princess', contains Tennyson's solution of the problem of the true position of woman in society—a profound and vital question, upon the solution of which the future of civilisation depends. But at the time of its publication, the surface thought of England was intent solely upon Irish famines, corn-laws, and free-trade. It was only after many years that it became conscious of anything being wrong in the position of women. The idea was not relegated to America,[2] but originated there in the sweet visions of New England transcendentalists; and, long after, began in Old England to take practical shape in various ways, notably in collegiate education for females. No doubt such ideas were at the time 'in the air' in England, but the dominant practical Philistinism scoffed at them as ideas 'banished to America, that refuge for exploded European absurdities'.[3]

This passage, quoted in part by Hallam Tennyson in the *Memoir*, has been highly influential in two ways. It first suggests that Tennyson was prophetic about the 'theme' of women's higher education; and secondly, it advances the idea that the 'woman question' of which Tennyson's 'theme' was a part, was first debated in America. The founding of Queen's College, Harley Street, London, in 1848 would make us suspect

[1] *Study*, p. 8.
[2] An Edinburgh Reviewer in 1855 wrote that the poem was 'a brilliant serio-comic *jeu d'esprit* upon the noise about "women's rights", which even now ceases to make itself heard anywhere but in the refuge of exploded European absurdities beyond the Atlantic'.
[3] *Study*, p. 9.

15

the first claim: the second is simply untrue, and one wonders whether Dawson was entirely ignorant of the progress of feminism in Europe, or simply so piqued that America should have been slightingly referred to in the *Edinburgh Review* that he felt obliged to advance a counter-claim.

We may say then, that about the story and the form of the poem there has always been a problem, but that after the publication of Dawson's *Study* there was some doubt about the theme as well. Editors have, on the whole, done very little to elucidate either problem, and occasionally have added to the confusion by suggesting 'sources' not only for the tale as I outlined it earlier, but also for the theme, or what is worse, for both combined; of this Dawson was not guilty. He did not even venture any suggestion for a source of the tale.

One of the earliest editors, however, P. M. Wallace, was guilty, and he was followed by others. In his edition of 1892,[1] he was already able to write that much ingenuity had been exercised on the subject of the source from which Tennyson may have drawn the idea of the Ladies' College, and mentioned that some had traced it to a passage in *Rasselas* wherein Nekayah, herself a Princess, contemplates founding a College for women. He also mentioned Defoe's Project for an Academy for Women, and the Duchess of Newcastle's play *The Female Academy* (1662). For good measure he threw in *Love's Labour's Lost*. I think it will be agreed that in suggesting all these possibilities, the confusion of ideas could hardly be exceeded, for no distinction is made between the theme and the tale. He assumed, with Dawson, that the theme of women's higher education was not a public preoccupation when the poem was written, and consequently was just as probably borrowed as was the romantic tale illustrating it. Yet Wallace partly realized the improbability of Tennyson's being indebted to any literary forebear for the theme, by also suggesting that the poem was prompted by 'a wild and hysterical clamour' on the subject of women's rights which had succeeded the sound principles laid down by Mary Wollstonecraft. He gave no examples, save of the efforts of Amelia Bloomer in America (and here we see the influence of Dawson, no doubt),

[1] *Tennyson: The Princess*, ed. P. M. Wallace (1892).

16

and observed that the emancipation that women had come to enjoy during the previous forty years (1850–90) was due in part to the efforts of Auguste Comte 'who was working out his system of ideal social organization, just at the time when Tennyson was engaged upon this poem'; he quotes the *System of Positive Polity* in support of his view.[1] Neither of these remarks is true. Mrs. Bloomer's agitation did not commence until after the poem was published, and Auguste Comte's work can have contributed little to practical reform in the rights of women.

A little later, in 1901, Andrew Lang contributed a biography of the poet to the 'Modern English Writers' series. In this he boldly seized upon Dawson's conciliatory remark that the question of women's education may have been 'in the air' at the time *The Princess* was published, even if it was not of much importance in the public eye, and roundly asserted that in fact this was *not* so; the woman question was quite unheard of. Indeed he deduced that it was because of the public indifference to feminine education that the poem was 'not of a nature to increase Tennyson's fame and success', and thus sold badly at first! This extreme view, which was really Dawson's put more plainly, was not accepted by John Churton Collins, who published an introduction to the poem in the next year (in his *In Memoriam, The Princess and Maud*). He pointed out that after 1830, the ' "woman question" as it was called' had been brought into prominence by several writers— Bentham, the Westminster Reviewers, Lady Morgan, Mrs. Jameson, Miss Martineau and others. He even suggested that Tennyson discussed the education question with his friend F. D. Maurice, founder of the women's academy, Queen's College, Harley Street. Collins, in fact, went back to Wallace's view that there *was* contemporary agitation (which he discusses more accurately), and even borrowed Wallace's 'sources', again overlooking the fact that only *Love's Labour's Lost* in any way provides a suggestion for the *plot*, which is all that a source need supply.

[1] Comte's *Système de Politique positive* appeared in 1852–4. A brief account of the part Comte thought women should play in society is given by Basil Willey, *Nineteenth Century Studies* (1949), p. 198.

Facts and Problems

The confusion of theme and source is one which will be reconsidered when the possible source of the tale is described in Chapter X. For the moment, it will suffice to say that there can be no doubt that the theme of marriage and the higher education for women treated in the poem was suggested to Tennyson by contemporary theories and events; and that this is tacitly corroborated by all those early critics, of whom Forster has been selected as representative, who on the poem's appearance suggested that he had not seriously and suitably addressed himself to the topic he had selected. From this it is clear that Dawson's argument that Tennyson was 'prophetic' is not true in the sense that he intended: and that while feminism in America did have important repercussions in this country, there is no need to look across the Atlantic to understand why Tennyson wrote when he did. The poet himself provides a hint of where we are to look if we are to seek abroad. It will be recalled that the story of the Princess who put learning before marriage was related by a group of undergraduates staying at a country house in Kent. When the story was concluded and the story-tellers have quitted the Abbey-ruin in the grounds, the poet-speaker and his friends climbed the slope to the house,

> and turning saw
> The happy valleys, half in light, and half
> Far-shadowing from the west, a land of peace;
> Gray halls alone among their massive groves;
> Trim hamlets; here and there a rustic tower
> Half-lost in belts of hop and breadths of wheat;
> The shimmering glimpses of a stream; the seas;
> A red sail, or a white; and far beyond,
> Imagined more than seen, the skirts of France.

It was in France, victim of political spasms which the English could congratulate themselves on avoiding, that feminism received its most ardent expression in Tennyson's youth. When the poet-speaker's companion, 'the Tory member's elder son', speaks scornfully of French political wildness, he is rebuked:

> 'Have patience,' I replied, 'ourselves are full
> Of social wrong; and maybe wildest dreams
> Are but the needful preludes of the truth . . .'

This might well be the poet Leonard speaking, and Leonard voiced, it would seem, Tennyson's own views. And here, I think, Tennyson was acknowledging his debt to French social theorists for having anticipated some of his own concern with the lot of women. He was far from alone in being under an obligation to the Socialists, the nature of whose thinking will be discussed in the next chapter.

CHAPTER II

The Saint-Simonians and the New Feminism

ESPITE Hallam Tennyson's mention of Mary Wollstonecraft in connection with *The Princess* when discussing
the poem in the *Memoir*, her book must not be regarded
as being directly influential with Tennyson and his readers.
The feminist agitation which they were familiar with formed
part of a later stage in the varying fortunes of the struggle for
emancipation, that promoted by another Revolution, not political this time, but social. Mary Wollstonecraft did no more than
fulminate against hereditary wealth, standing armies and the
worship of Mammon; she fully recognized that before women
could hope to lead the fuller lives she wished to see, social
conditions would have to be radically changed. Moreover,
contrary to popular belief, she did not adopt the position of
hostility to men and marriage which, as I hope to show in
Chapter VII, is an essential part not only of the attitude
which Tennyson sought to condemn in *The Princess*, but also
of feminist agitation in the years immediately preceding its
publication.

The social revolution Mary Wollstonecraft looked forward
to was initiated by the appearance of a new concept of the
aims and consequent structure of society which found expression in the Socialist doctrines of Saint-Simon in France. These
came to public notice there at the time of the 1830 Revolution, but had been long preparing. So too had the generally
similar views of Fourier and Robert Owen. These men and
their followers advocated an entirely new form of society, to
be brought into being not by political decrees, but by the conversion of the minds of men from the old concepts of political
economy (namely, the inalienable right to amass property,
inheritance, free markets and competition), to new beliefs in

the importance to society of work, social purpose, co-operation and association. These were the ideals for a new society
to which Mary Wollstonecraft could have looked for improvement in the lot of women, and all three systems had much to
say on their place in the new order. Indeed the Saint-Simonians
eventually foundered on the very question of where a woman
could be discovered capable of adequately representing the
almost mystical ideal of womanhood which they desired to
worship. The reverential attitude to women would not have
appealed to her strongly Protestant mind; but a religious tone
was not a monopoly of the Saint-Simonians, for Robert
Owen's Socialism eventually became the 'Rational Religion',
with Owen as its 'Father'. Enfantin, the leader of the Saint-
Simonians, became 'Père Enfantin', and his followers claimed
that in their religion of humanity, they had supplanted Christianity. The connection between the new concepts of society,
religion and feminism reposes in the fact that they all shared
the central doctrine that love should guide the actions of men,
who should show their love for each other by co-operation
rather than by competition; they should manifest it by wor-
shipping the highest ideal of humanity, abandoning the outworn creeds which embodied irresoluble antinomies affronting
man's moral sense; and finally they should respect woman,
since she, more than man, had a talent for loving. This complex of ideas was present in the poetry of Shelley, and the resemblances to Socialist doctrines in his work were remarked
by the Owenist journals.

The reaction to the total doctrine in England was complicated by the presence in individual minds of varying degrees
of opposition to its parts. Some who were interested in the
economic views were repelled by the claims to be in possession
of a 'new Christianity'; others found the ardent feminism
either incomprehensible or ridiculous. But at any rate, there
was no possibility of the English newspaper-reader who interested himself in politics and related topics being unaware
of what the Socialists in France had in mind. Just at this
time, Tennyson was among his friends at Cambridge, discussing with them political questions, as well as morals and
religion.

The Saint-Simonians

These discussions were over-shadowed by the conviction that upon the sagacity of the young men of their age and station would largely depend their country's chance of surviving real and imminent perils. The years immediately before the Reform Bill of 1832, during which Tennyson and his friends were together at Cambridge, were extremely troubled both at home and abroad. The state of Ireland, the sufferings and unrest of the poor, the free expression of radical opinions, the insurrections in Spain and Belgium, the Revolution in France —all these questions are discussed in their correspondence, and are generally viewed with disquiet and premonitions of worse to come, Arthur Hallam and R. C. Trench taking a particularly gloomy view of affairs. Tennyson's position was that of an interested and sympathetic onlooker, fearful of extremes, and particularly concerned lest the pursuit of freedom might lead to anarchy. Consequently, we see him supporting the Anti-slavery Convention and even advocating the measure for abolishing subscription to the Thirty-nine Articles;[1] yet at the same time he was clearly unwilling to go quite as far as Sterling, as will be seen from his unpublished lines of this period:

> I, loving Freedom for herself,
> And much of that which is her form,
> Wed to no faction in the state,
> A voice before the storm,
> I mourn in spirit when I think
> The year, that comes, may come with shame,
> Lured by the cuckoo-voice that loves
> To babble its own name.[2]

The society of the 'Apostles', who discussed religion and politics, provided an airing-ground for the latest views; Sterling saw them 'waxing daily in religion and radicalism'.[3] In *In Memoriam* Tennyson makes a passing allusion to the topics they discussed:

> . . . we held debate, a band
> Of youthful friends, on mind and art,
> And labour, and the changing mart,
> And all the framework of the land.

[1] *Memoir*, i, p. 41.   [2] ibid.   [3] ibid., pp. 42–3.

22

Tennyson was deeply moved, like the rest of his circle, by the plight of the poor, and felt that real reforms were necessary; Blakesley in 1830 suggested to the poet that he should consider writing poetry which might contribute to the reform of the times:

> A volume of poetry written in a proper spirit, a spirit like that which a vigorous mind indues by the study of Wordsworth and Shelley, would be, at the present juncture, the greatest benefit the world could receive. And more benefit would accrue from it than from all the exertions of the Jeremy Benthamites and Millians, if they were to continue for ever and a day.[1]

He goes on to mention the sympathy Sterling once felt with Shelley's advocacy of the 'lopping off those institutions in which that selfish spirit shows itself'; but suggests that he later saw with Wordsworth that this was not so effective as the implanting of new and opposite principles in the minds of men.

Shelley, at the period of Tennyson's sojourn at Cambridge, was much admired, and it is of interest to see Blakesley connecting him with a specific attitude to reform in 1830; but in view of the nature of contemporary political agitation, it is hardly surprising. One of the questions debated by the Apostles, and a very pertinent one if the religious as well as political interests of the society are considered, was 'Have Shelley's poems an immoral tendency?', to which Tennyson voted 'No'.[2] Hallam's interest in the poet may be inferred from the leading part he took in the publication of *Adonais* in England.[3]

After Tennyson left Cambridge in February 1831 he kept up a correspondence with the Apostles and, of course, with Arthur Hallam, who since 1830 had been engaged to Emily, his sister. Hallam was studying law in London at this time. The subjects of their discussion included literary topics, and especially Tennyson's own poems; but still, and inevitably, the

[1] ibid., p. 68.   [2] ibid., i, p. 44 n. 1.
[3] See the letter from W. B. Donne to R. C. Trench, endorsed December 1829 in Trench, i, p. 42. Arthur Hallam, soon after going up to Cambridge in 1828, wrote: 'At the present day, *Shelley* is the idol before which we are to be shorn by the knees.' From a letter quoted by Shannon, p. 22.

state of politics occupied their thoughts, and among other matters they discussed the Saint-Simonians, who in 1831 were attracting much attention in England by their 'religion' of social regeneration. One of the correspondents wrote that the new party's opinions on many points 'resembled those of Shelley, although they were much more practical'.[1]

The connection of Saint-Simonism with Shelley gives a glimpse of the pattern of associations in the minds of Tennyson and Hallam. While Tennyson saw no immorality in Shelley, and clearly indicated his dissatisfaction with conventional Christianity in such poems as 'To J.M.K.' (John Mitchell Kemble), yet we may take it, on the evidence of his later development, that he would have resisted any encroachment upon the Christian interpretation of the duties of men, and would indeed subscribe with Sterling to the Wordsworthian rather than the Shelleyan treatment of even political reform. All the same, Tennyson was bent upon reconciling the discoveries and advances of the 'Mother-age' with the central faith, and it is probable that some at least of the daring ideas of Saint-Simonism would have appealed to his mind, imbued as it was with a consciousness of the deplorable materialism of the age and the sufferings of so many of his fellow-men. In 1832 he wrote to Mrs. Russell, his aunt:

What think you of the state of affairs in Europe? Burking and cholera have ceased to create much alarm. They are our least evils, but reform and St. Simonism are, and will continue to be, subjects of the highest interest. The future is so dark in the prospect that I am ready to call out with the poet:

> The empty thrones call out for kings,
> But kings are cheap as summer dust.
> The good old time hath taken wings,
> And with it taken faith and trust,
> And solid hope of better things.

Reform (not the measure, but the instigating spirit of reform which is likely to subsist among the people long after the measure has past into a law) will bring on the confiscation of Church property, and maybe the downfall of the Church altogether: but the existence of the sect of the St. Simonists is at once a proof of the immense

---

[1] *Memoir*, i, p. 82.

mass of evil that is extant in the nineteenth century, and a focus which gathers all its rays. This sect is rapidly spreading in France, Germany and Italy, and they have missionaries in London. But I hope and trust that there are hearts as true and pure as steel in old England, that will never brook the sight of Baal in the sanctuary, and St. Simon in the Church of Christ.[1]

This somewhat cryptic letter reveals one thing—Tennyson's mind looked forward beyond the events of the moment to their consequences. The reforming spirit would next turn to the Church's right to property: if it were dispossessed, it might collapse. Nevertheless, he quite obviously felt that the interests of reform in the secular field were paramount. Religion would have to survive as best it could, because social evils would not wait longer for remedy. This interpretation of the words of his letter applies even more pertinently to Saint-Simonism, which he links with 'reform' as 'subjects of the highest interest'. When he says that the 'existence of the sect of the St. Simonists is at once a proof of the immense amount of evil that is extant in the nineteenth century, and a focus which gathers all its rays', he is saying no more than that Saint-Simonism is both a product of the social evils abounding at the time and an attempt to solve them. He is no more antagonistic to it, it may be inferred, than to reform, which likewise wins his support, even though it is also a two-edged instrument, capable of striking at established religion while lopping deformed institutions. The Saint-Simonians, at this time, were openly asserting that they inherited the role of Christ in the redemption of the world, and it is clear that it was this side of their creed which Tennyson could not be easy about. But this does not mean that much else of what they were saying did not earn his approval. Their vision of a society deriving its unity from a common belief in the value of co-operative labour, and its strength from the liberated energies of the two helot classes of mankind—the workers and women —could not have failed to excite him if we may judge from what he wrote.

The views of Arthur Hallam and R. C. Trench, and the way in which they were disseminated among the group of friends, are

[1] ibid., i, p. 98.

The Saint-Simonians

illustrated in a letter written by Hallam to W. B. Donne on 29 January 1831, when a Saint-Simonian 'mission' was in England seeking converts:

The life I have always desired is the very one you seem to be leading, a wife and a library—what more can man, being rational, require, unless it be a cigar? I am not, however, without my fears that the season for such luxuries is gone or going by: in the tempests of the days that are coming, it may be smoking, and wiving, and reading will be affairs of anxiety and apprehension.

Trench considers a man, who reads Cicero or Bacon nowadays, much as he would a man who goes asleep on the ledge of a mad torrent, and dreams of a garden of cucumbers . . . He tells me he has awakened you to some alarm concerning the St. Simonians those prophets of a false Future, to be built on the annihilation of the Past in the confusion of the Present. I too am alarmed at this gigantic organisation, and the facility with which France appears to imbibe the poison, but I cannot but confide yet in English good sense that it will repel them from these shores with indignant scorn. Should it be otherwise, better will it be for Chorazin and Bethsaida in the day of judgement than for us. The mission is come however and according to their instructions they are to call upon Sir Francis Burdet and 'the chief of the aristocracy', to tell them that 'humanity marches'! Bless their five wits—what incurable fools Frenchmen are![1]

John Mitchell Kemble also believed that the fearful weapon the Saint-Simonians had made from the evil spirit of Industrialism might possibly be found ineffectual in England: but if not it would be overcome by the bigotry of Spain, and bigotry, in his view, promised more than 'Liberalism and Infidelity'.[2]

Many people besides Arthur Hallam took the view that the Saint-Simonians were fools; and more were actively hostile to the claims they advanced that their religion of humanity supplanted the Christian faith. It is clear that Hallam was much less beset by religious doubt than Tennyson, and that he clung tenaciously to the Christian faith; and in other ways the Apostles differed from one another to a remarkable degree.

[1] Donne, p. 8.
[2] From an unpublished letter to W. B. Donne dated 2 January 1832. The copyright of this letter belongs to Mrs. Barham Johnson, to whom I owe thanks for permission to quote it.

Trench was thoroughly alarmist about the Saint-Simonians, as we have seen. He was no enthusiast for the Reform Bill either, but resigned himself to it as inevitable in view of the dreadfulness of the times. He wrote to W. B. Donne on 6 December 1831 as follows:

> What think you of the St. Simonians? To me they seem the most perfect expression of the spirit now at work. Primogeniture, aristocracy, heredity, all that rested on a spiritual relation, which relation will no longer be recognized, must be swept away before the new industrial principle, *à chacun selon ses œuvres*.[1]

Trench knew Tennyson very little at this time, a circumstance which Hallam regretted, though he thought that the bents of their minds were quite different. We need not infer that he could have influenced Tennyson on this subject as he is thought to have done in the suggestion for 'The Palace of Art'.

A little later, on 19 February 1832, John Sterling wrote to Trench on the subject of the sect:

> With St. Simonism and some of its disciples I am tolerably familiar. They tried to convert me at Paris a few years ago. I was taken suddenly to one of their meetings, where I was the only Gentile, and the first thing I heard was that religion is one of the fine arts ... There is one obstacle to their success which will meet them throughout Europe, and more especially in England, viz. that potent spirit of individuality which may be regarded as the shadow of the Gospel extending to vast regions and millions of minds altogether ignorant of the substance. Ages ago, the Chinese were St. Simonists in theory, and that is as much as any man or people can ever be.[2]

In London, the Saint-Simonian emissaries may indeed have made less impression than they would have wished, but in the industrial centres of the north, where Robert Owen's influence

---

[1] Trench, i, p. 103. Charles Merivale, writing from Cambridge on 11 November 1831, reported that the Saint-Simonians were 'all the rage' there then, and that Trench had come up to keep a term 'full of the most horrid' misgivings about the co-operative religion. 'We look upon it here very much as the Catholics of the sixteenth century looked upon the Reformation, and nobody but myself seems inclined to sacrifice the prospects of the present age to the chance of alteration for the better a century hence.'—*Autobiography and Letters of Charles Merivale, Dean of Ely*, ed. Judith A. Merivale (Oxford, privately printed, 1898), p. 169.

[2] ibid., p. 110.

was also greater, they reported more success. The reactions of the Cambridge men quoted show that among intellectuals too, their activities caused considerable disquiet. This is hardly surprising, for in 1830 and 1831 their notoriety was at its height: indeed, as Tennyson wrote, Saint-Simonism seemed a focus which gathered all the rays from the mass of evil extant in the nineteenth century. It will perhaps be helpful to look at what the new sect was saying.

In the first place, they believed history to teach a great lesson, namely, that man is perpetually in a state of spiritual development: in the words of an historian of the movement, they believed that:

> Properly understood, history is an exact science whose laws, once understood in relation to the past, cast brilliant light upon the present and the future. It shows three states to succeed one another: the theological, the metaphysical and the positive; it teaches us that the peoples have marched from isolation to union, from war to peace, from antagonism to association.[1]

This interpretation of history as humanity's progression from one distinct stage to another is fundamental to an understanding of the movement.[2] Indeed, Georges Weill remarks that in insisting that man had now reached a stage wherein he was to contribute positively to his destiny by using his own faculties, and the scientific method in particular (humanity being considered as susceptible of constant improvement), the Saint-Simonians had substituted for individual immortality an

---

[1] Weill, p. 4. On p. 31 he writes of the Saint-Simonian system: 'It rests in its entirety upon the philosophy of history. This new study was then in favour; the works of Herder and of Vico were being translated . . . and philosophers of all schools believed that exact historical laws allowed of predictions about the future.' This idea that civilisation moved through phases or epochs of a distinct character was not therefore peculiar to the Saint-Simonians. For a discussion, see George Boas, 'Il faut être de son temps', in *Wingless Pegasus* (Baltimore, 1950), and J. S. Mill, *The Spirit of the Age*, opening paragraph.

[2] The idea of development by stages was developed by Auguste Comte in his *Cours de Philosophie positive* (1830–42): and it was also he who contributed the notion to the Saint-Simonians by way of an earlier version of his *Système de Politique positive* (1824) first published in 1822 as part of Saint-Simon's *Catéchisme des industriels*. See F. A. von Hayek's introduction to his edition of J. S. Mill's *The Spirit of the Age* (Chicago 1942), p. xviii.

eternal life for the human race, a theory which was a social counterpart to evolution in the field of biology.[1]

The grand concept of the school derived from this reading of history was, however, economic co-operation in place of competition. The time was past when the exploitation (their word) of the worker could be permitted: the need was to exploit the world's resources to benefit society as a whole, and this could only be done by co-operation, an idea made familiar by Robert Owen and Fourier as well. This was to be achieved by reorganizing society to permit government to come into the hands of the three main classes of society—workers, *savants* and artists; all men must work, and all were to receive according to their usefulness. (The emphasis upon the importance of work in the new society and the objectionableness of idleness sprang from Saint-Simon directly. He had asked which would cause the most harm to France, the loss of the Court and government or the best artisans in each trade. He was nearly imprisoned for his tactlessness.) The object before everybody must be to advance society morally and spiritually. Science must be planned and co-ordinated. As for the fine arts:

. . . today they drag along in a state of impotence, as is shown by the interest taken in the vain disputes between the romantics and classics; the big subjects, the profound results of inspiration, are not to be seen because art has withdrawn into a proud isolation, and refuses to mix itself in contemporary life. Art is worthless unless it expresses the ideas and beliefs of its age, exciting warm feelings. The artists of the future will understand their mission; the poet will sing the conquests of science, the end of war, universal association.[2]

In 1827, the movement had taken a religious turn, almost in deference to the Romantic spirit. French society seemed to

[1] Weill, p. 291.

[2] ibid., p. 6. See F. A. von Hayek's 'The Counter-Revolution of Science', in *Economica*, n.s. viii (1941), p. 282, where he observes that the influence of the Saint-Simonians was often greatest in literary and artistic circles; 'The demand that all art should be tendentious, that it should serve social criticism and for this purpose represent life as it is in all its ugliness led to a veritable revolution in letters'. He is referring of course only to France, but Tennyson's 'The Palace of Art' makes a similar case.

29

be yearning for a religious revival, and the apostles of Saint-Simon had good precedent in their master's *magnum opus, Le Nouveau Christianisme*,[1] for endeavouring to supply the need; nevertheless, some of the most important of the original members opposed this innovation, Auguste Comte among them. (Ironically, he was later on to reach independently a religious sanction for his philosophy in the *Système de Politique positive*.) They broke away, to leave two rivals, Enfantin and Bazard, in undisputed control of a 'church' which aimed at 'rehabilitating matter and the flesh', or in other words ending the dualism on which Christianity is founded. Matter and the body were not evil and to be rejected, but as worthy of divine love as the human spirit. They saw industry and science as part of divine activity, worthy to be thought of as religious activities: 'tous les hommes sont fonctionnaires de la société, la fonction de chacun est sainte'.

The new 'church' gained converts of two main categories, scientists from the École Polytechnique and those in search of religious faith. It was soon obliged to extend its doctrine. Enfantin, who sought constantly to elevate the new system of thought to the highest regions of religious aspiration, advocated that the 'clergy' should be both male and female, but nevertheless entirely celibate: this sprang from Saint-Simon's dictum that those devoted to the advancement of humanity should take humanity for their family. This was the beginning of the sect's interest in the woman question, a question unheeded by Saint-Simon himself.

The Revolution of 1830 tempted the Saint-Simonians to try a *coup d'état*, but the time was not ripe; the popular movement benefited them however, and supplied many converts among artists, including Liszt and Heine:[2] but their often eloquent addresses were primarily intended to procure an improvement in the condition of the labouring poor by evoking sympathy among the *bourgeoisie* rather than to incite revolution and antagonism between the classes. The movement spread abroad, and to the provinces; in England, its emissaries d'Eichtal and Duveyrier in February 1832 met the supporters of Owen, but

[1] This was translated, but not published, by Carlyle.
[2] Weill, p. 47.

had less success with others than with J. S. Mill, who was already a sympathizer, having corresponded with d'Eichtal. These were the missionaries of the sect to whom Tennyson and Hallam refer in the letters previously quoted.[1] On 18 July 1831, the liberal newspaper, *Le Globe*, of which Sainte-Beuve was one of the editors, passed into the control of the Saint-Simonians through the conversion to their principles of Pierre Leroux; the paper bore an epigraph which broadly expressed the views of the sect at this time:

> All social institutions must have as their object the moral, intellectual and physical improvement of the largest and poorest class. All privileges of birth are without exception abolished. To everyone according to his ability, and to each ability according to its works.[2]

This journal concerned itself not with the future but with the present, and intervened forcefully over international affairs: it even advocated an alliance of France, Prussia and England to form a kind of *bloc* for peace;[3] this was a practical demonstration of the Saint-Simonian ambition to effect an improvement in the conditions of the labouring classes (*artistes, savants, industriels*) through co-operation and peace, even at the expense of war in the first instance. In art, *Le Globe* criticised Scott for mediaevalism, Vigny for despair, Balzac for 'entertainment', but praised Victor Hugo for an awakening social conscience.[4]

But while this propaganda flourished, the two fathers of the Saint-Simonian Church, Enfantin, a religious dreamer, and Bazard, a realistic social critic, were meeting difficulties over the attitude which the group should adopt towards women. In Enfantin's exalted dreams there was always a strong element of mysticism, a sense of *culte*; and in allowing his mind to dwell upon the position of women in the new Saint-Simonian society, he reached conclusions which, though innocent enough in intention, could not fail to cause widespread misunderstanding. So acute was the crisis that finally the society suffered a serious rupture, and under Enfantin's single government took

---

[1] For an interesting account of the Saint-Simonians in England, see Richard K. Pankhurst's article 'Saint-Simonism in England', in the *Twentieth Century*, clii, no. 910 (December 1952), p. 449, and cliii, no. 911 (January 1953), p. 47. I am indebted to it for a number of matters.
[2] Weill, p. 65.   [3] ibid., p. 68.   [4] ibid., p. 85.

a course which led to its final collapse, not without derision from many, despite the supreme eloquence with which the defence in the public prosecution which followed was conducted. The Saint-Simonians had early subscribed to the policy of 'freeing woman' as a necessary accompaniment to freeing the proletariat. They rejected the 'stale' Christian idea of female subordination to man: they believed that woman should be granted independence and education in order to share in the progress of the new society based upon universal co-operation. The offices of life were to be conducted by 'couples', and from this it was properly inferred that the sect's intention was to sanctify and almost to exact marriage between the 'couples'. As already narrated, Enfantin, a *catholique manqué*, believed that priests and priestesses should co-operate only on a spiritual plane, 'separés par un nuage d'encens', to use his own words. But, in time, he believed that since the flesh was as holy as spirit, superiors 'pouvaient avoir des relations sexuelles avec les inférieures pour les mieux diriger'. Romantic notions of free love are not without support in the writings of Blake and Shelley, but probably had never before been advanced for such a remarkable reason. But Enfantin plunged on, divided men into 'Othellos' and 'Don Juans', the constant and the 'progressive' types of lovers, and referred to the historical precedents of paganism. His blunt confrère, Bazard, condemned the doctrine unequivocally. For him, Christianity had 'créé la poésie de l'amour individuel'; only it had regarded the woman 'comme un subalterne'. Equality was the means of improvement, and marriage should remain hallowed. The rift grew serious; the party was thought to advocate the community of women. All-night discussions raged among the volatile expositors of rival views; some found themselves inspired; Bazard collapsed, and finally submitted. On 19 and 21 November 1831, Enfantin announced that he did not intend to impose his views, which were only provisional. Those of women on this subject were necessary, and were to be awaited.

Thereafter, a constant advocacy of the cause of women was kept up, the Father of the movement, Enfantin, keeping beside his own a vacant chair to be filled by the representative

Woman, for whom diligent search was made. (Saint-Simon himself had offered marriage to Mme de Stael on principles approximating those of Enfantin.)

After the party finally collapsed when prosecuted in the courts, Enfantin was imprisoned, and the other members dispersed, many to become highly influential in various walks of life. Some adopted Fourierism, the natural inheritor of the collectivist ideas of Saint-Simon; some of the women founded a newspaper advancing views tending to the emancipation of women.[1]

Saint-Simonism, without a leader, was an almost spent force. Nevertheless, on the minds of those who had accepted its doctrines with all the enthusiasm of religious conversion, it left an indelible impression. The short-lived movement unquestionably began that agitation on the condition of the labouring classes which took active expression in the Revolution of 1848, a fact which was perceived in England. In an article published in that year, showing remarkable sympathy with the sect,[2] a writer observed that the Revolution was connected with the new social ideas called 'communist', a vague term indicating repugnance, both intellectual and sentimental, to the doctrines of Adam Smith and Malthus, and favour for association in place of competition, views disseminated by the Saint-Simonians. He then summarized the teachings of the Saint-Simonians on the woman question:

On the subject of the rights of women, they professed that what they aimed at was the complete emancipation of the sex, so that woman might reveal her powers, whatever they are, to the utmost, and perform her full part in the social evolution. The law of marriage, however, by which one man was conjoined with one woman, so as to form a social unit, they regarded as holy; and all the modifications they would make of it would be for the facilitation, in certain cases, of divorce . . . Never was Saint Simonianism more prosperous than in 1830 and 1831.[3]

[1] *La Femme libre*, later *La Femme de l'Avenir*, and finally *La Femme nouvelle*.
[2] *The North British Review*, ix (May–August 1848), pp. 213 f. Note the reviewer's use of the term 'social evolution'.
[3] p. 229.

D   33

He then discussed the ideas introduced by the Saint-Simonians (and Fourierists) which contributed to the events of 1848, namely that an industrial crisis was inevitable, and that it would be met by the organization of labour into compact bodies—neither idea being opposed to good sense or Christian belief. But this was in 1848, when England felt herself no longer involved, but only a bystander of the struggle in France. Not unnaturally, the view of the movement taken by Englishmen in the early eighteen-thirties was sometimes less detached. Robert Southey, for instance, contributing to the *Quarterly Review* in 1831,[1] did his best to influence its readers against the Saint-Simonians by giving a sketch of alleged French religious fickleness going back to Henri IV. He nevertheless found it rather difficult to make the sect look absolutely devoid of reason in its doctrines, and indeed went so far as grudgingly to approve of their intentions.[2] To Southey in 1831, the sect was but one of a number of extremely worrying movements bent on forming a 'new state of society', some pretending to be within the church, others like the Saint-Simonians expressing startlingly unorthodox views with remarkable moderation. His words are not without value in setting the mood of the hour:

> Perhaps there is no more alarming symptom in these portentous times than the general persuasion, which every man must have observed, that we are on the eve of some great crisis: a restlessness in the public mind, like that which, in individuals, is often the first indication of some rapid and fatal disease,—a blind and uneasy and helpless prescience such as dogs and birds manifest before the shock of an earthquake.[3]

Southey makes the obvious allusion to the Owenist movement, in which the Saint-Simonians were themselves interested, and quotes from an extremely outspoken journal which fully justifies his anxiety. He observes that

---

[1] *Quarterly Review*, xlv (April–July 1831), p. 407; von Hayek, *Economica*, loc. cit., p. 283 n. 1.

[2] For example, he writes, p. 447: 'The Saint-Simonites . . . address themselves to the understanding, and, as far as they understand it, to the heart of man: and no system which has been advanced under cover of pious fraud has ever been presented to the world so temperately, so reasonably, nor with so much ability as theirs.'

[3] p. 447; see also p. 448.

. . . Saint Simon has conceived a new science, a science as positive as any which has gained that title: it is the Science of the Human Race, and the method employed in it is the same as is followed in astronomy and in physic, that of classing facts, and arranging them by generalization and particularization. It follows from this science that the tendency of the human race is from a state of antagonism to that of an universal peaceful association—from the dominating influence of the military spirit to that of the *industrial* one: from what they call *l'exploitation de l'homme par l'homme* to the *exploitation* of the globe by industry . . . Universal association,—behold the future.[1]

He continues:

The rights of women are fully acknowledged by the Saint Simonites. Having been charged with pleading for a community of women as well as of goods, they repel the first charge as indignantly as the other, but they proclaim that women are to be delivered from that domination, that pupilage, that eternal minority, which all existing institutions impose upon them, but which are incompatible with the social state that is about to commence. Christianity, they say, has raised the sex from servitude, but has condemned them to *subalternity*, and throughout Christian Europe they are still under an interdict, religious, political and civil. The Saint Simonites announce their definite enfranchisement, their complete emancipation, not abolishing the holy law of marriage, but fulfilling it by giving it a new sanction, and adding to the strength of the inviolability of the union which it consecrates. 'They demand, with the Christians, that one man shall be united to one woman, but they teach that the wife ought to be equal with the husband, and that, according to the peculiar grace which God has conferred upon her sex, she ought to be associated with him in the exercise of the triple functions of the church, the state, and the family: so that the *social individual*, which has hitherto been the *man* alone, henceforth shall be the *man and wife*', presenting politically thus the perfect Androgyne of philosophical fable. 'What the religion of Saint Simon puts an end to is that shameful traffic, that legal prostitution, which so often, under the name of marriage, consecrates the monstrous union of devotedness with selfishness, of intelligence with ignorance, of youth with decrepitude.'[2]

It may be well to remember that Tennyson registers his dislike of 'that shameful traffic, that legal prostitution, which so often,

[1] p. 429. [2] p. 443.

under the name of marriage, consecrates the monstrous union of devotedness with selfishness, of intelligence with ignorance, of youth with decrepitude', in his poem 'Locksley Hall'. The year in which this poem was composed is unknown, but it would appear to have been *completed* after 1837, when Tennyson's reading of Pringle's *Travels* provided him with the image of the lion drawing near to the watch-fires; but the expression 'ringing grooves of time' was struck out in 1830. A few lines from the poem will illustrate the parallel now being made. The speaker is addressing his cousin Amy, who has been obliged to marry a wealthy rival:

Is it well to wish thee happy?—having known me—to decline
On a range of lower feelings and a narrower heart than mine!

Yet it shall be; thou shalt lower to his level day by day,
What is fine within thee growing coarse to sympathize with clay . . .

It may be my lord is weary, that his brain is overwrought;
Soothe him with thy finer fancies, touch him with thy lighter thought . . .

Cursed be the social wants that sin against the strength of youth!
Cursed be the social lies that warp us from the living truth!

The fickleness of cousin Amy is clearly the literary projection of a dislike of one of the social consequences of a state of society founded upon acquisitiveness. The poem is curiously inconsequential, and one feels that it expresses something at least of the poet's personal views. (The speaker's boyish delight and more mature despondency are akin to Tennyson's own case. The temptation to quit the modern world of human strife for the languor of the tropics, and the determination to see it through after all is expressed in 'You ask me, why, tho' ill at ease', and we know from the *Memoir* that the poet seriously considered, at one time, quitting the unsympathetic atmosphere of England for Jersey, the south of France, or Italy.[1]

[1] *Memoir*, i, p. 97.

The same tendency of mind is illustrated by 'The Lotos Eaters'.) In 'Locksley Hall', Tennyson makes the speaker seek to forget his personal grief in the recovery of his earlier optimism. This takes a form curiously like that which formed the ideal of the Saint-Simonians; we see the same interest in a society founded upon labour:

> Men, my brothers, men the workers, ever reaping something
> new;
> That which they have done but earnest of the things that they
> shall do.

The commercial development of the world by all the means open to scientific discovery (*l'exploitation du monde*) is picturesquely described:

> Saw the heavens fill with commerce, argosies of magic sails,
> Pilots of the purple twilight, dropping down with costly bales.

Eventually war is brought to an end, and the era of 'universal association' begins:

> Till the war-drum throbb'd no longer, and the battle-flags were
> furl'd
> In the Parliament of man, the Federation of the world.

The Saint-Simonian notion of a *bloc* able to impose peace seems indicated in:

> There the common sense of most shall hold a fretful realm in awe,
> And the kindly earth shall slumber, lapt in universal law.

It is, of course, true that the ideas of 'association' and the scientific (or positivist) attitude to social problems were at this period beginning to emerge as part of the European system of thought; yet it is hard to believe that Tennyson did not owe something to the leading exponents of a new, and indeed, revolutionary, social theory when such a degree of coincidence of ideas is apparent. Of his familiarity with the tenets of the sect there can be no doubt, in view of his mention of it in the letter of 1832 quoted earlier, and, moreover, it would be surprising if the political side of their programme did not appeal to him if only because it was founded upon a notion of development in humanity, which, as we shall see, his scientific reading at this period and later, inclined him to believe in. It is possible that Carlyle, whose debt to the Saint-Simonians is well known,[1] and whose *Sartor Resartus* was composed during his correspondence with the society, may have had an influence, though it could hardly be personal; for although Carlyle knew Tennyson before, he does not seem to have become intimate with him till after 1842.[2] Tennyson's poem, too, emphasises more of the grandeur than the moral equity of the 'Vision of the world'.

If Tennyson was familiar with the political aspect of Saint-Simonism as is suggested by the evidence I have adduced, he could by no means be unaware of the sect's preoccupation with the woman question, for in the words of a Westminster Reviewer of 1863,[3] Enfantin 'was the genius of progress and peace come to emancipate labour and women'. It would be going too far, perhaps, to suggest that it is significant that 'Locksley Hall' deals with the failure of a woman to live up to the ideals of an aspirant to the 'new state of society'; but upon the author of 'A Dream of Fair Women', the French party's concern with elevating the status of the subaltern sex must have had its effect. Indeed, the press united in abusing the Saint-Simonian emissaries, and gave particular attention to the sect's views on women, *The Times* taking a virtuous tone for the occasion. No reader could fail to be at least aware of the question. The sect found staunch supporters in Robert Owen's followers.[4]

The *Westminster Review* addressed itself to the Saint-Simonians in an article for April 1832,[5] which also noticed two Owenist pamphlets and a work on political economy. The article is hostile, and indeed rather narrow, but it makes a damaging attack on the practical weaknesses of the doctrines, demonstrating that the means would defeat the ends. The writer gives a full account of the discussions held by the sect

[1] See David Brooks Cofer, *Saint-Simonism in the Radicalism of Thomas Carlyle* (1931), wherein is reprinted his correspondence with the Society.
[2] See *Memoir*, i, p. 188.
[3] *The Westminster Review*, N.S. xxiv (July–October 1863), p. 122.
[4] See Owen's paper *The Crisis*, iii, p. 92 (16 November 1833) for a spirited defence.
[5] *The Westminster Review*, xvi (January–April 1832), p. 272.

on 19 and 21 November 1831 (which had been published as a pamphlet) on the subject of woman's social position, which, revealing as they did the internal dissensions provoked by the woman question, were very injurious to the party's reputation for temperate discussion. He concludes, very significantly:

> There can be no doubt that the political inequality of woman is a remnant of the barbarous state, which will be removed exactly as that state is receded from, and that a time will come when the equal rights of women will be made a powerful lever by somebody. But Father Enfantin is manifestly not the man.[1]

So much for Father Enfantin! The studied tone of superiority in this comment is perhaps justified, but the reviewer nevertheless achieves his air of sagacity at the cost of a most interesting statement: 'There can be no doubt that the political inequality of women is a remnant of the barbarous state.'

One might think that the seeming absurdity of the lengths to which Enfantin took the search for the 'new woman' in 1830 and 1831 would have evoked ridicule enough to destroy any hopes of further feminist activity by Socialist parties. The political enemies of the movement could attach scandal to the principle of association by hinting that a community of women was intended. But feminism and the new social theories were so closely connected that the survival of the political programme preserved feminism with it. Moreover, it seems certain that, although Saint-Simon had in fact enunciated a theory of the 'rehabilitation of the flesh' which in a sense justified something of the feminism manifested by Enfantin his disciple, Enfantin had really been led to the extreme form he adopted by another social thinker, Charles Fourier.[2]

We have already seen that this dangerous doctrine finally broke up the Saint-Simonian order (for so it must be termed in this religious phase, during which it went into 'retreat' at Ménilmontant); but by a curious irony, Fourier's doctrines

---

[1] p. 313. Carlyle, too, thought very ill of the 'femme libre' interests of the Saint-Simonians. See Cofer, op. cit., p. 15. On the other hand, J. S. Mill 'honoured them most of all for what they have been most cried down for'. *Autobiography*, p. 167.

[2] See Marguerite Thibert, *Le Féminisme dans le Socialisme français (1830–1850)* (Paris, 1926), pp. 31 f.

gained an able champion, Victor Considérant,[1] at this very time, and on the break-up of the Saint-Simonians, the Fourierist circle received a number of most valuable recruits and engaged in several publications, including a newspaper, *Le Phalanstère*,[2] founded in 1832; they even attempted to found a Phalange or community, just as Owen had established communities at Orbiston and New Harmony earlier.

As might be expected, Considérant was anxious to dissociate the new movement as much as possible from the extravagances to which the 'Apostolat de la Femme' had led Saint-Simonism.[3] Consequently he concentrated particularly upon the more practical possibilities of industrial association, and left alone that part of Fourier's doctrine dealing with feminism, although it was really the central part. Fourier was outraged at the oppression of women, and made their condition the criterion of the true state of culture in society—*le pivot de mécanique*—but Considérant and his colleagues very carefully avoided everything in Fourier's teaching which might not appear *positive*. When the emancipation of women was spoken of, it was in terms of the independence which employment would afford. Despite this circumspection, the Fourierists nevertheless seized every opportunity of advancing the feminist cause in articles in the *Phalanstère* and its successors, the *Phalange* and the *Démocratie pacifique* and other reviews, and women writers like George Sand and Flora Tristan received favourable notices.[4]

By 1840, according to an historian of the movement, it seemed as if the emancipation of women was a natural part of the Socialist programmes:

. . . the founding of a new world, founded upon principles of absolute justice, presupposed that women should participate to the full in all human rights. No new order would be possible if the arbitrary privileges of one sex should withhold half of society from its common rights . . . the public was so accustomed to seeing the same men espousing the causes of both women and the people, that

[1] His *Destinée sociale* (1835–54) is the classic statement of Fourierist doctrine.

[2] Its alternative title was *La Réforme industrielle*.

[3] Thibert, op. cit., p. 122.　　[4] ibid., p. 135.

and the New Feminism

the reactionary parties regarded socialism and feminism with a like aversion.[1]

This is an important fact, and in Chapter VII I shall show that Tennyson was probably aware of the state of society in France at about this time, when he had already considered the plan of *The Princess*, and may have begun writing. As may be imagined, the opponents of Socialism in France were not slow to see the tactical advantage this association in the public mind had for them. The legend of the 'femme libre' was unreservedly reviled in the knowledge that the Socialists would suffer in like measure. Between 1836 and 1849 Daumier's caricatures in *Charivari* ridiculed blue-stockings absorbed in literary meditation while their husbands did the housework, and poked fun at Leroux and Considérant. By this means they suggested that the reformers were really the enemies of marriage and normal morality, and feminist views stamped their holder as a reformer of society.

I hope to have shown that agitation on the woman question, although it was also present in the writings of the Owenists, was very much before the public eye in France if not in England. There it was part of a Socialist reform movement which played a far greater part in French political thought than did Owen's socialism in English politics,[2] a fact fully recognized by the English reviews of the time, which as we have seen gave considerable space to discussions about the activities of the Saint-Simonians. We should be prepared therefore, to consider the possibility that it was not so much feminism in America which prompted Tennyson to consider the subject for a poem as the doings of the Socialists in France. The paucity of clear evidence on the point obliges us to consider testimony of a more general sort. As we shall see, J. S. Mill was led to reflect upon the rights of women partly by his disagreement with his father over the question of their political

[1] ibid., pp. 167–8
[2] When Dr. Elizabeth Blackwell, who graduated in medicine at Geneva (N.Y.) Medical College, visited Paris, the medical fraternity assumed that she was a Socialist of the most rabid sort, and that her undertaking so unusual a profession was the beginning of a systematic attack on society by the whole sex. See *The History of Woman Suffrage*, ed. Elizabeth Cady Stanton and others (1881–1922), i, p. 94.

representation. Lest it be thought that his notable championing of their cause should have been due entirely to this early formation of his opinions, or to the exclusive influence of Mrs. Taylor, the following passage from a letter written by Mill to Dr. Cazelles, the translator of *The Subjection of Women*, is adduced. It is dated 30 May 1869.

D'abord il me semble que vous ne rendez pas pleine justice aux St. Simoniens et aux Fourieristes, que vous désignez clairement sans les nommer. Je condamne comme vous beaucoup de leurs doctrines et surtout le gouvernementalisme à outrance des St. Simoniens. Cependant je trouve que les uns et les autres ont rendu de grands services: et notamment sur la question des femmes, le St. Simonisme surtout ayant jeté dans les hautes régions de la vie intellectuelle et pratique, un grand nombre d'esprits supérieurs, désabusés aujourd'hui de ce qu'il y avait de faux ou d'exaggéré dans leurs systèmes, mais conservant ce qu'ils avaient de bon, y compris l'égalité des femmes. Les St. Simoniens avaient d'ailleurs le bon esprit déclarer toujours qu'on ne peut prononcer sur la fonction des femmes sans elles, et que la loi qui les droit régir ne peut être donnée que par des femmes ou par une femme.[1]

This tribute to the success of the French Socialists in forming enlightened views on the part in life to be played by women— by one who might be forgiven for forgetting it at the moment when his own contribution to the subject was published—is an indication of their importance to a writer like Tennyson who was treating it twenty years before. This is, I believe, acknowledged by the poet himself in the passage added to the Conclusion in the third edition, 1851, which I quoted at the end of my first chapter. Referring to the events of 1848—which as I showed earlier were seen at that time to spring from Saint-Simonian thinking—'the Tory member's elder son' derisively points a finger across the narrow seas to the coast of France, and utters with typically English impatience his condemnation of the French passion for acting upon their progressive ideas, even at the expense of social stability:

> 'The gravest citizen seems to lose his head,
> The king is scared, the soldier will not fight,

---

[1] *The Letters of John Stuart Mill*, ed. Hugh S. R. Elliot (1910), ii, p. 204.

and the New Feminism

> The little boys begin to shoot and stab . . .
> Revolts, republics, revolutions, most
> No graver than a schoolboys' barring out;
> Too comic for the solemn things they are,
> Too solemn for the comic touches in them,
> Like our wild Princess with as wise a dream
> As some of theirs—God bless the narrow seas!
> I wish they were a whole Atlantic broad.'

But his poet-companion is made to chide this complacency.

> 'Have patience,' I replied, 'ourselves are full
> Of social wrong; and maybe wildest dreams
> Are but the needful preludes of the truth . . .'

Tennyson, the author of 'Locksley Hall' and 'The Golden Year', poems of social visions similar to those of the Saint-Simonians, was teaching his public to see reform in the structure of both marriage and political institutions to be worth more than a careless dismissal out of a sense of content with peace and prosperity.

CHAPTER III

Robert Owen, Feminism and the
Mechanics' Institutions

DISCUSSIONS in the Reviews of the Saint-Simonians almost invariably mentioned Robert Owen,[1] and very frequently Fourier, whose supporters in France had sometimes been earlier influenced by Saint-Simonism. The claim to priority in certain of the similar principles they severally adopted is difficult to determine: there can be little doubt, indeed, that similar ideas, long germinating, had presented themselves to different minds more or less simultaneously. The fundamental ideas of association and the emancipation of workers and women are common to all three parties. A contributor to the *Monthly Magazine* of an article called 'Socialism in France', believed to be 'Shepherd' Smith, wrote:

> Owen has certainly the honour, if honour it be, of having first filled the columns of the daily papers with his doctrines, and disseminated over Europe the knowledge of his name. St. Simon first appeared as an author in 1801; but his views were not then fully developed: he directed his thoughts to scientific unity before he entered upon the career of political or industrial agitation . . . In 1814 he brought his scientific theory into politics, and in 1819 he published his celebrated parable, for which he was tried and acquitted, by jury, in 1820. The latter date is the epoch of St. Simon's notoriety. Owen was well known to all Europe three years

[1] Owen met the Saint-Simonian 'missionaries' in London in 1832. They were well aware that the ground had been prepared for them by his efforts, and those of the political economists (who at least centred attention upon the economic aspects of political doctrine). They wrote early in 1832: 'Today England has arrived at the eve of a revolution which resembles in no way the revolutions of the past: its people aspire to a new life. . . . The tendency to the political organisation of the worker is everywhere manifest because the industrial population has grown considerable.' See Richard K. Pankhurst, 'Saint-Simonism in England', *Twentieth Century*, cliii, no. 911 (January 1953), p. 48.

before this (1817). He bought the London press—spent several thousand pounds in a few weeks upon newspapers only—and so loaded the mail-coaches with the new social ideas, that the directors of the post-office entered a complaint against him to the Government. Amongst the crimes laid to his charge, was that of having, on one occasion, delayed the departure of the mail twenty minutes—this was in 1817. Fourier published his first work in 1808: but the work in which the science of association is reduced to a form and subjected to a severely critical and laborious analysis, is the *Association Domestique Agricole*, published in 1822. It is therefore impossible to determine to which of the trio the priority belongs, for each is prior in one sense, and posterior in another.

St. Simonism made a brilliant attempt to hatch the new social system in 1830, but ere two years had passed, the sect was politically extinct . . .[1]

Fourierism had its supporters in England, but of course the followers of Owen were much more influential and numerous, and branches of his association were formed throughout England. Lectures and public debates as well as newspapers (*The Crisis* and *The New Moral World*) served to spread their doctrines, and incidentally those of the Saint-Simonians. Robert Owen's indefatigable industry and the steady opposition of the Church did much to enhance the reputation of the movement among the free-thinking section of the community—the literate poor. It bent its energies towards bringing about national education, the abolition of property, community life and many other revolutionary projects which are sufficiently familiar. There can be no doubt that Tennyson must have been acquainted with the agitation of the supporters of Owen in view of his political interests and sympathies: he may well have disliked its anti-clericalism.[2]

What is of interest to the present study is the intense preoccupation the Owenists had with the position of women in society, and their strenuous propaganda to bring the question before the public under its widest aspect.

[1] Quoted in *The New Moral World*, vi, p. 609 (20 July 1839).

[2] There are numerous accounts of the life and thought of Owen, among which A. J. Booth's *Robert Owen* (1869) may be mentioned. See *Memoir*, ii, p. 339 for Hallam Tennyson's testimony for his father's 'great belief' in the Co-operative movements of the day, from the 'Rochdale pioneers' onwards.

Robert Owen, Feminism

It is well known how the simple suggestion of self-supporting 'communities' for agriculture and manufacture combined, originally intended as an alternative to Poor Relief, grew in his mind as a pattern for future society as a whole; he went so far as to recommend the immediate establishment of a voluntary community on these lines, and opened enrolment books at the principal booksellers, publicizing his views in letters to the newspapers, of which he purchased no less than forty thousand for free distribution. In 1825, at Orbiston, near Glasgow, the first attempt at a Community was made, though necessarily of a transitional type, and another was founded at Harmony, the Rappist settlement in Indiana, afterwards called New Harmony. This Owen himself founded and visited. At New Harmony Robert Owen may have assimilated a doctrine originally propounded by Frances Wright who had established at Nashoba a philanthropic settlement on Owenist lines, but this time for negroes.[1] This was that the legal form of marriage was tyrannous, because contrary to human nature. In April 1826 a couple were married at New Harmony by simple declaration. The *New Harmony Gazette* commented upon 'the absurdity of the present form of marriage, according to which the future husband and wife are compelled solemnly to promise to love each other during their whole lives, while at the same time they are conscious that their affections do not depend for one hour upon themselves'. In the same journal, Owen himself published an article which showed that he had decided to introduce this idea into his social philosophy; he added Marriage to Private Property and Religion in his list of

[1] The doctrine *may* have emanated from William Thompson, who probably originated much Owenist theory. Frances Wright later became Mme D'Arusmont; see *DNB*. She became a supporter of the women's suffrage movement in the U.S.A., and at one time corresponded with Mrs. Shelley upon reform in marriage. In Paris she became familiar with Saint-Simonian feminist doctrine; in London, she lectured for Owen. 'Fanny' Wright is thus a link between the Socialist and feminist movements of Owen in England, the Saint-Simonians in Paris and the similar, but much less significant movement in the U.S.A. That she should also have been associated with anti-slavery activities is quite consistent with her interest in marriage reform and the woman question, as I hope later remarks will show. See A. J. G. Perkins and Theresa Wolfson, *Frances Wright, Free Enquirer; the Study of a Temperament* (New York, 1939).

evil customs distressing society.[1] This was the beginning of a long campaign on the woman question conducted by both himself and his followers with great vigour over a number of years.

In 1828 Owen retired from the New Lanark Mills to devote himself entirely to advocating his system of reform. This was based upon principles which came to be enunciated in his *Book of the New Moral World*,[2] in which he boldly asserted that men were now destined to enter a new stage in their development. He maintained, moreover, that the transition could be painlessly accelerated if the rulers of Europe would recognise the truth about human nature as Owen saw it. This is that men are made what they are by their youthful experiences, and since they cannot be held responsible either for their existence or for the opinions they entertain, society must, in its own interest, take care that opinions are moulded by education. In the Introduction to Part I he remarks, concerning the life possible when these matters are understood:

The impurities of the present system, arising from human laws opposed to nature's laws, will be unknown. The immense mass of degradation of character, and of heart-rending suffering, experienced by both sexes, but especially by women, will be altogether prevented,—and the characters of all women will, by a superior yet natural training, be elevated to become lovely, good and intellectual. Of this state of purity and felicity, few of the present generation have been trained to form any correct or rational conception.[3]

At present, man arrogantly takes it upon himself to say to Nature,

I am more wise and holy than thou, and I will therefore oppose thy laws with all my might, and endeavour to frustrate thy weak and foolish decrees. I will force into union according to my notions, bodies and minds, contrary to thy laws, and compel the continuance of the union however thy laws may repel or loathe the connection. [Man has also] decreed that men and women, whose natural sympathies and affections unite them at one time, and repel each other at another, shall speak and act in opposition to

[1] Quoted by Booth, op. cit., pp. 121–2.
[2] In seven parts, 1836–44.
[3] *The Book of the New Moral World*, Part I (1836), p. xxv.

these unavoidable feelings; and thus he has produced hypocrisy, crime, and misery, beyond the powers of language to express . . . It is in reality, therefore, the greatest crime against nature to prevent organized beings from uniting with those objects or other organized beings, with which nature has created in them a desire to unite . . .

The objection to Christian marriage contained in these words is explicit; but it may be observed that nothing is said about possible alternatives. A similar vagueness is to be found in another and more lengthy treatment of the subject, published as *Lectures on the Marriages of the Priesthood of the Old Immoral World*,[1] the lectures in question having been delivered in 1835; it appears from the Preface to the work that Owen had lectured on similar lines in 1830 and published in 1833 the laws by which marriages should be regulated in the New State of Society (in his *Charter of the Rights of Humanity*). From these 'laws' we can easily see that Owen required, not the abolition of marriage altogether, as his *Lectures* seemed to imply and his opponents inferred, but the substitution of marriage without religious oaths, and a simple, cheap system of divorce at the wish of even one partner.[2] The *Lectures*, which are tediously repetitive, are decidedly anti-clerical in tone; and Owen met stiff opposition. Some querulous voices were raised even in his own ranks. But Owen was a man not easily abashed; he was seemingly possessed of religious faith in his own principles, and indeed the Radical System, in 1835, became the Radical Religion, with Owen as 'Our Social Father' on lines sadly reminiscent of Enfantin.

Clerical opposition was naturally forthcoming. The Rev. Mr. Bowes met on 27 May 1840 at Liverpool Mr. Lloyd Jones, a leading figure of the Socialist movement to discuss marriage 'as advocated by Robert Owen'.[3] Bowes endeavoured to prove that Socialism inculcated a doctrine not only adulterous but murderous. Jones in reply charged his opponent with a want

---

[1] The fourth edition, 1840, is the one I have consulted.

[2] This was made explicit in 1833 in a report of a lecture delivered by Owen. See *The Crisis*, 11 and 18 May 1833, ii, pp. 143, 145.

[3] See the Report reprinted from the *Liverpool Journal* as *Report of the Discussion on Marriage as advocated by Mr. Robert Owen between L. Jones and J. Bowes* (Liverpool, 1840).

of candour, and the argument went on in a spirit of some acrimony, the audience eventually awarding the palm to the Socialist, who received two-thirds of the votes. John Brindley, an inveterate enemy of the Socialists, who toured the country counter-lecturing in a rather uninhibited manner, published in 1840 a tract called *The Immoralities of Socialism, being an exposure of Mr. Owen's attack upon Marriage.* In it he made plentiful use of exclamation marks and damaging quotation, of which Owen had provided a plentiful garner. He concluded by quoting from another pamphlet, called *The Overthrow of Infidel Socialism* by Joseph Barker, in which numerous allegations of immorality were made against members of the association. But it is not to be supposed that there were not supporters for Owen's ideas. Mrs. Frances Morrison delivered a lecture on 2 September 1838 at Manchester, which she published under the title *The Influence of the Present Marriage System, upon the Character and Interests of Females contrasted with that of Robert Owen Esq.* It begins thus:

Poets have sung in praise of female beauty. Our reverend divines have extolled the virtuous chastity of the sex. The historian has dwelt with rapture upon deeds of female heroism. And even the stern moralist has refused to censure the little foibles of woman— choosing rather to condemn in silence, than to reprove at the expense of gallantry. But it remained for a philosopher of our own times (Robert Owen) to found a system, calculated to free the sex from social bondage, and to elevate the female to an equality with man. Hitherto, as we have lately shown, the rights of woman have been culpably and cruelly overlooked: so much so, that it has become even *fashionable* to scorn and neglect her. She has therefore, now but one alternative, amid the accumulating wrongs that press upon her, namely, to arouse herself at once from the lethargy in which she has so long been slumbering, and to point the attention of her fellow-sufferers to the only system which promises them protection, independence and happiness.

The lecture continues on Owenist lines, complaining of the foolish education of women, the heartless condemnation of large numbers of women to prostitution as a means of survival, the wickedness of a dual code of morality, the cruelty of the means of 'redemption' undertaken by the church; and recommends community, equality of the sexes and the abolition of the present laws of marriage.

But although good use was made of the spoken word in disseminating the doctrine of emancipation, Owen was not slow to realize the power of the press, as we have seen. It was in April 1832 that he had founded the penny newspaper *The Crisis*, which ran until 23 August 1834. It was associated with the Institution of the Industrious Classes in Gray's Inn Road (and its successor in Charlotte Street, Fitzroy Square) where great point was made of 'Social Festivals' to give variety to lectures. As was explained in *The Crisis*, these were meant to provide *rational* amusement, 'the diffusion of the most useful knowledge, and the promotion of better feelings among all classes'.[1] The Socialist movement always sought the closest connection with Mechanics' Institutions, themselves bent on useful instruction.

The Crisis, like *The New Moral World* which succeeded it, contained numerous articles on the social position of women. Robert Dale Owen, Robert's son, wrote on 29 December 1832[2] on the great interest being shown in France in the improved education of women and the poor, a matter hitherto (and still, in England) entirely neglected. 'Concordia' denounced the folly of making women playthings of men instead of rational companions.[3] Mrs. Anna Wheeler translated from a French journal a powerful demand for equality—'*Let us reject as a husband any man* who is not sufficiently generous to consent to share with us all the rights he himself enjoys.'[4] The Saint-Simonian *Tribune des Femmes* obliged by translating one of 'Concordia's' articles, a fact duly noted in *The Crisis*.[5] Another contributor sees women as slaves,[6] and 'Concordia' resumed the attack with the favourite nineteenth-century topic 'The influence of women'.[7] Occasionally articles from journals of a quite different complexion were reprinted with or without comment.

One of these received very special approbation. It was an article called 'Men and Women' which had appeared in *Tait's*

[1] i, p. 29.   [2] i, p. 171.   [3] ii, p. 159.
[4] ii, p. 182.   [5] iii, p. 232.   [6] ii, p. 212.
[7] iii, p. 204.

Edinburgh Magazine for March 1834.[1] It was initialled M.L.G., standing almost certainly for Mary Leman Grimstone, a feminist contributor of Owen's next paper, and a novelist both under her own name and under the *nom de guerre* 'Oscar'.[2] This article makes a number of striking points in support of a reformed education for women, arguing that if men are right in asserting that they are volatile, superficial and so on, then their need of a superior education is all the greater. Certain remarks in the article clearly indicate her Owenist sympathies; apparently feminist writers of such leanings took what opportunities they could to infiltrate into other periodicals. She is certainly to be given credit for boldly asserting what did not become a popular belief for some years:

> For those women whom early widowhood, or other causes, consign to celibacy, I see not why civil offices should not be open, especially chairs of science in colleges endowed for the education of their own sex. Why should moral philosophy come with less power from the lips of woman than of man? Why may she not fill a professorship of poetry as well as he? . . . There is a spirit now shouting from hill and valley, and making mockery of his [man's] mistakes. Kings are crouching, and thrones tottering at the sound. A worker of iron has become a worker of wonders. There is a halo of genius around the head of a mechanic, that has rarely consecrated the brow of a monarch. The secret of true power is being revealed: the secret of its proper application will attend it; and real strength and equal justice will soon stand upon the ground from which they will push pretension and hypocrisy.

In making a claim for employment for women, Mrs. Grimstone showed her awareness of the problem which in a few years was to alter the whole attitude of society to the woman question.

The Crisis had no need as a rule to reprint material from other periodicals on the feminist side of its programme. Its own correspondents could keep up a steady supply of copy on all aspects of feminism. 'Justitia', for example, rebuked the Saint-Simonians in London for having criticised Owen for not

[1] *Tait's Edinburgh Magazine*, N.S. i, p. 101. *The Crisis*, iii, p. 236.
[2] Further reference will be made to her later. She frequently contributed to the *Monthly Repository* on various, including feminist, topics under these initials; see Francis E. Mineka, *The Dissidence of Dissent: The Monthly Repository 1806–38* (Chapel Hill, 1944), p. 410.

making the emancipation of women a more central part of his doctrine, pointing out that it can only consist 'in equal education and in equal participation in the laws by which she . . . is to be guided'.[1] 'Philia', anticipating Oscar Wilde, insisted that perhaps it was men who needed a better education, and not women after all.[2] 'Concordia' kept up a regular fusilade upon the readers.[3] 'Vesta' derided the useless cultivation of memory in women's education.[4] Letters, articles, and quotations, all are pressed into the service of the agitation. Then, in August 1834, the paper was abruptly discontinued, with a promise from Owen that another would later take its place.

The explanation of this is that Owen had quarrelled with his editor, the Rev. James E. Smith. Smith was later to become well known as 'Shepherd' Smith, on account of his editorship of *The Shepherd*. He also edited the *Family Herald*. A few words here about the sources of his opinions will perhaps show the manner in which the feminist parties in France and England were, so to speak, cross-fertilized by each other's opinions. The followers of John Wroe,[5] who were for a time adherents of Joanna Southcott, but after 1831 became independent, believed in a female Messiah. Smith was a convert to this so-called 'Doctrine of the Woman'. On joining Owen's movement however, he adopted the brand of feminism Owen favoured, and, as we have seen, included articles in *The Crisis* translated from French journals, which reciprocated the service. One of these articles was supplied as already noted, by Mrs. Anna Wheeler.[6] Mrs. Wheeler had become acquainted with Smith through attending his public lectures in London; he called her 'a woman of great talent, quite a high-born aristocrat'.[7] She

[1] iii, p. 246.   [2] iii, p. 258.
[3] iv, pp. 31, 67, 75, for example.   [4] iv, p. 8.
[5] See the article on him in *DNB*.
[6] See also W. Anderson Smith: *'Shepherd' Smith the Universalist; the story of a mind* (1892), p. 102.
[7] ibid., p. 90. She was the mother of Rosina Wheeler, whom Edward Bulwer married against his mother's wishes in 1827. A good deal of information about Mrs. Wheeler is supplied by Michael Sadleir in *Bulwer and his Wife, a Panorama 1803–1836* (1931). She seems to have caused Bulwer to interest himself in Saint-Simonism and feminism during the very early years of his marriage. See p. 80. He contributed an article 'On the influence and education of women' to *The New Monthly Magazine*, xxxiv (1832), p. 227.

had been a member of a Saint-Simonian circle at Caen as early as 1818, and in addition to being a Socialist and in good relations with Bentham, Robert Owen, William Thompson and Charles Fourier, was an ardent propagandist for the emancipation of women.[1] It is not surprising that she should have introduced the Saint-Simonian emissaries in London to Smith, and initiated him into the doctrines of Fourier and Owen. So remarkable and first-hand an education into the various feminist causes of his day made it certain that on breaking with Owen in 1834 he would not remain silent on the woman question. Of his later doings I shall say something in Chapter V.

On Saturday, 1 November 1834, Owen issued the first number of *The New Moral World*, a paper similar to *The Crisis*, which continued without break, though with changes of format and place of publication, until 1841. A regular flow of articles on various aspects of women's supposed rights was kept up during the whole period of its existence, and many of these are of the greatest interest for the account they give of the conditions objected to and the suggestions for reforming them. Some consist simply of telling extracts, as in *The Crisis*; others appear under more *noms de guerre*, the most notable of which is 'Kate'.[2] Many of the contributions are rhetorical appeals to women to cast off the yoke, to associate, to awaken from sloth, and so on, and are often decorated with elegant extracts from the poets; but others are more prosaic but none the less effective attempts to dismiss the various misapprehensions under which society labours when considering the woman question.

For example, the question of what is the true capacity of woman was frequently discussed, and much conjecture was hazarded in the absence of any real knowledge.[3] The phrenologists were referred to for expert advice, which seems not to have been unanimous, and consequently itself a source of

[1] See Richard K. Pankhurst, 'Saint-Simonism in England', pp. 47–8.
[2] Later Mrs. Goodwyn Barmby; see G. J. Holyoake, *History of Co-operation in England* (1875/9), i, p. 379.
[3] J. S. Mill in *The Subjection of Women* emphasized the need for scientific inquiry into the subject. It was soon forthcoming, as will be seen from Viola Klein's study *The Feminine Character. History of an Ideology* (1946).

controversy.[1] (For example, a feminine faculty for 'adhesive-
ness' was observed by some phrenologists, but not by others
who took the view that if women were said to 'adhere' to
people, men could be equally justifiably charged with 'ad-
hesiveness' where money was concerned.) In *The Princess*,
Lady Psyche glances at the phrenologists:

> . . . some said their heads were less;
> Some men's were small, not they the least of men;
> For often fineness compensated size . . .

The indefatigable 'Kate' complained of 'Man's Legislation' in
a front-page article in the issue for 25 May 1839,[2] that it took
no account of expert opinion that the 'gift of mind is equally
bestowed' between the sexes. Feminist writers were in fact
always on the look-out for new scientific evidence on the mental capacity of women. Realization of this is of the greatest
importance for this study.

Another article on this theme was supplied by John Goodwyn Barmby, who was a frequent contributor. He expounded
a theory of the gradual ascendancy of 'woman-power' with the
evolution of society. In the progress of human life through the
epochs of patriarchalism, feudalism and the age of religion to
the present age of *political* civilization (note the language of
historical development here), the qualities of brute strength
associated with the male sex had given ground to gentler ones
normally possessed by women. This did not mean that women
nowadays had more influence, for demonstrably they had not.
'Woman-power' and 'man-power' are both possessed by individuals of either sex. It should be the aim of true Socialists to
bring the two components into a more satisfactory equilibrium
to form the 'man-woman'. Barmby exemplifies his novel terms
by citing Cromwell and Joan of Arc as examples of 'man-
power', Mrs. Hemans and William Cowper as specimens of
'woman-power', and Shelley and Mary Wollstonecraft as
special cases of 'woman-man-power'. The idea may seem fanci-
ful, but it was not uncommon. Tennyson seems to have had

---

[1] In general, phrenology and Owen's rationalism both tended to neces-
sitarianism, and there was little quarrel between them. See for example
i, pp. 180 ff.
[2] v, p. 481.

something of the sort in his mind when he wrote in *The Princess* that the sexual characters ought to converge:

> Yet in the long years liker must they grow;
> The man be more of woman, she of man;
> He gain in sweetness and in moral height,
> Nor lose the wrestling thews that throw the world;
> She mental breadth, nor fail in childward care,
> Nor lose the childlike in the larger mind.

I shall show later that Tennyson's attitude to the relation of the sexes in the final part of his poem was determined by his reading and reflection on the evidences which eventually led to the theory of evolution. Barmby's article strikingly exemplifies the way in which new ideas can have analogies in quite different departments of thought. His theory rests not upon any thinking about physical development but upon a belief in the progression of society through homogeneous epochs. I have already shown that this concept gave historical sanction to the Socialist and feminist doctrines of the Saint-Simonians. Later it was to re-emerge in the mature work of Auguste Comte. The second component of his theory, the increase of 'feminine' qualities in the social thinking of his age has obvious counterparts in the opinions of Enfantin, 'Shepherd' Smith and the Southcottians.

Another theme which greatly preoccupied the Socialists was the education of women, though we do not find anything very explicit. The positivist approach of the Owenists here uncovered abuses faster than means of remedying them. Mrs. Grimstone, quoted in *The New Moral World* for 21 February 1835,[1] under the title 'Female Education', saw the question still as a moral issue rather than as a practical problem, despite her earlier advocacy of female professors. She goes on to condemn as wickedness the keeping of woman so idle and ignorant that she is defenceless before a seducer's wiles and then holding her singly responsible for her degradation. This is no more than a means whereby men may indulge in wanton licence, and is thus indirectly responsible for widespread

---

[1] i, p. 132. The article first appeared in the *Monthly Repository*, N.S. ix (1835), pp. 106 f.

prostitution. The Socialists took great interest in the problem of prostitution and *The New Moral World* condemns the society which disregards the statistics of human misery at this time being compiled. In addition to the protests in the over-furnished manner of Mrs. Grimstone there were inserted elo-quent paragraphs giving figures of the estimated number of prostitutes in the respectable cities of England.[1]

Another article, signed W.W.P., and given great promi-nence, appeared in the paper on 12 January 1839, and a subse-quent issue. It was prefaced by a long quotation from Shelley's *The Revolt of Islam*: the paper was running a series of articles on Shelley at this time. This contribution was a general on-slaught on the *slavery* of women, arguing that the respect entertained for women is an index to the happiness of society in general.

On divorce, Milton was discovered to occupy a position con-genial to the Owenists; in fact the poets were carefully scanned for passages with which to decorate the fearful symmetry of the argument. At the head of one article by 'Kate', printed under the title 'Woman' in the issue for 4 March 1837,[2] there were inserted the following lines:

> In every land
> I saw, wherever light illumineth,
> Beauty and anguish walking hand in hand
> The downward slope of death.
>
> In every land I thought that, more or less,
> The stronger, sterner nature, overbore
> The softer, uncontroll'd by gentleness,
> And selfish evermore.
>
> ALFRED TENNYSON

These lines, taken a little inaccurately from 'A Dream of Fair Women' in the version which appeared in the *Poems* of 1833, show Tennyson joining the company of the poets who could be quoted by the Socialists in support of their feminist cru-

---

[1] See for example v, p. 159, where it is stated that there were in 1838 14,000 prostitutes under fifteen years of age in London alone.

[2] iii, p. 151.

sade.[1] The influences which led him to lament the fate of women the world over will be better understood when the feminism in the air at Cambridge has been discussed; for the moment it must suffice to say that his championship of the woman's cause was appreciated long before the appearance of *The Princess*.

Before leaving the Owenists' interest in feminism, I shall give some details of the workings of their organization, for these too are of particular relevance to *The Princess*. An important point of distinction between them and the Fourierists, for example, lay in the class to which appeal was made. The Fourierists, like the Saint-Simonians, addressed themselves to the middle class, and concentrated upon the problem of raising capital. The Owenists were much more interested in the working class. (In other important respects, the movements were similar, and the Owenists steadfastly avoided competing; they offered the hospitality of their columns to exponents of the Fourierist system, and printed a summary of Victor Considérant's *Social Destiny*.) Branches of the movement were set up wherever opportunity offered, though principally in the industrial centres. They numbered nearly ninety in 1840,[2] and, as mentioned earlier, were often associated with Mechanics' Institutions. A writer in the Tory *Coventry Standard* whose article was reprinted in *The New Moral World* for 19 May 1838,[3] commented upon these increasingly active institutions:

They have done more mischief in their day, as far as this country is concerned, than Voltaire and the whole tribe of Encyclopaedists did in theirs. They were established under a colour of disseminating information among the people,—an object worthy enough in itself, but in the hands of designing men, capable of being diverted into the most obnoxious channels of worse than useless knowledge . . . Their rise was rapid—and a single generation will witness their fall.

[1] See Newman I. White, 'Literature and the law of libel: Shelley and the radicals of 1840–2', *S.P.* xxii (1925), p. 34 and 'Shelley and the active radicals of the early nineteenth century', *South Atlantic Quarterly*, xxix (1930), p. 248.

[2] See 'Progress of Social Reform' in the index to vol. viii of *The New Moral World*.

[3] iv, p. 239. The article was entitled 'Beware of Mechanics' Institutions'.

They excluded religion and adopted Deism: for their morals, Owen has picked them up, and given them barbarism in exchange (*The New Moral World* is a very faithful offshoot of Mechanics' Institutions) . . .

At Manchester, Birmingham and other large towns, the Mechanics' Institutions have been almost entirely neglected for the *New Moral World*, or 'Social Institutions'.

The writer then gave an account of the activities carried on at the Social Institutions, in the course of which he observed that 'The evils of marriage are among the favourite topics: the women are told that they live in slavish dependence upon the men: the men are, in their turn, flattered that they are the producers of all wealth . . .'

On 5 June 1839, a new Social Institution was opened in Chelsea, and Owen himself gave an address. The report of the occasion ends thus:

> It is but right also to add, that Mr. Hetherington, immediately on being made acquainted with our wish to conjoin, with the usual objects of a Social Institution, those of a Mechanics' Institute, expressed his intention to make us a present of books for our library . . .[1]

The Owenist movement derived great strength from this large organization throughout the country. Not only could new members be recruited constantly among work-people, but they could be converted to Socialist doctrines, including Owenist teaching upon the new social role of women, by the team of energetic lecturers who moved from one lecture-hall to another. The newspaper was not, consequently, merely a means of delivering the doctrine; it was a channel of communication between the Branches, who reported their more successful doings for the benefit of others. As the Branches were ostensibly *Social* institutions, it is not surprising to find that one of the most common topics of the Branch Reports was the Social Festival. These Festivals were sometimes held indoors, but often in country surroundings. The Branch members could not go far in the single day of public holiday they could enjoy, and often they sought permission to disport

---

[1] *The New Moral World*, v, p. 555.

themselves in a neighbouring park, normally the secluded preserve of its aristocratic owner. (It will be remembered that the Festivals were not only intended to provide rational amusement, 'the diffusion of the most useful knowledge', but also to further 'the promotion of better feelings among all classes'.) They seem to have spent their day partly in revel, partly in watching demonstrations combining amusement with instruction; the pattern of the Festivals was quite uniform. The Branch Reports give a most interesting picture of the goings-on all over the country. Here is a rather long one from *The New Moral World* for 8 June 1839:[1]

The Social friends of Salford and Manchester, had, for a long time, anticipated the pleasures of having a rural fête in Whitsun week: and Friday the 24th, was the appointed day. Although the preceding part of the week had been cold and lowering, yet the day fixed upon turned out a most favourable one. Early in the morning, our friends were all on the *qui vive*, and at six o'clock many were on the ground waiting for our country brethren, who by seven o'clock, came in great numbers, after which they proceeded to the boats. One large boat was filled with the children of the school, with their teachers and the officers of the association; and by eight o'clock three or four boats were loaded with our friends. It was a complete bustle at the quay: there were crowds waiting to witness our embarking. We had a pleasant passage, and at our landing, we formed into a procession with our flowing banners and flags. After entering the park, our friends distributed themselves to partake of their refreshments. A broad even spot in front of the mansion was chosen whereon to commence our festivities. The trumpet was sounded, and our friends collected around our standard, which was a splendid green flag, near which were placed the musicians. There could not be less than one thousand persons then assembled. After forming a large circle, we commenced by singing the first festival song, 'O may this feast increase the union of the heart', which was sung with high spirit and delight. A short address was then given, and immediately afterwards the dancing began, and hundreds mingled in the mazes of the whirling dance, with such manifestations of innocent joyousness, as might have thawed the heart of the coldest misanthrope. At the termination of the dance, the friends distributed themselves among the sylvan scenes around, and commenced a variety of rural and cheerful games,

[1] ibid., p. 524. The park in question was Dunham Park.

whilst others threaded their way among the trees, to view the varied beauties of the park, which, in many of its aspects, bears a great similarity to Kensington Gardens, the late residence of our youthful Queen. Again the trumpet sounded, our friends collected, and other dances were performed. The crowd increased and on forming the ring, there were upwards of 1,500 persons witnessing and enjoying our pastimes; and, in fact, our party was the great attraction of the park. We had the steward of his lordship's domains on horseback overlooking us. He paid great attention to what was going on, and passed a high encomium on the dancing of our friends. He came several times to see us, and near the close, one of our most respectable friends went to him and asked his opinion of our festivities. He expressed himself highly satisfied and pleased at them, and of our good conduct during the day. It is by this manner of proceeding that we express our gratitude to his lordship, the Earl of Stamford and Warrington, for his kindness in continuing open the park for the enjoyment of the surrounding population, and more particularly of Manchester. Friends were present from all the surrounding branches, from Hyde, Mottram, Ashton, Stockport, Oldham and other neighbouring towns, in great numbers. Leeds, Huddersfield, Rochdale, Blackburn and Macclesfield furnished us with many visitors . . . We left the park about four o'clock, and proceeded homeward, where we arrived soon after seven. We then went to the hall which was prepared for our reception, and here we congregated to upwards of 800 persons. Our friends forgot the previous exertions of the day, they felt fresh vigour, and entered into the various amusements with high spirits and delight. Mr. Charles Junius Haslam had prepared a quantity of laughing gas, which was partly used in the park, and the remainder at night, which gave us some exhibitions, to the great pleasure of our young folks. The festivities terminated at twelve o'clock, and our friends returned home well-satisfied with their whole day's amusements. The night was beautiful and calm, and the bright shining moon lit the paths of many of our dear branch friends, who had to return home at the end of the holiday ten or twelve miles, wearied yet delighted, and anticipating the return of similar enjoyments next Whitsuntide.

I think it will be agreed that to unprejudiced eyes these innocent revels, earnestly designed to combine a joyous romp with simple instruction in a scientific experiment, can hardly be regarded as socially disruptive, as the *Coventry Standard* would have had us believe. The organizers were bent upon providing a small dole of pleasure to a class which we would nowadays think under-privileged. They were respectful to their social superiors, but happy in their own sorts of diversion. Perhaps the instruction given in their Institutions was less well-adapted to bring the classes together, though even there they taught the truth as they saw it. To show that this sort of large-scale *fête champêtre* went on all over the country, I give another report, but this time from a provincial newspaper not of Owenist allegiance, of a Social Festival held by an Institution in the south of England. In took place on 6 July 1842 in the park of a house near Maidstone, and was reported in the *Maidstone and Kentish Advertiser* for 12 July:[1]

MAIDSTONE MECHANICS' INSTITUTION

On Wednesday last the members of the above institution held their fourth annual festival, in the Park of E. L. Lushington, Esq., which had been most kindly granted for that purpose by the kind hearted owner. The company began to enter the grounds at 2 o'clock through a gate near Mr. Lushington's house, leading into the park nearest the Rochester Road. Dancing was soon commenced under the row of trees which formed the avenue leading to the old house. Two bands were engaged, one for quadrille, and one for country dancing. Cricketing, trap bat and ball, and various games were played in different parts of the ground, a cannon was occasionally fired off, ignited by a spark from an Electrical Machine at a distance of about 20 yards; at another part of the grounds a model of a steam engine was at work, turning a circular saw with great rapidity, and the model of a steam boat plying round a light house, a table spread with philosophical instruments, consisting of telescopes, microscopes, etc. etc., formed a very interesting source of amusement.

At 5 o'clock 800 persons sat down to tea, in a capacious booth erected for the occasion, and between 6 and 7 o'clock a large fire balloon ascended. The amusements were kept up without intermission, until half-past 8, when the bell was rung for the company to assemble on the summit of the hill in front of the house, the thanks of the meeting were then moved to E. L. Lushington, Esq.,

[1] I am grateful to the Borough Librarian of Maidstone for kindly procuring this report for me.

for his kindness in granting the use of the park, which was unani-
mously agreed to with great cheering, Mr. Lushington returned
thanks in an appropriate speech, expressing himself highly delighted with the interesting manner in which the company had
amused themselves, and the decorum which had prevailed throughout the day. The numerous assemblage then dispersed in the most
orderly manner.

This particular Festival has literary as well as social interest.
Edmund Lushington was a few months later to marry Tennyson's sister Cecilia. Moreover, Tennyson and his family were
also living at Boxley, near Maidstone, quite close to Lushington's house and park; on the day the Mechanics' Institution
held its festival there, the poet was also present.[1] When, five
years later, *The Princess* was published, the Prologue described
the incident very faithfully, as the following lines will show:

> Strange was the sight to me;
> For all the sloping pasture murmur'd, sown
> With happy faces and with holiday.
> There moved the multitude, a thousand heads;
> The patient leaders of their Institute
> Taught them with facts. One rear'd a font of stone
> And drew, from butts of water on the slope,
> The fountain of the moment, playing, now
> A twisted snake, and now a rain of pearls,
> Or steep-up spout whereon the gilded ball
> Danced like a wisp; and somewhat lower down
> A man with knobs and wires and vials fired
> A cannon; Echo answer'd in her sleep
> From hollow fields; and here were telescopes
> For azure views; and there a group of girls
> In circle waited, whom the electric shock
> Dislink'd with shrieks and laughter; round the lake
> A little clock-work steamer paddling plied
> And shook the lilies; perch'd about the knolls
> A dozen angry models jetted steam;
> A petty railway ran; a fire-balloon
> Rose gem-like up before the dusky groves
> And dropt a fairy parachute and past;
> And there thro' twenty posts of telegraph

[1] *Memoir*, i, p. 203.

They flash'd a saucy message to and fro
Between the mimic stations; so that sport
With science hand in hand went. Otherwhere
Pure sport; a herd of boys with clamour bowl'd
And stump'd the wicket; babies roll'd about
Like tumbled fruit in grass; and men and maids
Arranged a country dance, and flew thro' light
And shadow, while the twangling violin
Struck up with Soldier-laddie, and overhead
The broad ambrosial aisles of lofty lime
Made noise with bees and breeze from end to end.

Strange was the sight and smacking of the time;
And long we gazed . . .

The passage makes it clear that what struck Tennyson in
the scene was its strangeness; and it was doubtless in part on
that account that he included it in the Prologue. That part
of the poem is permeated with a curious, dreamlike air, as if
time and place were uncertain. The ostensible narrator of the
events at Vivian Place—for so the house and park where the
festival is held are called in the poem—is the poet-member of
the party of undergraduates on their visit. He falls under the
spell cast by his imagination dwelling upon what he reads in
an old chronicle, and the sight of strange objects collected by
the Vivian family:

Carved stones of the Abbey-ruin in the park,
Huge Ammonites, and the first bones of Time;
And on the tables every clime and age
Jumbled together; celts and calumets,
Claymore and snow-shoe, toys in lava, fans
Of sandal, amber, ancient rosaries,
Laborious orient ivory sphere in sphere,
The cursed Malayan crease, and battle-clubs
From the isles of palm; and higher on the walls,
Betwixt the monstrous horns of elk and deer,
His own forefathers' arms and armour hung.

This detritus of oddly-disparate cultures blends in his mind
with the sight of his surroundings, a 'Grecian' house 'set with
busts' and the ruins of an old abbey—a fit setting for the

63

recollections of the old, unhappy far-off things described in the chronicle he has been reading. The present moment and place become dim and insubstantial—the experiments and revels (strange medley!) going on among the crowds in the park assume an air almost of fantasy. Indeed, the park, though a modern 'fair field full of folk', a substantial nineteenth-century scene to prosaic eyes, is to the poet sounding with the voices of past and future.

In the Prologue to *The Princess*, Tennyson is seeking at one level to portray typical occurrences in modern life. (We recall his remark to de Vere in 1845 that 'a poem should reflect the time and place', and also his sensitiveness to the criticism that he was 'a tongue-tied poet in the feverous days'.) But over and above this he is concerned to follow the counsel he gave Emily Sellwood in 1839—'Annihilate within yourself these two dreams of Space and Time'.[1] Contemporary events are not to be viewed solely in their temporal context; they can be seen to contain within themselves hints and suggestions of wider import, and these the poet can elucidate by placing them in quite different settings, settings of a timeless kind like those to be found in romance and folk-tale. Only when disso-ciated from 'modernity' can the true significance of modern movements be grasped clearly. This, I think, partly explains why Tennyson treats the modern feminist movement as a 'fairy tale' in *The Princess*. The function of the Prologue is to conduct us imperceptibly to this view-point. What is described is to be thought of in different ways at one and the same time. The Festival of the Mechanics' Institution at the 'literal' level is a description of an actual Festival—but as we have seen, it was also typical. The diversions of the crowd are also intended to stand in contrast with the politer amusements of the leisured party picnicking among the Abbey ruins. More-over, they add to the air of strangeness I have mentioned. But all these good reasons for having it in the Prologue are not really sufficient, because the reader is conscious that it must have something to do with the theme of the whole poem, which after all is concerned with the effect upon sexual rela-tionships of granting women a new education for a different

[1] *Memoir*, i, p. 171.

role in life. Ida believes that she must do without marriage to achieve her ends; the Prince her suitor believes that in this, and only in this, she is mistaken. Whether the marriage-relationship could survive the fulfilment of women's aspirations is the real point at issue.

It was in this question, as I have shown, that the Owenists were deeply interested, Owen himself being ambiguous enough in what he wrote upon it to be thought to regard conventional marriage as an evil, to be cut out of the social body. We have seen that the teaching in the Mechanics' Institutions on the subject of reform in marriage was common knowledge. It is this circumstance, I suggest, which makes the description of a Festival of a Mechanics' Institution so appropriate to a scene also containing a party of young men and women discussing the legitimacy of women's aspirations. Women and the working-class were by many thought to be comparable in the matter of subalternity. Both the 'poet-speaker' and Lilia's aunt Elizabeth have something to say upon the need to improve the lot of the great mass of the people. The 'poet-speaker' asked

> Why should not these great sirs
> Give up their parks some dozen times a year
> To let the people breathe?

and Elizabeth

> Took this fair day for text, and from it preach'd
> An universal culture for the crowd,
> And all things great.

We might well believe that both shared something of Leonard's vision of 'the golden year',

> When wealth no more shall rest in mounded heaps,
> But smit with freer light shall slowly melt
> In many streams to fatten lower lands,
> And light shall spread, and man be liker man . . .

They both believe the 'crowd' to be capable of, as well as deserving, a richer life. But the youthful Lilia, whose equally idealistic vision of women's place in society gave occasion for the romantic tale, is less interested in the question of what are

F 65

the legitimate dues of the labouring classes; for her, the rights of women also depend upon first deciding what women are really capable of:

> ... she fixt
> A showery glance upon her aunt, and said,
> 'You—tell us what we are'—who might have told,
> For she was cramm'd with theories out of books.

I have tried to show in this chapter that her aunt could have formed her theories on the rights and capabilities of both women *and* the 'crowd' from writings which treated these questions as one, and that among the most important of them, a fact perhaps implied in the introduction of the Festival episode, were the publications of the devoted supporters of Robert Owen.

CHAPTER IV

Feminism at Cambridge

WE have seen how, with studied inconsequence, Tennyson carefully inserted into the Prologue and Conclusion of *The Princess* incidents directing the minds of contemporary readers towards the manifestations of social change, both in England in the shape of an invasion of a gentlemanly park by the workers, and in France by way of the events of 1848. The early signs of the social changes to come were probably discussed by the Apostles at Cambridge, and consequently it would not be impossible, on the face of it, that feminism was touched upon too. To a society of friends deliberating, as Tennyson tells us, upon 'labour and the changing mart' and deeply concerned with the fascinating doctrines of the Saint-Simonians, the closely-connected problem of the place women should occupy in society would, one imagines, hardly fail to occur. We cannot but notice that it was in his Cambridge days that Tennyson showed his concern with the life of women—in 'A Dream of Fair Women', a poem quoted with satisfaction by more than one feminist writer. Of course, it may well be that the poet was, like the prince in *The Princess*, temperamentally disposed to sympathy with the women's cause. But among the circle of his friends at Cambridge there were some who had feminist leanings for other reasons. It is difficult, naturally, to surmise what could have been discussed between them save from reconstructions from the small evidence available. But it seems clear that feminism did interest some undergraduates of Tennyson's day. In two circles at least we may safely infer that it was discussed—among the young followers of the elder Mill, and among the friends of Arthur Hallam, of whose direct influence upon the poet there can be no doubt. In addition it is probable that those who opposed Utilitarianism had something to say upon the subject.

Feminism at Cambridge

The Utilitarians in England were little occupied with social reforms of the sort which have been discussed hitherto, but the question of parliamentary representation inevitably brought them up against the awkward problem of deciding what rights women should have in elections. A pronouncement was necessary and was faithfully provided by James Mill in his 'Essay on Government', contributed in 1819 to the *Encyclopaedia Britannica* and reprinted for free distribution in 1820. In this article, Mill wrote:

> One thing is pretty clear, that all those individuals whose interests are indisputably included in those of other individuals, may be struck off from political rights without inconvenience. In this light may be viewed all children up to a certain age, whose interests are involved in those of their parents. In this light also, women may be regarded, the interest of almost all of whom is involved either in that of their fathers, or in that of their husbands.

This classification of women with children in regard to political rights was accepted by the great majority of people long after the passing of the Reform Act in 1832, despite a growing volume of protest at the absurdity of it. Lilia in *The Princess* is resentful that men should 'love to keep us children'; and Ida maintained that women

> had but been, she thought,
> As children; they must lose the child, assume
> The woman . . .

The young John Stuart Mill was not able to share his father's view on this question. We have already seen that in later years he attributed considerable influence to the Saint-Simonians in forming opinion on the feminist question; but 'early in 1825', four years before meeting Gustave d'Eichtal in 1829, when the Saint-Simonians had in any event hardly begun their meteoric flight, he had taken part in discussions with a group of Owenists at their meeting-place in Chancery Lane. Although at this time the Owenists' militant feminism had not appeared,[1] there can be little doubt that the political position of women at least was discussed. The reason for saying this is

[1] Owen was in this very year resolving to add it to his programme of social reform.

that speaking on the Owenist side was one whom **J. S.** Mill called 'a very estimable man', a Mr. William Thompson of Cork,[1] who had written a book on the subject which appeared in that very year.[2] It was called *Appeal of one half the Human Race, Women, against the pretensions of the other half, Men, to keep them in political, and thence in civil and domestic slavery,* and was usually known as *The Appeal of Women.* In this book, Thompson, a Socialist who had published the previous year a work called *The Distribution of Wealth,*[3] made a direct reply to the elder Mill's paragraph on women's suffrage; and it is a reply so admirably logical that if Thompson could speak as he wrote, one can easily understand why J. S. Mill thought highly of him. I shall not rehearse here Thompson's arguments; suffice it to say that they demonstrate first an error of fact and then a logical fallacy: the former is corrected by pointing out that in feminist matters women can in no sense be represented by their menfolk, who are their potential opponents: and that it does not follow that women should not be represented *at all* when the interest of only '*almost* all' (James Mill's own words) is involved in that of their husbands or fathers. What is of great interest to us is that the book is dedicated to the same Mrs. Anna Wheeler who introduced 'Shepherd' Smith to the Saint-Simonians in London, and to the theories of Owen and Fourier, and who was an ardent Socialist. Thompson says he was inspired to write the book by her, and was supplied by her with many of its arguments. Through her we may see a link between the social theories discussed in previous chapters on the one hand, and Utilitarianism on the other. The ideological convergence indirectly effected by Mrs. Wheeler between these highly inimical systems on the question of women's rights shows how inevitable some reform was in the years to follow.

Mill wrote in his *Autobiography* of a period near 1824 that

> there was by no means complete unanimity among any portion of us [Utilitarians], nor had any of us adopted implicitly all my father's opinions. For example, although his Essay on Government

---

[1] *Autobiography*, ed. Helen Taylor (1873), p. 125.

[2] The British Museum copy is signed by Thompson and dated 22 April 1825.

[3] See Leslie Stephen, *The English Utilitarians* (1900), ii, pp. 260–4.

was probably regarded by all of us as a masterpiece of political wisdom, our adhesion by no means extended to the paragraph in it, in which he maintains that women may consistently with good government, be excluded from the suffrage, because their interest is the same with that of men. From this doctrine, I, and all those who formed my chosen associates, most positively dissented. It is due to my father to say that he denied having intended to affirm that women *should* be excluded, any more than men under the age of forty, concerning whom he maintained, in the very next paragraph, the very same thesis . . . But I thought then, as I have always thought since, that the opinion which he acknowledged, no less than that which he disclaimed, is as great an error as any of those against which the Essay was directed: that the interest of women is included in that of men exactly as much and no more, as the interest of subjects is included in that of kings: and that every reason which exists for giving the suffrage to anybody, demands that it should not be withheld from women. This was also the opinion of the younger proselytes; and it is pleasant to be able to say that Mr. Bentham, on this important point, was wholly on our side.[1]

Support for female suffrage would have been one of the few grounds of concurrence between the Owenist speakers and Mill and his friends, for Mill does not appear to have been impressed by Socialist views until he met the Saint-Simonian variety. The circumstance that he was prepared for feminism before he was willing to accept the 'new social world', later to become an automatic corollary in France, is an interesting indication of English thought in general. For the present study it has a more particular interest. As may be imagined, Utilitarian views were freely canvassed at Cambridge by some undergraduates. Among these was Charles Buller, who entered Trinity College, Cambridge in 1824.[2] We may learn something of his activity from the following remarks of Mill:

It was my father's opinions which gave the distinguishing character to the Benthamic or utilitarian propagandism of that time. They fell singly, scattered from him in many directions, but they flowed from him in a continued stream principally in three channels.

[1] *Autobiography*, p. 104.
[2] W. W. Rouse Ball and J. A. Venn, *Admissions to Trinity College, Cambridge* (1911), iv, p. 243.

Feminism at Cambridge

One was through me . . . A second was through some of the Cambridge contemporaries of Charles Austin . . . The third channel was that of a younger generation of Cambridge undergraduates, contemporary not with Austin, but with Eyton Tooke, who were drawn to that estimable person by affinity of opinions, and introduced by him to my father; the most notable of these was Charles Buller . . .[1]

Buller was a frequent speaker at Union debates on political subjects;[2] but he took his degree in 1828, and in the winter of 1829, while studying law, attended early-morning discussions on Metaphysics and Mental Philosophy at the house of George Grote in company with Mill, J. A. Roebuck, Eyton Tooke and others.[3] The consequence is that Tennyson could have only known him for a short time—from the time he first entered Cambridge in October 1827[4] until Buller went down next year. That he did know him we have on the authority of Hallam's *Memoir*.[5] From this we may think it possible that Tennyson heard Buller espouse the cause of female suffrage at Cambridge, for if he were making converts as Mill says he was, it is most unlikely that he would have had nothing to say on the one point on which he demurred from the elder Mill's teaching. Moreover, he seems not to have been alone in adding feminism to his radicalism. Mrs. Brookfield wrote of Henry Lushington (to whom *The Princess* was dedicated) that 'He had in politics a leaning towards Liberal, even Radical, opinions; he enthusiastically welcomed the accomplishment of Catholic Emancipation; he applauded the French Revolution of 1830; and he

---

[1] *Autobiography*, p. 102.
[2] See *The Life, Letters and Literary Remains of Edward Bulwer, Lord Lytton*, by his Son (1883), i, p. 232. Arthur Hallam wrote from Trinity College on 8 November 1828, shortly after going up to Cambridge, that Utilitarianism was the 'ascendant politics' of the Cambridge Union, and that the influence of the Union was very much felt, even among reading men who took no part in its doings. The letter was published by Shannon, p. 22.
[3] Mrs. [Harriet] Grote, *The Personal Life of George Grote* (1873), p. 59.
[4] The arguments for this date are given by W. D. Paden, *Tennyson in Egypt*, pp. 112 f.
[5] i, p. 36. Tennyson may have met Buller after he left Cambridge. In the summer of 1834, there was a meeting of former Apostles at Spencer House—C. H. E. and F. M. Brookfield, *Mrs. Brookfield and her circle* (1906), p. 11.

approved of the Reform Bill and voted for the grant to Maynooth'. For saying this she had the authority of a memoir written by Lushington's best friend, G. S. Venables. She herself adds, however: 'In his political leanings, the opinions of all the "Apostles" stand revealed—they seem to have been at one over all these questions—though some of them in addition espoused the vexed cause of Women's Suffrage.'[1] What authority Mrs. Brookfield had for saying this is uncertain. Her facts are sometimes demonstrably wrong. We have seen that the Apostles were not at one over these questions—Trench, for example, opposed the Reform Bill. But the interest in women's suffrage she mentions may well have been shown by Buller and friends of like mind, as we have seen already to be probable; and it seems unlikely that she would have made special mention of this circumstance without evidence, which she had unusual opportunities for obtaining.

Mrs. Brookfield elsewhere[2] says that F. D. Maurice was joined at Cambridge by Arthur Hallam, Tennyson and Milnes, though this she herself shows to be untrue by quoting Hallam's well-known recommendation to Gladstone at Oxford that he should seek out Maurice, whom he declares he had never met personally.[3] One might have deduced a great deal from Tennyson's having met at Cambridge the man who was to do so much towards founding the first women's college in England only a year after the publication of *The Princess*; but they clearly did not meet. Nevertheless, although Maurice had left Cambridge before Tennyson could have met him, his influence lingered on, not a little by virtue of his creation of the spirit, if not the form, of the society of the Apostles. It is accordingly not without interest that Maurice was deeply concerned, while at Cambridge, with the education of women.

Maurice's interest in it had been aroused by his sister, and took a form which may have brought it to the notice of those friends (like J. M. Kemble) who also later knew Tennyson at Cambridge. Together with Charles Shapland Whitmore he

[1] Frances M. Brookfield, *The Cambridge 'Apostles'* (1906), p. 196. The first of the sentences quoted is very closely based upon one occurring on p. xxi of Venables's Memoir prefaced to *The Italian War 1848-9* by Henry Lushington, published (posthumously) in 1859.

[2] ibid., p. 203.   [3] ibid., p. 212.

Feminism at Cambridge

edited *The Metropolitan Quarterly Magazine*, which first appeared in November 1825: in it he wrote an article called 'Female Education'.[1] This article was ostensibly supplementary to an earlier one on the question of the best mode of educating the middle and upper classes, in which a position extremely hostile to the *Westminster Review*'s is taken. At this date discussions on education were numerous: the older Universities were being attacked, a controversy was arising over the founding of a University in London: the *Westminster Review* was advocating the Chrestomathic principles of Jeremy Bentham.[2] It was this which Maurice in the *Metropolitan Quarterly Magazine* looked upon with abhorrence, for he saw the attempt to initiate the young into a large number of practically useful studies at the expense of solid effort upon the classics as contributing to that 'age of folly' described in the journal's first number. The education of women was of little public concern; but Maurice points out that women, having no professional avocations to prepare for, should be able to learn to contribute to that general culture of society which the journal had earlier suggested was the true purpose of education. He then proceeds to anatomize the rules of women's education in order to show how utterly unrelated it is to the end. The article is perhaps the most slashing attack on the 'young ladies' establishment' that appeared in the first half of the century.

In fairness to the *Westminster Review*, it must be said that Maurice could not charge it in 1825 with neglect of the cause of women, for J. S. Mill went further than merely supporting female suffrage in opposition to what his father had written. In the second number,[3] he attacked the *Edinburgh Review* for supporting the code of dual morality and the subalternity of

[1] ii, p. 265. Maurice's authorship is established in *The Life of Frederick Denison Maurice*, ed. Frederick Maurice (3rd edn. 1884), i, p. 66.
[2] Bentham's *Chrestomathia* tabulated a formidable list of studies through which the pupil progressed in ordered stages; its object was strictly utilitarian.
[3] i, p. 525 (April 1824). He quotes the *Edinburgh Review* as saying 'Shakespeare has expressed the very perfection of the female character, existing only for others, and leaning for support on the strength of its affections'. He adds: 'A character which has nothing to lean upon but the strength of its affections must be a helpless character indeed.'

women. He suggested that it was because men derived satisfaction from the sense of power afforded by the dependence of women upon them that they would not agree to the education of women on male lines. The young Benthamites at Cambridge would have found this doctrine, put out in their own new journal, rather novel but entirely in keeping with Utilitarian principles: women were being denied legitimate happiness.

We can see, therefore, that from Benthamites like Buller and anti-Benthamites like Maurice, feminist views were introduced into Cambridge thinking in the years immediately preceding and during Tennyson's residence. The society of the Apostles ensured that new doctrines, political and religious, circulated quickly. It was a free association of different minds which was of the greatest value to all its members, who recognized the fact by going on meeting long after they had gone down from Cambridge. So close was the association that one can feel reasonably sure that the views of one member could easily come to influence those of another.[1] Those I have hitherto discussed in this chapter were the objective conclusions of minds particularly sensitive to the feminist problem because they had a thorough grasp of fresh educational or political principles. Arthur Hallam, who came to be Tennyson's closest friend, thought on different lines, yet his feminism was equally ardent.

It is not difficult to see how easily Tennyson could have come to share one of Hallam's most cherished beliefs, when that belief occupies so large a place in the poems he wrote and intended to publish jointly with Tennyson. It was a sympathetic reading of Plato and Dante which gave this principle peculiar force in Hallam's mind, though there can be little doubt that he owed a good deal to Shelley's splendid account in *A Defence of Poetry* of the way in which the 'poetry of sexual love' manifested itself in the work of Petrarch and Dante. It also appears in his prose writings, and although the

---

[1] See *Memoir*, i, p. 43. The friends met almost daily in one another's rooms. A rather striking example of this sort of influence is to be seen in Charles Merivale's setting himself to learn Anglo-Saxon under J. M. Kemble's instruction. See *Autobiography and Letters of Charles Merivale, Dean of Ely*, ed. Judith Anne Merivale (Oxford, privately printed, 1898), p. 161.

majority of these were undertaken after the surviving verse was completed, I wish to consider them first because they provide explicit statements of the philosophical principles to which he was sympathetic. These were certainly in his mind some time before he expressed them, and may therefore be used for a commentary on the earlier poems. I should perhaps add that although Tennyson went down from Cambridge before most of the prose papers were written, Hallam sent them to him when they were not able to meet.[1]

The first we may consider is an 'Essay on the Philosophical Writings of Cicero', which was awarded a Trinity College prize in 1831 and was printed in pamphlet form early in 1832.[2] It is an elegantly-written and cool assessment of Cicero's philosophy to which I am unable to do justice here, for my purpose is to single out what I might call the cardinal idea in his work. In Cicero's philosophical writings he finds much to admire, but cannot refrain from viewing his ethical system as seriously defective:

> His praises of friendship, as one of the duties as well as ornaments of life, never seem to have suggested to his thoughts any resemblance of that solemn idea which alone solves the enigma of our feelings, and while it supplies a meaning to conscience, explains the destination of man. That he had read Plato with delight, we see abundant tokens, and his expressions of admiration and gratitude to that great man remain as indications of a noble temper; but that he had read him with right discernment can hardly be supposed, since he prefers the sanctions of morality provided by the latter Grecian schools to the sublime principle of love as taught by the founder of the Academy . . .[3]

It was Plato's supreme aim to communicate to our nature the highest kind of love, the love of a worthy object; upon this aim, Hallam dilates in a passage which is of special interest for this study:

> Hence his constant presentation of morality under the aspect of beauty, a practice favoured by the language of his country, where from an early period the same το καλόν had comprehended them

[1] *Memoir*, i, p. 88.
[2] Motter, p. 142, where all the relevant authorities are cited.
[3] ibid., p. 157.

both. Hence that frequent commendation of a more lively sentiment than has existed in other times between man and man, the
misunderstanding of which has repelled several from the deep
tenderness and splendid imaginations of the Phaedrus and the
Symposium, but which was evidently resorted to by Plato, *on
account of the social prejudices which at that time depressed woman
below her natural station*, and which, even had the philosopher himself entirely surmounted them, would have rendered it perhaps impossible to persuade an Athenian audience that a female mind,
especially if restrained within the limits of chastity and modest
obedience, could ever possess attractions at all worthy to fix the
regard, much less exhaust the capacities of this highest and purest
manly love.

There was also another reason. The soul of man was considered
the best object of ἔρως, because it partook most of the presumed
nature of Divinity.

To this Hallam added a note:

When a general admiration for Plato revived with the revival of
arts and learning, the difference of social manners, which had been
the gradual effect of Christianity, led men naturally to fix the
reverential and ideal affection on the female character. The expressions of Petrarch and Dante have been accused as frigid and un-
natural, because they flow from a state of feeling which belonged to
very peculiar circumstances of knowledge and social position, and
which are not easily comprehended by us who live at a different
period.[1]

The theme of woman's high role was taken up by Hallam
again in an oration delivered on 16 December 1831 entitled
'The Influence of Italian upon English Literature'. In this
beautifully-written essay, Hallam discusses the 'romantic
spirit' in terms of four moving principles which he calls Christian, Teutonic, Roman and Oriental.

The four moving principles consolidated their energies in two
great results: enthusiasm for individual prowess, and enthusiasm
for the female character. Imagination clothed these with form, and
that form was chivalry . . . In the midst of a general dissolution of
manners (the greater part being alike ignorant of a comprehensive
morality and neglectful of religious injunctions . . .), the orient light

[1] ibid., p. 159. The italics are mine.

of Poetry threw a full radiance on the natural heart of woman, and, as in the other sex, created the high sense of honour it pretended to find.

I have said that all the four agencies I have mentioned had their share in impressing this direction on the resurgent genius of Europe. Can it be doubted that the spirit of revealed religion, however little understood, wrought in the heart of man a reverence for the weaker sex, both as teaching him to consider their equality with him in the sight of God, and the privileges of Christian life, and as encouraging in himself those mild and tender qualities which are the especial glory of womanhood? Can it be doubted that if this were the tendency of Christianity, yet more emphatically it was the tendency of Catholicism?[1]

Hallam's admiration of the Catholic worship of the Virgin and the female saints, as showing a reverence towards the female sex, does not extend to its doctrines, which he condemned as unscriptural; but he could not withhold a tribute to the faith which together with the work of the Provençal poets he regarded as the inspiration of Italian love-poetry, 'which dwells like a star apart'.

Its base is undoubtedly the Troubadour poetry, of which I have already spoken, but upon this they have reared a splendid edifice of Platonism, and surmounted it with the banner of the cross . . .

But it was not in scattered sonnets that the whole magnificence of that idea could be manifested, which represents love as at once the base and pyramidal point of the entire universe, and teaches us to regard the earthly union of souls, not as a thing accidental, transitory and dependent upon the condition of human society, but with far higher import, as the best and the appointed symbol of our relations with God, and through them with his own ineffable essence. In the Divine Comedy, this idea received its full completeness of form.[2]

From these passages we can see how the original Platonic 'principle of love' was modified in Hallam's mind by a sympathy and admiration for the Christian adaptation of it to the love for women, as represented in Italian, and particularly in Dante's poetry. This modification supplements the adaptation he earlier made in grafting upon it modern psychological concepts derived from Hartley and Mackintosh. He gives a more

[1] ibid., p. 218.   [2] ibid., p. 224.

detailed exposition of his belief in the importance of Christian responsibility for rightly directing the spirit of love towards women in a pamphlet published anonymously by Moxon in 1832, called 'Remarks on Professor Rossetti's "Disquisizioni Sullo Spirito Antipapale" '. Rossetti's work suggested that the *Divine Comedy* and *Vita Nuova* were cabalistic documents intended to foster opposition to the Pope and support for the Empire: but Hallam, in the course of a delicate rejection of this remarkable view, expresses his own opinion that Dante found in Beatrice an embodiment of that ideal love which was the principal attribute of God in the Christian faith. Christianity sought to present to men objects of love to inspire them to virtue, and it would, in his view, be remarkable not to find in the supreme poet of the Middle Ages a treatment of a religious subject in some such amatory form, for

sufficient causes may be found in the change of manners occasioned by Christianity, to explain the increased respect for the female character, which tempered passion with reverence, and lent an ideal colour to the daily realities of life. While women were degraded from their natural position in society, it could not be expected that the passions which regard them would be in high esteem among moralists, or should be considered capable of any philosophical application.

The sages of the ancient world despised love as a weakness. Calm reason, energetic will—these alone could make a man sovereign over himself; the softer feelings were fit only to make slaves . . .

But with Christianity came a new era. Human nature was to undergo a different development. A Christendom was to succeed an empire; and the proud αὐτάρκεια of male virtues was to be tempered with feminine softness. Women were no longer obliged to step out of the boundaries of their sex,—to become Portias and Arrias, in order to conciliate the admiration of the wise. They appeared in their natural guise, simple and dignified, 'As one intended first, not after made Occasionally'.

This great alteration of social manners produced a corresponding change in the tone of morality. The church too did its utmost for the ladies. The calendar swelled as fast from one sex as from the other . . . The worship of the Virgin soon accustomed Catholic minds to contemplate perfection in a female form. And what is that worship itself, but the exponent of a restless longing in man's

78

unsatisfied soul, which must ever find a personal shape, wherein to embody his moral ideas, and will chuse for that shape, where he can, a nature not too remote from his own, but resembling in dissimilitude, and flattering at once his vanity by the likeness, and his pride by the difference?[1]

He then proceeds to demonstrate that whereas Hebrew religion and literature were pervaded by what he terms 'a sentiment of erotic devotion', so likewise, Christianity, 'mater pulchra, filia pulchrior', carried on a belief in a God who had like passions with men, 'requiring heart for heart, and capable of inspiring affection because capable of feeling and returning it'.[2] A perusal of Thomas à Kempis's *Imitation of Christ*, he avers,

will be sufficient to convince us that the influence of Christianity, in elevating the idea of love to the position it occupied at the dawn of our new civilization, was not merely indirect or collateral. A passion from which religion has condescended to borrow her most solemn phrases, her sublimest hopes, and her most serious modes of operation, could not fail of acquiring new dignity in the eyes of Catholic Christians. It was to be expected that in this, as in all things, the Visible would vindicate its rights, and the sentiments whose origin was in the constitution of earthly nature, would lay hold on an earthly object as their natural possession.[3]

The importance of love, humanly considered, in Arthur Hallam's philosophy will, I hope, have been sufficiently established by this brief examination of his prose writings. The influence of Dante and Plato is so apparent that one might infer that his practical experience was not greatly called upon. This is not so. Hallam resided for nine months in Italy before entering Trinity College, Cambridge, in October 1828, and there fell in love with Anna Mildred Wintour. One of the most ambitious of his poems, 'A Farewell to the South' probably written on his return from Italy in June 1828, celebrates his love for Anna, and its profound effect upon him.

This poem of nearly seven hundred lines is of great interest for the knowledge it provides of Hallam's thought at the time he met Tennyson.[4] He published it in 1830, by which time it

---

[1]ibid., pp. 268–9.   [2] ibid., p. 269.   [3] ibid., p. 274.
[4] Seemingly in April 1829: see T. H. Vail Motter, 'When did Tennyson meet Hallam?', *MLN*, lvii (1942), p. 209.

must have been known to Tennyson; Hallam drew upon it slightly for his own 'Timbuctoo', which yielded the palm to his friend's poem. Although it adapts his experience of falling in love with Anna Wintour, it is principally concerned with a great theme, which 'fitlier from great Plato might be heard', or from 'our English boast'—namely, the ennobling influence of women. The belief that women exerted such an influence upon men was very common at this period, as will appear from the following chapters; it was the constantly reiterated theme of many works published by 'ladies' for 'ladies', and persisted long, despite a growing opposition to it by those reformers who saw it as a sop thrown to women while their true rights were being silently usurped. What distinguishes Arthur Hallam from the ruck of conventionally-minded men and women of his day is that his high ideal of woman sprang fresh from the mediaeval source in Dante. While at Cambridge he planned an edition of the *Vita Nuova* in which Tennyson was also much interested;[1] but even before that, his poem on 'the ennobling influence of women' proclaims his love for Anna Wintour to be a manifestation of that same divine grace which fell upon Dante when he felt an ideal love for Beatrice. In the poem he tries, however, to make explicit the gracious function of women which in Dante is idealized. In doing this, he shows once more the way he had of bringing up to date the doctrines of his masters, Plato and Dante. The fine quality of his religious and conservative nature is revealed by an eager submission to their difficult teachings. For him 'sexual love exerts an ennobling spiritual power upon the lover'.[2]

From the inspiration he received from Anna he drew a conclusion which he asserted in the 'Theodicaea Novissima', namely, that 'lovers who have acquired philosophy' feel that the 'erotic feeling is of origin peculiarly divine, and raises the soul to heights of existence, which no other passion is permitted to attain':

> Oh, were I born
> Beneath a loftier star, no natural terror
> Should bar me from th'essayed development
> Of this high mystery, which rarely a hearer

[1] *Memoir*, i, p. 44.   [2] Motter, p. 116.

Feminism at Cambridge

Can find below: That Woman's Love was sent
  To heal man's tainted heart, and chasten him for Heaven.
  But as I am, my visual power doth faint . . .
            Nor the word
  May from my lips gain worthy utterance,
  Which fitlier from great Plato might be heard,
Or him, our English boast, who in defense
  Of liberty, laid down the joy of light . . .
                                  (421 ff.)

As he looked upon Anna, standing by his side in the Palazzo
Barberini, he felt himself strangely stirred;

                     and I knew
  A power, upraising thought, as winds the ocean,
Within me, but not of me: for it grew
  Unto my spirit, striking root, as moved
  By some supernal influence, breathing through
The medium of the being that I loved!
                                  (483 ff.)

This sense of inspiration can be explained, though not to all.
The splendour of the light of sunset falling upon the many
ranges of the Alps evokes in one possessed of a yearning for
spiritual purity a feeling of devotion and joy.

  How much the rather must that bodiless ray
  Of spiritual radiance, downward sent
From its own home of unapproached day
  By HIM whose name is LOVE, to win the soul
  With a more suasive influence, should its way
Through Woman's heart be taken! . . .
  Or is not Woman worthy to awake
Our primal thoughts of innocence, and share
  With us that wisdom—she, whom ne'er estrange
  The turmoil, and the war-cry from the glare
Of hot Rule dwelling far: but sightlier range
  Of meditation pleaseth, in the shrine
  Not made with hands (which never chance nor change
May harm) her inward reason, communing
  With Faith, and Hope, and godliest Charity.
                                  (528 ff.)

Is this idea of Woman's being an instrument for conveying
God's love to men so difficult to conceive? Some, looking on

the frivolous women of their day, will wonder if it could be possible:

> 'Can she merit
> This reverence,' such may say, 'whom still we see in
> Full many a sprightly mood scatt'ring away
> Hour after hour, all thought's deep travail fleeing?'
> Go, read my answer in the lightsome play
> Of the green leaves around the holm-oak's might . . .
> (565 ff.)

Beneath woman's soft exterior lies a fund of strength; her seeming inferiority in intellect must also be thought of in the light of men's misuse of his vaunted superiority in this respect:

> . . . if still amid this spreading blaze
> Of manifold improvement, which the land
> Rings with from coast to coast, no moral power
> Accedes to th'human mind; and still the hand
> Of vice lies heavy on us, as before,
> Perchance e'en heavier, wherefore do I err
> In that I stoop to rise, and deem the lore,
> Which profiteth to strength, may best from her
> Be learnt, who draws each breath in purity—
> That inmost valour, that bright character,
> Of Godhead, stamped on woman's soul—that we,
> Whose paths are in the perilous mist, may take
> Its impress, and be safe?
> (591 ff.)

The poem concludes with an address to Anna, who is figured throughout as Nina. Though his path is through the perilous mist, the idea of her will give him a charmed life, invulnerable to despair, and he uses his new strength to make a resolution, a resolution much needed in the days to come in the melting-pot of opinions at Cambridge.

> I have an oath,
> Graven in the heart, that I will never drift
> Before the varying gale in aimless sloth
> Of purpose, like a battered wreck: but firm
> Intendment on the base of my young troth,
> My winter's tale, my Tuscan feelings warm,
> Shall rear the fabric of a thinking life.
> (630 ff.)

82

Feminism at Cambridge

Tennyson's sympathetic feelings must have been evoked by
more than one passage in this poem, and by others which develop the central idea. I do not wish in saying this to suggest
that he later consciously elaborated his friend's doctrine, but
I think it hardly possible that he was not influenced by it. *In
Memoriam* is, among other things, a record of doubts (finally
resolved) concerning the truth of the claim that God is Love,
doubts created by the death of Hallam and the findings of
science. It is significant that both 'The Two Voices' and *In
Memoriam* conclude with pictures of marriages, which assuage
the bitterest pangs and leave the speaker reconciled with life,
'all passion spent'. I hope later to show that *The Princess* is
not without echoes of Tennyson's themes in *In Memoriam*,
and that the airy romance carries stronger implications than
may at first be realized.

That one whom Tennyson later viewed as a noble forerunner
of 'the crowning race' of men should have felt so deeply, yet
so philosophically, concerning the role of women in elevating
man's spiritual nature must have caused him to reflect upon
their actual position, a position which the young Utilitarians
at Cambridge were pointing out to be more in need of reform
than that of men, at least where politics were concerned. For
the majority, subordination in marriage might be enough, just
as lowly employment suited most men. But what of the rarer
spirits, the independent, heroic women? Were they not
repressed and undervalued? Heroic women appealed to Tennyson before he enshrined two in *The Princess*; 'A Dream of Fair
Women' is a misleading title, for the women we meet in the
poem have something besides beauty in common—they are
all associated with war or violent death in ways that leave them
renowned. In the poem as it originally appeared in the 1833
volume,[1] it was made plain that it was women

Whose *glory* will not die

who were to be celebrated. It will be recalled that Tennyson

[1] *The Early Poems of Alfred, Lord Tennyson*, ed. J. Churton Collins
(1900), p. 116. See also *Memoir*, i, pp. 82, 90, 121, 504. The poem was
partly composed at Somersby, and certain phrases (like 'the hollow
dark', 'Joyful and free from blame') derive from early unpublished
poems: see Sir Charles Tennyson, *Tennyson's Unpublished Early Poems*
(1931), and his article in the *Nineteenth Century*, cix (1931), p. 506.

'frames' his own poem by presenting it as a dream suggested by reading Chaucer's *Legend of Good Women*: only the know-ledge of Chaucer's art held him above the subject, though, to quote his own words,

> my heart,
> Brimful of those wild tales,

> Charged both mine eyes with tears. In every land
> I saw, wherever light illumineth,
> Beauty and anguish walking hand in hand
> The downward slope to death.

It was the picture of women everywhere oppressed that led him to the first stage of his dream. In verses omitted in the 1842 version of the poem, doubtless because *The Princess* was to be a development of them, he introduced it thus:

> In every land I thought that, more or less,
> The stronger sterner nature overbore
> The softer, uncontrolled by gentleness
> And selfish evermore:

> And whether there were any means whereby,
> In some far aftertime, the gentler mind
> Might reassume its just and full degree
> Of rule among mankind.

He first dreamed of the 'far-renowned brides of ancient song' surrounded by the horrors of war and the instruments of a violent death; this Goyaesque scene slowly gave way to the Wood of Memory wherein he meets in succession Helen, Iphigeneia and others. But before the nightmare faded, he dreamt he saw a town besieged in the Great Rebellion:

> I started once, or seem'd to start in pain,
> Resolved on noble things, and strove to speak,
> As when a great thought strikes along the brain
> And flushes all the cheek.

> And once my arm was lifted to hew down
> A cavalier from off his saddle-bow,
> That bore a lady from a leaguer'd town . . .

84

Feminism at Cambridge

One can easily imagine what were the noble things he resolved upon that led him to try to intervene, in his dream, at the siege of a Cromwellian stronghold: principally, no doubt, to do his best to adopt the principles of the chivalry his friend Hallam so much admired. As we shall see later, some of his contemporary readers who were bent on advancing the cause of women were not slow to see that Tennyson was expressing in poetry what they were attempting more prosaically through newspapers and prefaces.

CHAPTER V

The Feminist Controversy in England prior to 'The Princess'—I

Dawson's challenging remarks on the indifference of the English public to the position of women in society, though unacceptable to a scholar like John Churton Collins, have never been seriously examined by subsequent editors and critics. In fact, as has already been shown, the Socialists gave a central place in their programmes to feminism, and men like J. S. Mill, F. D. Maurice and Arthur Hallam all advanced new views of the question with very little regard to Mary Wollstonecraft and other writers of the period of the French Revolution. The most progressive thinkers at about the time of Tennyson's sojourn at Cambridge all saw the question in a fresh light, and the Socialists in particular related it to a crisis in human affairs generally.

After this time and up to 1847, the relationship of women both to men and to society at large slowly underwent a change, and this change was far from being disregarded by the public. Literature on the 'woman question' abounds, exposing to our view a shift in sympathy, a knowledge of which is valuable for understanding the position of other writers than Tennyson. Books giving advice to young women on how to conform to the established ideal for woman, a creature pious, self-sacrificing and long-suffering had, naturally, appeared at intervals in the period from the French Revolution up to 1830, and sustained a tradition which lived on for many more years to come. This ideal grew up in the eighteenth century, and was very strong when Mary Wollstonecraft wrote *A Vindication of the Rights of Woman*: her castigation of the principles announced in the sermons of Dr. Fordyce and Dr. Gregory's *Legacy to his Daughters* was intended to rebut the notion that women should submit patiently to the role which had been fixed for them.

Her admonitions were largely unheeded, but after 1830, the old ideal and new ones existed side by side. They cannot be disengaged without some distortion; opposition to dominating ideals naturally exists at all times, and change is not a break but a shift of emphasis. Just as the standard ideal had its advocate in Dr. Fordyce many years before, so *opposed* ideals had their supporters too, and their writings likewise established traditional ways of approaching the subject.

Good examples of early 'models' for such writings appearing between 1830 and 1850 are easily found. First must come the claims for 'justice', modelled upon Mary Wollstonecraft's *Vindication*. Then some books of feminist tendency were presented as serious studies of the history of the status of women in many lands. A famous one was William Alexander's *The History of Women, from the earliest antiquity to the present time*, which was published in 1779, and reached a third edition in three years. When, as late as 1855, the *Westminster Review* considered the question of women's status, as brought before the public by Lady Morgan in the second edition (1855) of her *Woman and her Master*, William Alexander's work was also cited at the head of the page. The reason was that Lady Morgan's book followed the same historical method. A third 'traditional' way of treating the question was by way of biography, exemplified by George Ballard's *Memoirs of Several Ladies of Great Britain* (Oxford, 1752), and Mary Hays's *Female Biography* (1803). This was the method followed, for example, by a little book called *Tales of Female Heroism* (1846); it bore as its frontispiece an illustration of Lady Banks's heroic defence of Corfe Castle against a royalist onslaught with the aid of her daughters, female servants and five men, which might have served as a model for the incident of Tennyson's 'miracle of women' defending her walls in the Introduction to *The Princess*.[1] Another way in which feminist doctrines were advanced was by contributions to the political and literary Reviews. Among the first to follow this method was Sydney Smith, writing in the *Edinburgh Review* in 1810.[2] His article set a fashion for treating the woman question at

---

[1] The passage was expanded in the fifth edition to its present form.
[2] xv (October 1809–January 1810), p. 299.

large in Reviews; many of these articles are now of the greatest value in assessing the progress of thought on the subject. Sydney Smith characteristically brought humour and irony to his task of questioning the oft-repeated but little-considered idea that women were naturally inferior to men; his essay, though written so early, ranked as a masterpiece among feminist literature for years to come, and was constantly alluded to by his more militant successors.

Then again there were novels of a feminist tendency. An early specimen of these was James Lawrence's *The Empire of the Nairs; or the Rights of Women*, published in 1811. This 'Utopian Romance', as it was called, first appeared in Germany; Lawrence announced in the Advertisement that it was accepted for publication on the recommendation of Schiller. The interest of Schiller in this book is significant, for it may well have influenced his own work in a way which, I hope to show later, is not unconnected with *The Princess*. Of Shelley's reliance upon it there is less doubt, for *The Revolt of Islam* fairly certainly took over from it the episode dealing with the incarceration of women in the harem;[1] an eastern setting is often given to fictional treatments of the woman question and is present in *The Princess*. The novel describes a kingdom which is matriarchal in organization, in which marriage is regarded with disgust as being foreign to the needs of human nature. Free love is the rule, and chastity is not identified with celibacy.

In these five ways, the standard eighteenth-century ideal of womanhood was assailed in England. Frances Power Cobbe, in an essay 'The Final Cause of Women', contributed to *Woman's Work and Woman's Culture*[2] (which appeared in 1869, a little after, but independently of J. S. Mill's work), was sufficiently enlightened to see that the emancipation movement was really a process of substituting one or more new ideals for women in place of that which had satisfied the previous age. She thought it curious that there should have to be an ideal at all to which women should conform when men managed without one. On reflection, she thought that Lecky's theory,

[1] See Walter Graham, 'Shelley and the *Empire of the Nairs*', *PMLA*, xl (1925), pp. 881 ff.
[2] Ed. Josephine E. Butler.

that each age possessed a moral or religious ideal which powerfully influenced the character of the nations which adopted it,
could supply an explanation of the assumed characters of
women. Already, she wrote, new types of women were growing up, types which could be distinctly traced to Mrs. Fry and
Florence Nightingale. She even went so far as to suggest that
the transmission of acquired characters might tend to con-
serve a new type when once it was established!

As an important corollary to this view, some words of J. S.
Mill may be cited. They occur in a letter dated 6 October of
the same year, 1869:

> Indeed, in all societies which are not wholly demoralised, there
> is no occasion to fear that man will not try to idealise Woman.
> Nature will always contrive that he does so. But in this matter, as
> in all others, the ideal must not stand too far off from real condi-
> tions . . . but so it is with the ideal which many poets have sought
> to establish for women.[1]

In this passage lies the explanation why the ideal had to
change—it must always stand not too far off from real conditions; since these were undergoing a very great change from
1830 onwards, it was inevitable that in company with new
ideals for society as a whole, as most unreservedly expressed
in the writings of the Socialists, new ideals for women should
find utterance too. This fact has a curious bearing on the reception of Tennyson's poems.

As we have already seen, the years in which Tennyson was
at Cambridge were troubled, a fact to be borne in mind when
considering the attitude of the critics to his 1830 volume. A
review of the poems appeared in the *Westminster Review* for
January 1831; it seems to have been written by William Johnson Fox, the Unitarian, editor of *The Monthly Repository*.[2] It
was enthusiastic, and brought joy to the Apostles. Fox was
an ardent political reformer of Benthamite convictions, and it

[1] To Frédéric Mistral, from *Letters of John Stuart Mill*, ed. Hugh S. R.
Elliot (1910), ii, p. 217.

[2] xiv, p. 210. The evidence for seeing Fox as writer of the article is
supplied by W. D. Paden, in 'Tennyson and the Reviewers 1829–35',
in Univ. of Kansas Publications—Humanistic Studies vi, no. 4 (Lawrence, Kansas, 1940), p. 23.

is hardly surprising therefore that he thought poetry should be brought up to date by quitting outworn forms and sentiments which the 'utilitarian spirit in poetical criticism had happily ended'. He took pleasure in Tennyson's poetry, with certain reservations, exhorting him to remember that a poet could be a force in national life. He quoted 'The Burial of Love', and added:

Had we space we should discuss this topic. It is of incalculable importance to society. Upon what love is depends what woman is, and upon what woman is, depends what the world is, both in the present and the future. There is not a greater moral necessity in England than that of a reformation in female education. The boy is a son; the youth is a lover; and the man who thinks lightly of the elevation of character and the extension of happiness which woman's influence is capable of producing, and ought to be directed to the production of, in society, is neither the wisest of philosophers nor the best of patriots. How long will it be before we shall have read to better purpose the eloquent lessons, and the yet more eloquent history, of that gifted and glorious being, Mary Wollstonecraft?[1]

Mr. Shannon goes so far as to suggest that 'it is just possible' that the idea for a poem was lodged in the mind of the poet by this paragraph.[2] Certainly it must have proved of interest to the devoted friend of Arthur Hallam, though it is more likely that the suggestion for *The Princess* came at a date nearer 1839. The paragraph is not developed further in the Review, but it shows how even an early poem could be taken as a sign of the poet's awareness of the woman question. The Unitarians had long supported female emancipation. Mary Wollstonecraft, whom Fox so much praises, was herself a Unitarian, and her *Vindication* received a favourable notice in the short-lived Unitarian journal, *The Christian Remembrancer*.[3] The *Monthly Repository* continued the tradition, and one of Harriet Martineau's earliest contributions to this periodical was called 'On Female Education'.[4] In 1823 Fox had contributed a review of James Shergold Boone's *Men and*

[1] p. 221.   [2] Shannon, p. 93.
[3] See Francis E. Mineka, *The Dissidence of Dissent: The Monthly Repository 1806–38* (Chapel Hill, 1944), p. 158.
[4] ibid., p. 159. It appeared above the pseudonym 'Discipulus'.

The Feminist Controversy in England

Things in 1823 to the first number of the *Westminster Review*. In it he praised Robert Owen; and it seems that later on he was familiar with the feminism of the Owenists in England—indeed, it was his advocacy of the emancipation of women and the liberalizing of the divorce laws on lines reminiscent of Owen's which partly contributed to his eventual exclusion from the Unitarian hierarchy.[1] In 1832, he wrote an article for the *Monthly Repository* called 'A Political and Social Anomaly',[2] in which he dealt with the absurdity of allowing political power to devolve upon a queen while a well-educated woman was denied a vote in the election of (male) representatives. In the hurly-burly of the year preceding the passing of the Reform Act, we see, then, Tennyson reviewed by Fox, a leading figure in the feminist movement.

His periodical continued to air feminist doctrines. In 1833 there appeared an unsigned article 'On Female Education and Occupations'[3] which was approvingly quoted by Robert Owen's *The Crisis*. Its opening is typical of the time:

In a period like the present of mental activity and improving reason, when every ancient opinion is brought to the crucible, every established usage submitted to the test,—when prejudices, however hoary, superstitions, however venerable, are alike subjected to critical examination,—when a new era appears to be approaching, in which sages rather than conquerors shall govern the world, it seems but just and reasonable that more attention than has hitherto been bestowed, should be given to the claims of one-half of the human species, whose influence upon society and manners, though often misdirected, has never been denied.

The same note is struck by Junius Redivivus in another article of the same year called 'On the Condition of Women in England'.[4] It begins:

Far and near rings the loud shout of freedom, and the clang of the bursting fetters of bondsmen resolving to be free. Great moral truths are now stirring to the very depths of society, and half the world is plunged in the sea of politics, setting at nought all antique precedents, and looking only to the utility of those things which are to come. And this is well. But it would be still better, if those

[1] ibid., p. 188.   [2] N.S., vi (1832), p. 637. The article is unsigned.
[3] N.S., vii (1833), p. 489.   [4] ibid., p. 217.

engaged would reflect, that as that which is taken by the sword may be retaken by the sword, even so that which is won by the spirit—stirring excitement of political agitation, may be lost again in the revulsion, when the spirit shall be laid in slumber, or an excitement of a new kind shall prevail. Only by laying a firm groundwork of a just public opinion, can the causes of future strife be entirely removed: but to the very root of the evil, few have yet adverted. Well-intentioned men have frequently said, 'Give us the boys to educate, and we care not what you may do with the men'. There is a deeper depth than this. A philosopher would say: 'Give me the women to educate, and the whole world shall be fashioned after the pattern I may lay down.'

He too raised particular objection to modern marriages, and recommended, as did Robert Owen, that marriage should be made a civil contract, and divorce facilitated. In this he was pursuing a line of thought very much after the editor's heart, for Fox had contributed an article, again in 1833, entitled 'The Dissenting Marriage Question'.[1] In it he protested against solving the problem of the Dissenters' unwillingness to have their marriages celebrated by the clergy of the Anglican Church by allowing Dissenting ministers to perform the ceremony, and recommended civil marriages.

At the end of 1832, in a review of Tennyson's *Poems*, Fox again praised the earlier volume of 1830, describing how amidst the tumult of revolution in France, and Reform agitation in Britain, he had first read them, and felt that a poet had arisen in the land; he thought that 'there was hope for man in powers and principles and enjoyments which flow, a deep and everlasting undercurrent, beneath the stormy surface of political changes and conflicts'.[2] Thus Fox was responsible for placing favourable reviews of Tennyson's early poems in two periodicals, his own, *The Monthly Repository*, and the Benthamite *Westminster Review*. The first, as we have seen, was conducting a feminist campaign: the second especially praised Tennyson for a healthy approach to the woman question. Moreover, the *Westminster Review* being the organ wherein were expressed the opinions of the younger Benthamites, was itself an advocate of emancipation, as we might have

[1] ibid., pp. 136 f.   [2] ibid., N.S., vii (1833), p. 30.

expected from the Utilitarian talk on the subject at Cambridge already described. In July 1831, two issues after that in which Tennyson's *Poems, Chiefly Lyrical* was reviewed, there appeared in that journal an article entitled 'Education of Women—Madame Roland'.[1] The article stated that there were few practical questions that had given rise to more acrimony and strong discussions than the subject of 'Female Education', a bitter hostility which was only of recent date: 'This new question has divided the opinions of civilised society, and has introduced another and most potent cause of hatred and dissension.'[2] The writer described how one party of opinion justified the subalternity of women by maintaining that women were naturally endowed with an inferior intellect, and that consequently any woman who aspired to knowledge was a charlatan, and *ipso facto*, a hateful creature. Another class, the reviewer believed, now utterly opposed this traditional view, but had to overset 'a *beau idéal* which is supposed to be the highest point to which female nature can aspire':

Woman, they say, is formed to obey, and though she have an active and an exclusive part to perform, still she must perform it under submission to her lord. Her duties are confined to her home, and consist in ministering to the comfort of her husband, and in educating her children during their early years. To perform these duties well, she must have a docile, patient, and submissive spirit, she must possess no elevated description of knowledge; so she must be inferior to her attainments. Such is the creed of the great and overwhelming majority of society.[3]

The writer gives an account of the education of Mme Roland to demonstrate that a man's education such as she enjoyed in no way caused a woman to lose touch with domestic affairs; he insists, on the other hand, that the education which it is thought proper to bestow upon all young women of his day is calculated to render them utterly incapable of practical affairs, and consequently unable to conform even with the lowly ideal of the majority. A modern woman is not even taught domestic economy, which would at least enable her to attend to her

---

[1] *The Westminster Review*, xv (July–October 1831), p. 69. The author of this article is unknown.
[2] p. 71.   [3] p. 71.

husband's comfort. The article concludes with the following words: 'The task proposed in the present instance, will have been accomplished if we succeed in inducing the reader to believe that the subject of female education requires to be thoroughly re-considered.'

This article admirably illustrates the way in which the Reviews could bring the question before the public mind. We have seen already that J. S. Mill had earlier contributed feminist articles to the *Westminster Review*: for many years afterwards, the topic was kept before the public by this journal. As might be imagined, at the beginning of the eighteen-thirties, the aspect of the woman question of greatest interest to the Benthamites was female suffrage, the achievement of which was most accessible to political action: but at all times the *Westminster Review* was willing to broaden its attack to cover all sides of the question; the article I have referred to, published in 1831, taken with those of Mill, exemplifies this.[1] In other words, we may say that the two journals which first praised the poems of Tennyson were both conducting feminist campaigns;[2] moreover, one of the reviews of his work drew particular attention to the poet's awareness of the woman question. Even if we should hesitate to accept the view that 'it is just possible that the idea for a poem was lodged in the mind of the poet' by this circumstance alone, we are obliged, I think, at least to consider that he was encouraged to think of feminism as a topic of genuine importance in the minds of his contemporaries, and to keep abreast of changes in following years.

To determine exactly what changes may have led Tennyson to make a major experiment in poetic form to accommodate the subject, we must examine what changes in the attitude to the woman question actually occurred in the period from 1830 to the time of composing *The Princess*. I shall show that they were very great, and that they help to explain the appearance of the other poems on a feminist theme I mentioned earlier.

[1] The standard account of the early activities of the Review is George L. Nesbitt's *Benthamite Reviewing: the first twelve years of The Westminster Review, 1824–36* (Columbia U.P., 1934).

[2] The significance of the political allegiance of these periodicals for the criticism of Tennyson's early work is discussed by Shannon, p. 21.

The Feminist Controversy in England

In the eighteen-thirties, the books on womanhood (which Aurora Leigh read with so little satisfaction) show that the old ideal of womanly behaviour was in some danger from circumstances which seemed inexplicably to be at variance with it; but how precisely these circumstances had appeared was difficult to see; it was a case of *causa latet, vis est notissima*. The problem seemed to turn upon the fact that women's education had unaccountably moved out of step with the ideal that she should accept a retiring role. The instruction that young women received had a quite contrary aim, the development of social graces of which the exercise inevitably made their possessor enter the limelight; to play, sing, draw—all this was to ensure that admiration was forthcoming. The object is easy to see—to secure the married state so necessary to women denied other means of respectable support. For clearly, it was only when marriage had been achieved that the ideal could really be aspired to. Then it was that a woman was expected to assume a submissive part, at entire variance with that she had been prepared for by her education. For the excitement of a sort of power, she had to substitute something much duller.

This situation had seemingly arisen between 1800 and 1830, if we may trust the evidence of a writer of a book published in 1831:

Having already lived long enough to see the effects of a plan which has been pursued with little variation for the last thirty years, I feel a powerful inclination to question the wisdom which has directed it.

We may now see hundreds, nay, thousands of young women emerge from their schoolrooms, at the blooming age of seventeen, with the same portion of wisdom with which they entered into them at the innocent age of seven. That they have there imbibed a large stock of knowledge, and a great variety of accomplishments, I do not doubt. They may have gained, too, a considerable share of that experience which is gained from history and other books of instruction and information; and as much of the manners of the day as occasional visits to the drawing room on gala days and other days could afford. They have learned, too, perhaps, in proportion to the habits of the family, many duties, and many modes of exercising charity towards the poor . . . But with all this, there is a vapid sameness of character which prevails almost universally.[1]

The basis of this writer's objection is that no account is taken of natural ability: competent musicians are tortured and embarrassed by having not only to endure prodigious spells of musical entertainment but also to praise them. Indeed the stage had been reached when ability was looked upon as something of an impediment to exhibiting the triumph art could procure over nature at the behest of wealth. She substantiates the charge of the reviewer by saying that 'the *business* of female life, for some years past, has consisted of a cultivation of those resources which were formerly considered as its amusements'. In a sense, therefore, we may say that the *beau idéal* for women was itself compromised: the submissive qualities postulated as necessary for the perfect wife could not be exercised in the absence of a husband; and a husband could be won only by a degree of cultivation at odds with the first ideal.

The writers of books of this sort attempted to remedy the situation by piecemeal methods, and generally suggested the slightest of reforms. A good example is Mrs. Elizabeth Sandford, who wrote a very popular series of books on 'womanhood'. These were *Woman in her social and domestic character* (1831), *Lives of English female worthies* (1833), and *Female Improvement* (1836). The first of these exhibits an awareness that women have to face a change; it is perceived but not understood:

> It is thus, also, that the sentiment for women has undergone a change. The romantic passion, which once almost deified her, is on the decline; and it is by intrinsic qualities that she must now inspire respect. There is less of enthusiasm entertained for her, but the regard is more rational, and, perhaps, equally sincere; since it is in relation to happiness that she is principally appreciated.[2]

This timid recognition of a change in society irresistibly demanding reform had already in the early eighteen-thirties exacted the grudging admission that women had to be prepared by education for a different way of life; but whereas it

[1] *Females of the Present Day, considered as to their Influence on Society* (1831), by a Country Lady, p. 25.
[2] *Woman in her social and domestic character*, p. 1.

was felt fairly safe to reform the classroom—the vicious secondary product of the prevailing ideal—the ideal itself was clung to with the force of desperation. What the proposed reforms in education should lead to was carefully ignored; and a good indication of the state of opinion at this time is that the Birkbeck Literary and Scientific Institution was able, in 1833, unostentatiously to open its classes to women; yet any public discussion of possible consequences would certainly have provoked bitter controversy. Mrs. Sandford herself confined her educational aspirations to rigorous private study by women, the object of this study being unconnected with any practical activity. Occasionally, of course, a strident voice in favour of political justice was to be heard. In 1833, 'a lady' published from South Shields a book called *Female Rights Vindicated*. This book shows no doubt at all about the object of reform in women's education; it is to be a step in the overthrow of the old ideal and a means of allowing women to enter into a man's world on a footing of complete equality—in other words their education is to prepare them for the performance of public duties:

I acknowledge we might at first fill these employments somewhat awkwardly, and the transition would not a little surprise—but this would only be by reason of its novelty. If at the founding of states, and the regulation of the different employments which compose them, the women had been allotted their parts, they would have been equally accustomed to their execution as the men, and there would have been nothing more wonderful in their vocations.[1]

The writer of the book knew what sort of reception her claims would have: her openings words are:

The novelty and daringness of this performance cannot avoid drawing upon me the attention of the female world, and the criticisms of the male. To endeavour refuting an opinion of so long standing as that of the superiority of the men over the women with respect to genius and abilities, will no doubt appear to many a strange and impracticable attempt: and numbers, even of women, misled by prejudice and custom, may believe no one would be so quixotic as to list herself Champion of the sex upon this occasion;

[1] p. 44.

and that therefore this is nothing more than a ludicrous performance to turn the women into greater ridicule, and make them appear more contemptible than ever.

Her fears were fully justified. There were some ready to attack any aspirations of the sort which Mary Wollstoncraft held. In 1835 was published anonymously *Woman as she is and as she should be*. One would expect from the title a modest book in Mrs. Sandford's vein; but instead we find a virulent attack, in two volumes, upon even the mild reforms in education which we have been examining. Mrs. Sandford, for example, was, with many of her countrywomen, glad to keep up the belief that women, although without any real power, were silently influencing their male connections to better courses. All she hoped for in return was to be allowed to do away with an education designed to impose upon all women a harmful sexual character believed to be attractive to the male. The unknown author of *Woman as she is and as she should be* believed that the influence that they already had was excessive, and should be curtailed. He fully agreed with the reformers that the time had come when all established opinions must be examined, and if necessary rejected; he agreed too that 'the education of women, as at present conducted, is founded in mistaken principles, and tends to increase fearfully the sum of misery and error in both sexes'.[1] The reform he desired was a reduction in the misplaced admiration for women in England; they must be made to see their inferiority to men and to renounce all attempts to intervene in public affairs or in any other way to exert power:

In Woman, weakness itself is the true charter of power; it is an absolute attraction, and by no means a defect; it is the mysterious tie between the sexes, a tie as irresistible as it is captivating, and begetting an influence peculiar to itself—in short, *all independence is unfeminine*: the more dependent that sex becomes, the more will it be cherished . . . Let the only conquest aimed at be that of self; and let them not even *wish* to have a higher control of any kind than such as their condition legitimately allows them.[2]

The extreme one-sidedness of this suggestion, amounting almost to malice, is a remarkable example of the prejudice still

[1] He is quoting Mrs. Jameson.   [2] i, p. 37.

obtaining at this date: this writer even quoted Dr. Fordyce with approval. He asserted it as his belief that women have brains lacking one cell, and are capable of dealing only with *minutiae*, and are particularly hateful when pretending to learning ('it is somewhat difficult to regard the intellectual virago, notwithstanding her petticoats, in the light of a female'). Like the reformers proper, he too desired to see a change in the education dispensed in the boarding schools. To him they displayed a tendency to inculcate in young women a quite unjustified self-esteem. Their studies should be re-cast to ensure that she considers only the happiness of her menfolk, and on no account are they to be concerned with anything other than practical concerns, 'for whatever is unassayed or theoretical is as much beyond the reach and strength of the female mind, as it is out of the natural and healthy play of its machinery'.[1] To this he adds an interesting note:

The remarks ventured here will not be considered as ill-timed, or out of place, by any who have observed the presumption among our 'learned ladies' (so-called) of the present day. We *may* yet live to see such intellectual Amazons publicly styled 'Mistresses of *Arts*'—Our brethren of the West have, it is said, already established a College for ladies at Lexington, Kentucky. Here degrees are to be conferred,—M.P.L., Mistress of Polite Literature; M.I., Mistress of Instruction, etc., etc.[2]

This scornful reference to the award of degrees to women needs some elucidation. It is possible that the writer was really referring to the Oberlin Institute (in Ohio). Forms of co-education had existed in America in the eighteenth century, but the first *collegiate* education on this pattern was introduced at the Oberlin Institute, a college which set the pattern for much of the co-educational instruction in present-day colleges of the U.S.A. It aimed to produce potential ministers of the Church and 'pious teachers'; it very quickly achieved notoriety both for permitting anti-slavery discussion and, in 1835, the admission of negroes and women. This was 'the martyr age of the United States', as Harriet Martineau called it,[3] and soon

[1] ii, p. 258.   [2] ii, p. 267 n.10.
[3] *The London and Westminster Review*, xxxii (December 1838–April 1839), p. 1.

The Feminist Controversy in England

Oberlin was almost alone in not attempting to suppress abolitionist thought. Not surprisingly, the financial position of the Institute rapidly became grave, and an appeal was made to England, where the Abolitionists had very considerable support. Funds were made over to Oberlin in the full knowledge that they were intended to forward the political as well as the academic purposes of the Institute. Something of the agitation set up in the course of 'Oberlinising' England in 1839 may be seen in the extracts from Harriet Martineau's journal for that year given by Mrs. Maria Weston Chapman in her Memorials of Harriet Martineau.[1] How much knowledge was gained about the co-educational practice at Oberlin from the mission to England is difficult to say. Certainly it proved a great success. The interesting thing is that the inaugurators of so immensely significant an experiment had no feminist inclinations at all. They followed the course they did without the least belief in anything resembling 'women's rights'.

Although some were willing to adopt extreme positions on the woman question in the eighteen-thirties, the most general view seems to have been that of Mrs. Sandford, who thought that women should submit to their subalternity with a good grace, and by rigorous private study attempt to equip themselves to exert a benign influence within their families. Thus men might be able to regard them as sources of sweetness and light, or, as Meredith put it, ironically:

> The light which leads us from the paths of rue
> That light above us, never seen to swerve.

Mrs. Sandford's exhortation to her readers to seek to be angels, albeit ineffectual ones, was really only a counsel of despair, and derived from the hard, inescapable facts of the situation. Very probably the view would not have lived as long as it did had it not received the support of writers who advocated it on positive grounds.

In 1834 was published at Paris a work of very considerable influence. It was called *De L'Éducation des Mères de Famille*,

---

[1] Harriet Martineau, *Autobiography* (1877), iii, p. 226. See also Robert Samuel Fletcher, *A History of Oberlin College, from its foundation through the Civil War* (1943).

ou De la Civilisation du Genre Humain par les Femmes, and
was written by Louis Aimé-Martin. A revised and much expanded edition was published in 1838. It was awarded a prize
by the French Academy, and it was translated into English
by Edwin Lee, a medical man, in 1842,[1] though it was known
in England before that: George Eliot, for example, read it in
1840.[2]

The work began with a tribute to Rousseau[3] for having been
the first to emphazise the importance of the influence of women
in inculcating virtue into a state, an influence which the writer
believed to be so great that it was not too much to say that
what man makes of woman she will indirectly make of him.
As example he contrasted the characters of the eastern peoples
with European, and decided that the low state of civilization
in the Turkish empire was due to the absence of opportunity
under the system of the harem for the benign influence of
women to work upon the men. He would not admit that the
influence of women in Europe was confined to the home, for
society was only an aggregate of families, and the influence of
women in the family was reflected in the doings of men outside it.

If, then, there be an incontestable fact, it is that of the influence
of women: an influence exerted over the whole of life by means of
filial piety, pleasure and love. This being admitted, one is led to
ask oneself by what inconceivable oversight so powerful a lever
has been hitherto neglected—how moralists, instead of calling to
their aid the softest and the most energetic power, have laboured
to weaken it—and how legislators of every period have combined to
render it prejudicial to us? for it cannot be too often remarked that
all the evil which women have done us is derived from us, and all
the good which they do us comes from themselves.[4]

This is perhaps the classic statement of the doctrine of Female
Influence, which became an *idée fixe* of this period in England.

---

[1] *The Education of Mothers of Families,* 1842. I shall for convenience
cite this edition, despite its omission of parts of the original.

[2] J. W. Cross, *George Eliot's Life* (1885), i, p. 78.

[3] He later pays tribute to Fénélon's *De l'Éducation des Filles* as the
source of Rousseau's best ideas. The strength of French tradition in this
class of writing is apparent.

[4] Aimé-Martin, op. cit., trans. Lee, p. 21.

The Feminist Controversy in England

Aimé-Martin develops it to its greatest lengths: woman's influence is exerted in Christian marriage: therefore leave alone scholastic and social accomplishments, and educate women for marriage—not the conventional *mariage de convenance*, but marriage founded upon true knowledge of life and love. It is after marriage that woman should, however, devote herself to education: not by reading in the field of men's studies, even in the hope of benefiting her children; but by applying herself thoroughly to a study of moral philosophy and religion.

The book was reviewed in the issue for April 1835 of the *Westminster Review* and was welcomed for its high seriousness:

> Such purposes will be estimated highly in most countries; but in none be more sure of attention, nor more deserving of favour, than in France. The social power of women has long been greater there than elsewhere, although their influence has depended more on the graces of person, and force of character, than on correctness of conduct, or extent of intellectual attainments. The feverish interest which now pervades French society in regard to the position of women, is very remarkable. The press at this moment teems with projects of periodical and other works, devoted to their instruction and to their interest; the wildest opinions are afloat respecting their destination: and the St.-Simonians, among other strange aberrations, are actually gone towards the Holy Land to discover their type of the fair sex, a new *Magna Mater*.[1]

This passage gives an interesting estimate of the activity in France; it will be observed that the reviewer seems fully aware of the work of the feminist periodicals which sprang up in the wake of Socialist thought, and makes no mention of American activity.

In England, there was no comparably feverish interest in matters affecting women, as will be seen from the caustic remarks by Harriet Martineau on the reception accorded a proposal that the new House of Commons should contain a ladies' gallery:

> In July 1835, it was proposed in the House of Commons that accommodation should be provided in the new edifice for the presence of women at the debates. The proposal was made in a spirit and in language which went far to place every sensible woman

[1] xxii (January–April 1835), p. 504. See *Eothen*, chap. VIII.

on the same side of the question with Lord John Russell, when he declared his disinclination to debate the matter, and his intention to oppose the motion. Lord J. Russell was outvoted, however, and a committee was appointed to consider the subject. The whole proceeding had much the air of an ill-bred joke—the speech of the mover, the ostentatious eagerness to second it, the coarse mirth, and the large majority. On the next occasion, May 3rd 1836, matters were worse, the speeches more indecent, the mirth more flippant and unmanly, the majority larger in proportion. It seemed likely that the women of England might indeed be invited to be present at the deliberations of legislators whose method of invitation was an insult in itself, and who professed to wish for the presence of ladies, among other reasons, as a check upon intoxication and indecency of language . . . Those who advocated the admission of women in the gallery did not pretend to be thinking of the improvement of the women's knowledge, and the cultivation of their interest in subjects which concern every member of society— those who are waiting for political participation, as well as those who have it.[1]

We might infer from Harriet Martineau's remarks and from the appearance the year before of an influential work supporting Mrs. Sandford's general doctrine, that there was little hope of reform in 1835. This was certainly the view of 'Kate', writing in *The New Moral World* on 13 June of that year:[2]

If there is one object more deserving public attention than any other, one on which social, and, therefore, general happiness is more deeply involved, and on which any change which may be introduced is in a great measure dependent for its beneficial result —it is, the consideration of the present condition of woman, with a view to her future improvement. The neglect shown to a question of such vital import to humanity proves the very superficial manner in which discussions are carried on in society, and that a great degree of caution is necessary in placing reliance on the determinations that emanate from it.

The interest of society in France has been for some time past excited in favour of an improvement in the education of woman, while in that of England such is not even now the case, as is well known. It is not that the women of France are more advanced in

---

[1] Harriet Martineau, *History of the Thirty Years Peace* (1849–50). I have used the edition of 1877–8; see iii, p. 374.

[2] i, p. 263.

Intellectual attainments, in moral conduct, or, except in graces of
manner, are they our superiors: but it is the influence of external
circumstances, which as a mighty engine, acts on the tide of human
affairs, and leads, often by slow and tortuous steps, to human advancement. These circumstances have allowed them to see distinctly that any change in the social, political, or the religious
divisions of society must, as hitherto, remain unproductive of good,
unless the mental and moral freedom of woman is secured, through
the medium of a superior education.

Public opinion in France had indeed moved so far that Mrs.
Leman Grimstone, writing a little earlier in the same year, was
able to report that in the previous session of the French Chamber of Deputies the Minister of Public Instruction had been
requested to prepare a law to bring the standard of women's
education up to that of men's, since it was equally important.[1]

Though the situation seemed so gloomy in 1835, after this
date there is observable a distinct improvement, though it is
difficult to say to what it might be attributed. In 1837 there
occurred an event of which the effect was of the highest importance. The accession of Victoria provided feminism with
exactly the sort of glaring anomaly that Englishmen so often
need before an argument is felt to have any practical force.
Obviously it was the aspirants to *political* rights for women
who could make most of the point that it was absurd to allow
a woman to occupy the office which stood at the apex of
English constitutional government while every other member
of her sex could not cast a vote to decide what man should be
her parliamentary representative. But it is interesting to see
what a fillip it gave to feminists of all shades of opinion. The
Owenists did not even have to wait until the event to realize
the importance of having a young queen on the throne. Even
in the doldrum year, 1835, *The New Moral World* fondly
anticipated that with such a monarch there might be hope of
sympathy for their *social* reforms:

> The changes which are circulating with the vital currents of this
> country will mount upwards to the throne: but that will not be till
> a *young* branch waves its green honours there. Though no idolater
> of royalty, glad shall I be to see the day when I may bend in *heart*

[1] i, p. 132. The issue was that for 21 February 1835.

homage to the 'anointed head' of one who loves humanity—who looks upon a people with a wish to do much for them, not to make the most of them. So long as thrones be necessary, blest will be the lands which see them filled by such as rise to them in the spirit of the age in which they live, and of the people they are appointed to govern.[1]

'Shepherd' Smith had also realized that the fact that a woman was on the throne would make the aspirations of the Socialists look much more reasonable, and took the opportunity afforded by the coronation to remind his readers that the Saint-Simonians and Owenists had been preaching the doctrine that was now respectable on anyone's lips. Surely it was now the moment for them to do all they could to encourage the appearance of the right sort of woman to speak for the whole sex, as the Saint-Simonians had failed to do despite all their efforts:

It is with no small pleasure we reflect that the third volume of the *Shepherd* appears under the shadow of a woman's wing. We have always regarded woman as the representative of the moral department of Nature; as the end of progress, which finishes in the emancipation of her sex, and in the full development of her peculiar excellencies. These being cultivated by the male, and reflected upon him, at the same time elevate his character by his participation of the feminine virtues, which must ultimately put a check upon the horrid brawls of intellect, and the savage contentions of physical outrage and international warfare. This typical character is not a conceit; it is a principle of Nature. It was in following out this principle rather too eagerly ('He that believeth shall not make haste') that the St.-Simonians, under Enfantin, one of the most splendid doctrinists of the age, amused the French, and confounded themselves by looking out for what they call the Free Woman, the representative of the aspect material of industry and production. They longed to find such a woman: the very existence of their doctrine and system depended on such a woman. They could not find her—a sad confutation of the prejudgement of those who assert that impostors are easily found when a people is prepared to receive them. Here was a people—here was a vacant seat set apart for the purpose—but neither France nor England could furnish an occupant. To England they all looked for such a character. Their doctrine taught them that England must produce her . . . Now, all

[1] i, p. 101. The passage is quoted from an article by Mrs. Grimstone in *The Monthly Repository*.

The Feminist Controversy in England

England, the very government of England, is womanised. We are not augurs, neither do we regard omens—especially those on a small scale—when we are treating of great matters, but we like to trace analogies on a large scale when we are treating of large subjects; and now we say to both Saint-Simonians and Owenians, Now is your time, seek out this woman, for the spirit of woman has now ascended the throne of England. Is there a woman in England who can represent her sex? If there be, let her come forth, for be assured that until she appears, there is no salvation, even for man . . . We have many clever women amongst us—but what are they? Gossips who can prate well, syrens who can sing well and blue stockings who can write well on everything but salvation—women who write for personal fame, for money, or merely to give vent to their own vagaries. But there is scarcely a woman amongst them who writes for any great social purpose, in whom the selfish principle is absorbed in the social, and who seems willing to make a sacrifice of her fair fame for a time that she may ameliorate the condition of her sex and species. They are either not conscious of their degradation or they want the moral courage to assert their rights. Talent is not wanting. It is the faith in *the moral progression and final destiny of the species that they lack*.[1]

Smith's concluding words are of the greatest interest for this study, for I hope to show in later chapters that Tennyson's *The Princess* is closely connected with the sacrifice of her fair fame by one woman—the Hon. Mrs. Caroline Norton—and with the theme that the place of women in life is bound up with 'faith in the moral progression and final destiny of the species'.

I think that we may be reasonably certain that 'Shepherd' Smith would hardly have viewed Harriet Martineau as a fit person to raise the standards of feminism. But not a little of the credit for the awakened interest in the matter was due to her. Mention was made earlier of her contribution in 1823 of an article to the *Monthly Repository* called 'On Female Education'. But her main contribution to the new feminism came in 1837, in a book which was the outcome of a visit to America; it was called *Society in America*. This book was much more personal than the works which had already established her reputation. It was also frank and critical, and although many

[1] W. Anderson Smith, op. cit., pp. 65 ff. The italics are mine.

Americans could take the criticism to heart without rancour, others felt that it was almost a breach of hospitality. One thing, at any rate, is clear: she did not think that American society could teach her much about improving the lot of women.

Her remarks on the subject are of special interest because of her knowledge of the social mechanisms in England. Her concern with the woman question (*pace* 'Shepherd' Smith) was sincere but by no means the outcome of feeling personally misused by one man or many. She thought the position of women anomalous, and was not flattered by the masculine homage to her intellect (in the shape of a deluge of blue-books and respectful consultations) into proving renegade to her principles on the point. Her temperament was cool, yet energetic; she could disapprove of Mary Wollstonecraft and refuse a pension, yet very well see—and, we may consequently infer, feel—the hardships of working women. Her American tour took in the prisons and hospitals as well as drawing-rooms, and one might think she almost preferred the former. Deaf to chatter, she used her trumpet to invite confidences and statistics: and her eyes missed little of the important matters.

The passage she devotes to the political position of American women is short and brusque. She was familiar with James Mill's unfortunate utterance on female representation. Unhesitatingly she transferred Thompson's riposte to a similar pronouncement by Jefferson, with the advantage of being able to quote a written constitution. The Declaration of Independence established the principle that governments exercise their powers by the consent of the governed. Jefferson had said, however, that even if the state were a pure democracy, in the government of which all the citizens participated, women would still be excluded, 'to prevent depravation of morals and ambiguity of issue'.[1] In this disqualification they would share the fate of infants and slaves; and in Harriet's view, the true reasons were those applicable to the last category. She permits herself a little irony on despotism pretending to benevolence and concludes that the position of woman in society ought to be decided solely by reference to her powers, and not to a question-begging notion of a 'sphere'.

[1] i, p. 201.

The Feminist Controversy in England

The fearful and absurd images which are perpetually called up to perplex the question—images of women on woolsacks in England, and under canopies in America, have nothing to do with the matter . . . The kings of Europe would have laughed mightily, two centuries ago, at the idea of a commoner, without crown, robes or sceptre, stepping into the throne of a strong nation. Yet who dared to laugh when Washington's super-royal voice greeted the New World from the presidential chair, and the old world stood still to catch the echo?[1]

A whole chapter is devoted to Woman in the section entitled *Civilisation*. It is critical of American society in its attitude towards the sex, which is undoubtedly much indulged, but pays by foregoing rights. The education of women is much the same as in England, that is, a careful suppression of intellectual activity to prepare women for a life of no opportunity; the consequence is likewise the same, apathy or pedantry. Marriage is their highest expectation, women who enter into politics or literature being mercilessly pilloried. Heroic efforts are required of any woman who objects to negro slavery, for example. (She was not at this time aware of Oberlin; later she campaigned most energetically for it.) Her view was that American prosperity was perpetuating this evil state of things:

the prosperity of America is a circumstance unfavourable to its women. It will be long before they are put to the proof as to what they are capable of thinking and doing: a proof to which hundreds, perhaps thousands of Englishwomen have been put by adversity, and the result of which is a remarkable improvement in their social condition, even within the space of ten years. Persecution for opinion, punishment for all manifestations of intellectual and moral strength, are still as common as women who have opinions and manifest strength; but some things are easy, and many are possible of achievement, to women of ordinary powers, which it would have required genius to accomplish but a few years ago.[2]

This, then, was Harriet Martineau's view on the relative position of women in America and England; the last few years had shown an enormous improvement in their position in England; America's prosperity deferred the likelihood of any major improvement there. She was, as it happens, belied by events:

[1] i, p. 206.   [2] iii, p. 118.

she had overlooked the possibility of contact between American and English women.

The insistence that woman should *remain* in her 'sphere' was becoming more and more farcical when many women had no opportunity of entering it. I have suggested that the elaborate education of women in a glittering array of 'accomplishments' (for the almost undisguised purpose of capturing a husband) was really an admission that the old simple ideal of woman exercising a refining influence in her home was failing, a fact which was made manifest by the spectacle of both supporters and opponents of the ideal criticizing this form of education. It remained for Harriet Martineau, exercised in the laws of political economy, implicitly to reject the old ideal altogether and to substitute one wherein a woman might without indignity earn her own bread. America contributed no guidance in this. The country still retained the old chivalrous temper of Europe, where women were concerned. Men found their feelings wounded at the thought of a woman joining the labour market, but instead of helping her, this had the indirect effect of driving her into neglected occupations or prostitution. She pointed out accordingly, the terrible conditions suffered by governesses and sempstresses in America; and dispensing with any examination of women's occupations not as irrelevant, but as vain, she contented herself with a single exhortation:

I would only ask of philanthropists of all countries to inquire of physicians what is the state of health of sempstresses; and to judge thence whether it is not inconsistent with common humanity that women should depend for bread upon such employment. Let them inquire what is the recompence of this kind of labour, and then wonder if they can that the pleasures of the licentious are chiefly supplied from that class . . . During the present interval between the feudal age and the coming time, when life and its occupations will be freely thrown open to women as to men, the condition of the female working classes is such that if its sufferings were but made known, emotions of horror and shame would tremble through the whole of society.[1]

She had not long to wait before the revelations she desired were made—in England, at any rate—though it was Mrs.

[1] iii, p. 148.

The Feminist Controversy in England

Anna Jameson who gave herself the task of drawing the moral. In these circumstances it is ironical that Harriet Martineau spoke bitterly of this co-agitator: but she makes the reason clear. For neither Mary Wollstonecraft nor Mrs. Jameson (and certain others) could she feel sympathy, because she felt that they injured the woman's cause by making claims based upon their own misfortunes: '. . . their advocacy of Woman's cause becomes mere detriment, precisely in proportion to their personal reasons for unhappiness, unless they have fortitude enough (which loud complainants usually have not) to get their own troubles under their own feet, and leave them wholly out of the account in stating the state of the sex.'[1]

It is very doubtful whether Harriet Martineau was right. To Mrs. Jameson and to the Hon. Mrs. Caroline Norton, both *mal mariées*, much is owing also for the change in public feeling on the woman question soon after Victoria occupied the throne. Mrs. Jameson, like Miss Martineau, did much to make the reading public aware of what the true situation of women had become, and oddly enough, the work in which she astonished the public by her frank denunciation of the old ideal was also the outcome of a visit to the United States (and Canada), and appeared in the very next year, 1838. Like Miss Martineau too, Mrs. Jameson had occupied herself with feminism long before, but with her it was practically a passion, and a very great deal of her output, though varied, is to be seen as disguised feminist advocacy, but up to 1838 of a very polite sort.

She had first come before the public as early as 1825, with a work originally called *The Diary of a Lady*, published anonymously; but it was later renamed, and acknowledged, as *The Diary of an Ennuyée*. Like Lady Morgan, another Irishwoman and ardent feminist, she greatly admired Mme de Stael; though it seems likely that the form her feminism later took was greatly influenced by Lady Byron, to whom she was devotedly attached from 1834 down to 1852. Lady Byron was deeply interested in social schemes,[2] and especially in the

[1] *Autobiography*, i, p. 400. See also i, p. 352.
[2] See Mrs. Steuart Erskine, *Anna Jameson: Letters and Friendships, 1812–60* (1915), p. 165, and *Record*, i, p. 211.

conditions of employment of women; even Edward Trelawney became absorbed in feminism under her influence.[1]

In 1832 she published a book the title of which suggested one of the manuals of exhortation to women like those already discussed; it was called *Characteristics of Women, Moral, Poetical and Historical*. Only later did it become known (in many editions) by the more familiar title, *Shakespeare's Heroines*. The first title was not altogether misleading, for one reason for writing the book was clearly that which prompted her earlier book, *The Loves of the Poets*, namely to make a point in favour of women by the aid of literature. The book is prefaced with a 'polite conversation' between a certain lady, ALDA, writer of the book, and MEDON, a young gentleman acquaintance, sympathetic, but wise after the fashion of the world. Alda begins by making her purpose plain:

It appears to me that the condition of women in society, as at present constituted, is false in itself, and injurious to them,—that the education of women, as at present conducted, is founded in mistaken principles, and tends to increase fearfully the sum of error and misery in both sexes: but I do not choose presumptuously to fling these opinions in the face of the world, in the form of essays on morality, and treatises on education. I have rather chosen to illustrate certain positions by examples, and leave my readers to deduce the moral themselves, and draw their own inferences.[2]

The examples she chose were the heroines of Shakespeare's plays, who were regarded by everyone, she maintained, as real human beings. Every reader of Shakespeare was struck by the simplicity of his heroines, or at least of the women held up for our admiration. How unlike the young women of her own day! Alda has no doubt as to the reason:

ALDA

Blame then that *forcing* system of education, the most pernicious, the most mistaken, the most far-reaching in its miserable and mischievous effects, that ever prevailed in this world . . . a system

[1] 'We are earnestly at work on a work whose theme is divine, the *Wrongs of Women*, which we have the audacity to imagine we can lighten . . .' (from a letter dated 2 July 1838, quoted by Mrs. Steuart Erskine, op. cit., p. 165).

[2] *Characteristics of Women*, Introduction, p. viii.

of education which inundates us with hard, clever, sophisticated girls, trained by knowing mothers and all-accomplished governesses. Hence the strange anomalies of artificial society—girls of sixteen who are models of manner, miracles of prudence, marvels of learning, who sneer at sentiment, and laugh at the Juliets and the Imogens; and matrons of forty, who, when the passions should be tame and wait upon the judgment, amaze the world, and put us to confusion with their doings.[1]

In the body of the book occur remarks like this: 'A woman constituted like Portia, and placed in this age, and in the actual state of society, would find society armed against her; and instead of being like Portia, a gracious, happy, beloved and loving creature, would be a victim, immolated in fire to that multitudinous Moloch termed Opinion.'[2] Generally, however, the book is not rendered oppressive by an unremitting insistence upon the moral, and although one can, like Arthur Hallam, be 'bewildered with similes about groves and violets' (the quality of Portia is distinguished by the scent of attar of roses, whereas Isabella suggests incense, and Rosalind 'cotton dipped in aromatic vinegar'), there is some sensitive criticism too. One must confess that the purport of the book would hardly have been apparent had not the Introduction made it explicit.

I hope that these few remarks about *Characteristics of Women*, a book which achieved an enormous popularity through the rest of the century, will have shown how typical a production it is of its date, 1832, considered from the feminist point of view. It deals with literature rather than with life, denounces the educational system, but only suggests as a reform an education which will fit women for their 'future destination as the *mothers and nurses* of legislators and statesmen'—neatly anticipating Aimé-Martin's programme for 'l'éducation des mères', which likewise leaves the ideal itself unassailed. Yet the writer of the distasteful *Woman as she is and as she should be* in 1835 attacked Mrs. Jameson for publishing even this mild argument.

In 1833, Mrs. Jameson visited Germany, and on her return published (in 1834) a book of impressions and reflections which

[1] ibid., p. xliii.   [2] ibid., p. 32.

she entitled *Visits and Sketches*.[1] This work is introduced by another dialogue between Alda and Medon leading directly into the main body of the work. Medon presses her to give her general impression of German women; although she sees them as more natural than English women, she is obliged to quote Tennyson's 'A Dream of Fair Women' in the 1833 version adequately to express her view of their condition:

> In every land
> I saw, wherever light illumineth,
> Beauty and anguish walking hand in hand,
> The downward slope to death.
>
> In every land I thought that, more or less,
> The stronger, sterner nature overbore
> The softer, uncontroll'd by gentleness,
> And selfish evermore!

These lines had appealed to an Owenist writer on the woman question too; Tennyson's poem had a special appeal, we might say, to feminists of very different brands.

Mrs. Jameson reluctantly joined her husband in Canada shortly after this. The outcome of her experiences was *Winter Studies and Summer Rambles in Canada*, published in 1838. If Mrs. Jameson's little foible about women's rights had been overlooked before, the new book gave its readers pause. On its appearance it was, according to Mrs. Proctor, universally *relished*, but the men, she reported, were much alarmed by certain speculations about women and, she added, 'well they may, for when the horse and ass begin to think and argue, adieu to riding and driving'.[2]

One of the books Mrs. Jameson had read, Eckermann's *Life of Goethe*, arrested her attention by expressing exactly what she herself had thought. Goethe's physician was quoted as saying that the poetical talent in women was 'ein Art von geistigem Geschlechtstrielb', an 'intellectual impulse of sex'. He observed that women who distinguished themselves in literature, poetry especially, were almost universally women who had

---

[1] Later known as *Sketches of Germany*. I have used the edition of 1837.
[2] Mrs. Steuart Erskine, op. cit., p. 170.

been disappointed in their best affections, and sought in this direction a sort of compensation. Mrs. Jameson, who could well feel the possible truth of this, was willing to concede that three fourths of women distinguished in literature found themselves, for one reason or another 'placed in a painful or a false position'.[1] '. . . it is also most certain that in these days when society is becoming every day more artificial and more complex, and marriage, as the gentlemen assure us, more and more expensive, hazardous, and inexpedient, women *must* find means to fill up the void of existence.' To perpetuate, as men seem to desire, the old ideal of woman as a tender, shrinking, sensitive creature is surely 'to cultivate a taste for sunshine and roses in those we send to pass their lives in an arctic zone' (an apt analogy in Mrs. Jameson's experience).

We have gone away from nature, and we must,—if we can,— substitute another nature. Art, literature and science remain to us . . . The cruel prejudices which would have shut us out from nobler compensation and occupations have ceased in great part, and will soon be remembered only as the rude, coarse barbarism of a by-gone age. Let us then have no more caricatures of methodistical, card-playing, and acrimonious old maids . . . Coleridge, as you will remember, has asserted that the perfection of a woman's character is to be *characterless*. 'Every man', said he, 'would like to have an Ophelia or a Desdemona for his wife.' No doubt: the sentiment is truly a masculine one; and what was *their* fate? What would now be the fate of such unresisting and confiding angels? Is this the age of Arcadia? Do we live among Paladins and Sir Charles Grandisons, and are our weakness, and our innocence and our ignorance, safe-guards—or snares? Do we indeed find our account in being

'Fine by defect, and beautifully weak?'

No, no; women need in these times *character* beyond everything else; the qualities which will enable them to endure and to resist evil; the self-governed, the cultivated, active mind, to protect and to maintain ourselves.

She adds what she says she has never hitherto been able to say—that the ideal of woman being simply 'a happy wife and mother' is dangerous and even wicked: '. . . we know that hundreds, that thousands of women are not happy wives and

---

[1] i, p. 202.

mothers—are never either wives or mothers at all.' In a series
of anecdotes she calls into question many of the old prejudices
—describing the heroism of negro women, a new law to pena-
lize seduction, the failure of European educational methods to
train women to settle easily in Canada. She describes her surprise at learning that in the New World two-thirds of the
misery which came to the notice of a popular minister of religion 'arose from the infelicity of the conjugal relations'; and
that there, as in Europe, any attempt to discuss it met with
violent opposition. It will be observed that she does not find
America has much to teach her on the subject.

The part of the book which doubtless proved most interesting was that describing Mrs. Jameson's travels among the
Indian tribes, who dubbed her 'the woman of the white foam'
for her courage in shooting the Sault Ste Marie in a canoe. She
concludes her account of her summer travels by making some
observations upon the condition of Indian women, which
most travellers had hitherto condemned in scandalized tones:
'The women, they say, are "drudges", "slaves", "beasts of
burden", victims, martyrs, degraded, abject, oppressed . . . ;
and they seem to consider no expression of disapprobation,
and even abhorrence, too strong for the occasion . . .'[1] She
agrees that they are indeed, drudges; but holds that it should
not be overlooked that the Indians are at a different stage of
civilization, wherein the women are necessarily obliged to
occupy an inferior station, simply because they lack the
physical strength needed in the endless struggle to gain food
by hunting. She has a fine contempt for the ordinary notions
on this topic:

> When it is said, in general terms, that the men do nothing but
> *hunt* all day, while the women are engaged in perpetual *toil*, I sup-
> pose this suggests to civilised readers the idea of a party of gentle-
> men at Melton or a turn-out of Mr. Meynell's hounds;—or at most
> a deer-stalking excursion to the Highlands—a holiday affair; while
> the women, poor souls! must sit at home and sew, and spin, and
> cook victuals.[2]

She goes on to explain that the Indian hunter must in reality
face danger and racking toil merely to live, and consequently

[1] iii, p. 299. [2] iii, p. 300.

115

the women are obliged, in such circumstances, to assist their husbands in ways unfamiliar to a traveller accustomed to the delicacy of European ladies. For example the carrying of burdens by the women while the men go unladen has a simple explanation in the fact that the men must be free to use their weapons in the common defence. With the course of time, porterage had become a task which appears effeminate for a man to undertake, a source of shame to a wife who wishes her man to be as other men. Consequently, Indian women may be o'er-laboured—but at least their position is not false. And it had to be remembered that it is only one of drudgery and servitude in comparison with the refined leisure of an elegant woman in the higher classes of our society; compare it with that of a servant-maid of all work, or a factory girl, and it was gracious in comparison, dignified by domestic feelings, and a sense of equality with all her sex.

If women are to be exempted from toil in reverence to the sex, and as *women*, I can understand this, though I think it unreasonable; but if it be merely a privilege of station, and confined to a certain set, while the great primeval penalty is doubled on the rest, then I do not see where is the great gallantry and consistency of this our Christendom, nor what right we have to look down upon the barbarism of the Indian savages who make *drudges* of their women.[1]

Here we encounter an argument never met with in the conventional books. Most of them make two points clear: that their authoresses are 'ladies', and that they write for the middle class. Mrs. Jameson's conscience led her to prefer to see her sex as women first and ladies perhaps; she had taken the trouble to anatomize society, and the tone of her book was no longer set by references to attar of roses and incense: it has force and vigour, for she looked upon the workings of the social mass and was unafraid to say what she found there. European writers might lift their eyebrows at the low esteem in which chastity is held by the Indians:

. . . what right have civilised *men* to exclaim, and look sublime and self-complacent about the matter? If they do not exactly imi-

[1] iii, p. 305.

tate this fashion of the Indians, their exceeding and jealous reverence for the virtue of women is indulged in at a very cheap rate to themselves. If the chastity of women be a virtue, and respectable in the eyes of the community, for its own sake, well and good; if it be a mere matter of expediency, and valuable only as it affects property,[1] guarded by men just as far as it concerns their honour —as far as it regards ours, a jest,—if this be the masculine creed of right and wrong—the fiat promulgated by our lords and masters— then I should be inclined to answer, as the French girl answered the Prince de Conti, 'Pour Dieu! monseigneur, votre altesse royale est par trop insolente' . . . Such women as those poor perverted sacrificed creatures who haunt our streets, or lead as guilty lives in lavish splendour, are utterly unknown among the Indians.[2]

She makes some interesting comments on Indian tribes that do not live by hunting. Ottawas, who pursue agriculture, have much more favourable conditions for their women; while a tribe of Missouri Indians in which labour for subsistence is small, allow their women a rank and influence higher than any known elsewhere.

These, then, were the views which shocked readers in 1838. The stock estimate of one of the races whose sexual depravity bolstered the self-esteem of Englishmen (although the oriental peoples were even more deplored), had been overthrown; and more than that, European manners themselves were shown to be not merely superficially, but really, depraved and barbarous.

We can safely infer from the introductory dialogue to her next book[3] that Mrs. Jameson's published opinions of 1838 had not escaped the opprobrious sort of censure levelled at women-writers at this time. In print at least she was watching her words, though in her private correspondence she was unabashed. In a few years, however, the 'woman-question' was suddenly and dramatically brought before the public eye again in a way which justified her extremest strictures in that work. She took the opportunity, and once again entered upon the dangerous topic in 1843, this time by way of journalism. In 1842 had appeared the report of the Royal Commission on

[1] She refers to Dr. Johnson's famous dictum on female chastity.
[2] iii, p. 307.
[3] *Social Life in Germany, illustrated in the acted dramas of H.R.H. the Princess Amelia of Saxony* (1840).

the employment of women and young people in mines. Its revelations concerning the working-conditions of women and girls underground provided factual evidence directly support-ing the case of Miss Martineau and Mrs. Jameson exactly as the former had foreseen. In the following year *The Athenaeum* devoted a series of illustrated articles to the terrible revela-tions of the Commissioners, the third of which (on the Com-missioners' second report) was contributed by Mrs. Jameson. In this she summed up and moralized upon the findings; she regarded them as evidence of a dangerous neglect of educa-tion, particularly of women's education. Her old spirit of revolt was fired, and she once more spoke in the vein of *Win-ter Studies and Summer Rambles*, and castigated the blindness of those who retained the old ideal of women in face of glaring anomalies. Women needed employment, yet society brazenly questioned the propriety of a few girls learning the elements of design in a building occupied by boys—three storeys away. In 1846 she published a revised version of the article, under the title 'Woman's Mission and Woman's Position', in her *Memoirs and Essays*:[1] she prefaced it with the story of Donna Maria d'Escobar, who planted a few grains of wheat in her garden in Lima, and thence produced all the wheat in Peru; one is reminded of Tennyson's lyric in *The Princess*:

> Our enemies have fallen, have fallen: the seed,
> The little seed they laugh'd at in the dark,
> Has risen and cleft the soil . . .

She introduces the discussion about educating women for em-ployment by saying: 'After all that has been written, sung, and said of women, one has the perception that neither in prose nor in verse has she ever appeared as the *labourer*. All at once people are startled at being obliged to consider her under this point of view, and no other.'[2] Tennyson was too early committed to his theme to be able to write a poem on woman considered as the labourer, but in 1848 Clough's *The Bothie of Tober-na-Vuolich* (as it was later entitled), struck the new note; and in 1856, Mrs. Browning's *Aurora Leigh* pre-sented the same topic again.

[1] 1846.   [2] p. 213.

The Feminist Controversy in England

Mrs. Jameson's writings over ten years very faithfully reflect the general fortunes of feminism at a critical time. In 1832 she voiced a typically 'lady-like' view which did not challenge the old ideal. In 1838, however, she shared the credit for having uttered a forthright condemnation of the inhumanity of society's attitude to women, taking real life instead of literature for text. We then see her chastened by some occurrence or other which is enigmatically referred to in terms of 'shadows' falling upon her.[1] Then, in 1843, encouraged by the public's shocked recognition of the true situation of women obliged to support themselves by their own labour, she again spoke out, and decided that so great had been the change in general opinion that the woman question was now regarded in a quite different light; the old ideal had been severely shaken, and a new one was in course of being adopted.

[1] In a letter of November 1839, given in Gerardine Macpherson, *Memoirs of the life of Anna Jackson* (1878), p. 162.

CHAPTER VI

The Feminist Controversy in England prior to 'The Princess'—II

THE previous chapter has shown how the ideal of woman's role in English life underwent a remarkable change in the eighteen-thirties. 'Kate', the Owenist writer who in 1835 deplored the neglect of the woman question, was able to write in 1839:

> It may, indeed, be well regarded as one of the most favourable signs of the times, that the sentiments entertained for woman, (and which yet, unfortunately, exist in the great majority), have, by the enlightened few, undergone a change. To those who have anatomised society, and have looked at the workings of the social mass, not through the prism of passion of any kind, but from the single wish of seeing truth, the evils which arise from allowing woman to maintain a position so false and imperfect, are no less astounding in their nature than they are convincing in their effects.[1]

But though the appeals of Harriet Martineau and Mrs. Jameson were eloquent, other writers were equally strongly asserting opposite opinions. *Woman's Mission*, for example, which Mrs. Jameson called 'a beautiful little book', in 1839 transferred to England the almost mystical sentiments concerning 'woman's influence' which had been so ardently expressed in Aimé-Martin's *L'Éducation des Mères*. Moreover, in the same year, the fourth of the six volumes making up Auguste Comte's *Cours de Philosophie positive* appeared, and this too supported the older doctrine on women's position—surprising though this may seem in the work of one of the architects of Saint-Simonian theory. For Comte, attempts to reform the status of women came too close to an attack upon traditional marriage to be welcome, and he argued that the discoveries in biology, particularly those of Gall, showed that there were

[1] *The New Moral World*, v, p. 372.

radical differences, not only physical but also moral, between the sexes, and that these were properly recognized by the institution of marriage as at present constituted. Women's minds, in his view, were undeveloped because their brains were incapable of inductive reasoning; but they were compensated by possessing special powers of sympathy:

> Il est incontestable, en effet . . . que les femmes sont, en général, aussi supérieures aux hommes par un plus grand essor spontané de la sympathie et de la sociabilité, qu'elles leur sont inférieures quant à l'intelligence et à la raison. Ainsi, leur fonction propre et essentielle, dans l'économie fondamentale de la famille, et par suite de la société, doit être spontanément de modifier sans cesse, par une plus énergique et plus touchante excitation immédiate de l'instinct social, la direction générale toujours primitivement émanée, de toute nécessité, de la raison trop froide ou trop grossière qui caractérise habituellement le sexe prépondérant.[1]

Here we see Aimé-Martin's concept of women's influence sustained on 'scientific' grounds. Woman is undeveloped man, whose deficiency of intelligence acts as a check upon man's naturally exclusive and anti-social reasoning.[2]

Similar positions are taken in English works. *Woman's Rights and Duties*, published in 1840, supports Aimé-Martin. Mrs. Sarah Ellis's *The Daughters of England* (one of a popular series) contains the following:

> I must now take it for granted, that the youthful reader of these pages has reflected seriously upon her position in society as a woman, has acknowledged her inferiority to man, has examined her own nature, and found there a capability of feeling, a quickness of perception, and a facility of adaptation, beyond what he possesses, and which, consequently, fit her for a distinct and separate sphere; and I would also gladly persuade myself, that the same individual, as a Christian woman, has made her decision not to live for herself, so much as for others; but, above all, not to live for this world, so much as for eternity.[3]

---

[1] p. 573.
[2] In *The Princess*, the Prince rejects this notion:
> '. . . woman is not undevelopt man
> But diverse.'
[3] p. 16.

The Feminist Controversy in England

Even after the revelations of 1842, books could appear recommending women to subscribe to the old doctrine of self-sacrifice. A good example is *Woman's Worth, or hints to raise the female character*,[1] which condemned all forms of education which did not have the same end as that enjoyed by their 'respected grandmothers'.

Nevertheless, after this date, a decided swing in sympathy is observable. Signs of the change appear earlier. In 1840, for example, Lady Morgan, whose interest in feminism had been displayed as long ago as 1809 in a book called *Woman, or Ida of Athens*, published *Woman and her Master*, a thorough historical survey of women famous and infamous from early classical times to the coming of Christianity. Its feminist purpose is made explicit in its first chapter, which shows Lady Morgan to have been among the first non-Socialist writers on a feminist topic to argue in a positivist spirit. She believed science and the scientific attitude to be the key to men's future; it would oblige them to alter all their old concepts, moral, political and social:

Under this mighty influence, the relations of time and space to human power have been changed, till minutes comprise the labours of days; facts have been substituted for figments, and experiment for learning: and, above all, the intellectual machine itself, released from its scholastic trammels . . . realises, with certainty and precision, effects which the combined exertions of past ages were inadequate to accomplish. Mind, the universal mind, is now everywhere in action, producing new and endless combinations, political, moral and material: and, though the interests of a few, or the lingering prejudices of the many, may oppose and delay its march, still (as the martyr of physical truth was heard to mutter when he left the tribunal of his inquisitors for his dungeon), *e pure si muove*.[2]

So overwhelmingly rapid has been the march of mind in all fields of human interest and activity, that society has advanced in complexity more rapidly than philosophy and legislation can follow. Much suffering, for example, still exists in the midst of civilized societies, untouched by science, unmitigated by laws.

Crimes, necessitated and inevitable, are still committed with a fearful regularity, and in pre-assignable proportions. The arithmetic

[1] 1844.   [2] i, pp. 5, 6.

of statistics can foreshew the numbers of the victims of violence, and determine the instruments of its perpetration.[1] It can calculate the minds that must degrade, the hearts which must break, the felons who must suffer, the suicides who must perish. The future murderer, while yet smiling in innocence on his mother's bosom, is already surrounded by the circumstances which foredoom him to crime: and the fair and blooming hope of many a parent's heart must tread her fated path to shame and reprobation, because institutions are still unexplored, and laws are at war with the ends for which they were enacted.[2]

Lady Morgan introduced this seeming digression on the application of statistics to social workings in order to suggest that it should be possible to overcome many social ills at present entirely neglected because not understood.

There are, then, still unmastered, some great impediments to the working of the social machinery; there are unfitnesses and incongruities obstructing its play, and clogging its movements, that are yet scarcely suspected . . . In the great and general progress of knowledge, much has been neglected, much overstepped, and amidst the most beneficial reforms and sagacious improvements, great moral incoherences still linger, which require to be eliminated, before the interests of humanity can be based upon a system, consonant with nature, and conducive to general happiness.

But where lies the oversight? Can it be one, astounding in its obviousness, and all-important in its mischiefs? While codes have been reformed, institutes rationalised, and the interests of orders and classes have been minutely attended to, has one half of the human species been left, even to the present moment, where the first rude arrangements of a barbarous society and its barbarous laws, had placed it [?] Is woman still a thing of sufferance, and not of rights, as in the ignorant infancy of early aggregation, when the law of the strongest was the only law acted on? and in the great impulsion to a regenerating reform, has that most applicable and intelligible instrument of social improvement and national well-being, has Woman, been forgotten?[3]

[1] Lady Morgan is here referring to the social statistics published by L. A. J. Quetelet, Astronomer Royal at Brussels, in his *Sur l'homme et le développement de ses facultés, ou essai de physique sociale* (Paris, 1835). This work was an important illustration of the usefulness of statistics in social planning; it was consulted by Robert Chambers for his book *Vestiges of Creation*, which is to be discussed in Chapter XI.

[2] i, p. 7.   [3] i, p. 8.

Lady Morgan is here adapting a scientific method to feminism in order to reach a conclusion exactly opposite to Comte's. It is the resort to *practical* inquiry and *practical* reforms that distinguishes the feminism of the forties from that of the preceding decade; what was for a time lacking was suitable scientific evidence to decide whether the claims for greater opportunities for women were justified or not. Lady Morgan did the best she could with the findings of social statistics, but they were inconclusive; and so, for the most part, her book is on the lines of William Alexander's in ostensibly being an historical examination of the place of women in earlier cultures, from which the only conclusion is that her secret influence has invariably been behind man's intellectual achievements. (Here she again turns the tables on Comte; it is not woman, but man, who is intellectually retarded.)

She has, in various ages, given her secret services to her taskmaster, without partaking in his triumph, or sharing in his success. Her subtlety has insinuated views which man has shrunk from exposing, and her adroitness found favour for doctrines, which he had the genius to conceive but not the art to divulge. Priestess, prophetess, the oracle of the tripod, the sybil of the cave, the veiled idol of the temple, the shrouded teacher of the academy, the martyr or missionary of a spiritual truth, the armed champion of a political cause, she has been covertly used for every purpose, by which man, when he has failed to reason his species into truth, has endeavoured to fanaticise it into good; whenever mind has triumphed by indirect means over the inertia of masses.[1]

Lady Morgan might have pointed to an overt example of women's influence in an event which took place in the year that her book was published, 1840. At the Freemasons' Hall in London was held an Anti-Slavery Convention where an American delegation met a large number of English sympathizers. Lady Byron, Mrs. Jameson, Elizabeth Fry, William and Mary Howitt, Ann Knight, Harriet Martineau and Robert Owen were among those they met either publicly or in private. Unexpectedly, this delegation was found to include two women, Mrs. Lucretia Mott and Mrs. Elizabeth Stanton; and to the annoyance of many present, they were excluded from

[1] i, pp. 16–17.

the deliberations by a vote taken at the meeting. William Howitt denounced this as religious bigotry,[1] and William Lloyd Garrison, the leader of the American delegation, sat silent in the gallery as a protest.

This episode clearly illustrates that despite the signs of a more enlightened attitude at the beginning of the forties, the old one was by no means dead. The Reviews reflect this very clearly. A writer in the *Edinburgh Review* for April 1841,[2] in the course of an article discussing the more important works I have mentioned, stated his belief that the prejudice against allowing women an improved education had so much subsided since Sydney Smith's essay appeared in the same periodical thirty years before that it would be supererogatory to discuss it further. Nevertheless, he had small sympathy with women's claim to equal political rights, and denounced the assumption that since women's status had improved as civilization had progressed, there was reason to think that in time complete equality would result. In his view woman's constitution was such as to prevent her achieving eminence in any field of male endeavour; men's greater vigour caused them to go on educating themselves long after their schooldays were over; many a genius revealed his powers despite great obstacles; but where were the women artists and writers?

The *Westminster Review* also reviewed a selection of recent feminist literature at the beginning of 1841, but, as might be expected, in a quite different spirit.[3] It bore witness that feminism was now a question of the hour, and education was one aspect of it in which opinion had shown a material advance: 'On the subject of intellectual education, public opinion and practice have undergone a complete change within a very few years, so that the distinguishing and opprobrious epithet of blue-stocking grows as obsolete and obscure in origin as Whig or Tory.' The writer of the article pointed out that manufactures had supplanted many of the domestic tasks performed by women in the past. Furthermore, even conservatives had admitted at last that for the performance of the remaining

---

[1] *The History of Woman Suffrage*, i, p. 434.
[2] lxxiii (April–July 1841), p. 189.
[3] xxxv (January–April 1841), p. 24.

domestic duties, notably the rearing of children, education was no impediment, but an absolute necessity. He warmly praised Mrs. Jameson's words on the subject, describing them as 'acute and profound, displaying an intimate acquaintance with life (ladies' life especially) and a pretty exact appreciation of the point that society had attained in refinement, conventional or real'.[1] He used her views upon the need of many women to find employment to question the assumptions of books like those of Mrs. Ellis: female modesty would in no way be injured if English women were to undertake the duties of shopkeeping, as was universally seen in France; nor would it long seem improper, if the example of Miss Martineau were followed, for women to engage in literary work. He gave special praise to her *Society in America*, observing that:

> Should the claims of women to representation be any where admitted, we incline to think that they will be so first in our old aristocratic, over-taxed, over-populous, broken down country of England, rather than in young, free, democratic, thriving America, where representatives in husbands may be easily obtained, and where 'helps' (finding also representatives) can with difficulty be procured.[2]

I think that it will be seen that between 1839 and 1842, opinion stood in remarkable equipoise. Indeed, the Report of the Commissioners on the employment of women could not have come at a more opportune moment to tip the balance. Other writers than Mrs. Jameson reacted to the shocking accounts it contained of the life of English working women. Indeed indirectly it had the effect of revealing that the woman question, an issue hitherto seen in broken lights as an involved and apparently irresoluble complex of social problems, was really bedevilled by a single false assumption which had silently operated to cause the position of women to move more and more out of step with the facts of nineteenth-century life. This was that a woman's part in life was to be that of wife and mother exclusively, and that her engaging in gainful work rightly caused her to forfeit, partly at least, the respect and protection of society. The Report showed that many women had no choice but to work, and that their consequent sufferings

[1] p. 31.   [2] p. 48.

deserved pity rather than contumely. The growth from about 1800 onwards of an educational system for girls resembling, as one writer put it, a 'refined inquisition', accompanied by the rise of a governess class[1] to regulate it, could now be seen for what it was—a piece of self-inflicted torture on society's part in an attempt to conform with this futile (because out-moded) belief. After 1842 it was widely recognized that the social stigma had to be removed from women's educating themselves to take part in the work of the world, even if this resulted in a further problem—what would be the new relationship between men and women, and how would traditional marriage fit in? This, of course, appeared at this date rather remote, but the fact that Tennyson treated this theme rather than the narrower one of employment shows that he was aware of the more fundamental problem.

One of the writers who took account of the revelations of the Commissioners' reports was Mrs. Hugo Reid, who published in 1843 a book which she called *A Plea for Women*. She pointed out that thousands of women and children were forced to engage in manual labour in order to subsist, and that many women were driven to prostitution by economic hardship. She demanded equal rights because they would soon do much to relieve the terrible condition of the 'thousands upon thousands' of unprotected women, conveniently overlooked by the exponents of the 'woman's sphere' theory. It might be an accident that such large numbers of women should be outside male protection, but that was not sufficient reason for continuing a prejudice which made it 'next to a loss of caste for any woman to attempt earning an honest and independent livelihood'. Men, she maintained, were retaining their unmerited pre-eminence by disbursing public money upon boys' schools only. Women needed as good an education as men, and if they were truly weaker, they needed a better:

Besides the want of any public attention to the providing of first-rate elementary schools for girls, there is a great want of such

[1] Mrs. Jameson attempted to win sympathy for the plight of governesses in an essay published in her *Memoirs and Essays*. She observed that some thought was at last being given to the matter after fifty years. The book appeared in 1846.

127

institutions as colleges for the young women of the higher ranks who have plenty of leisure; and even of the lower ranks who have a strong desire to pursue their studies diligently and with little liability to interruption. The want of any institutions such as these, where women might pursue in quiet retirement the cultivation of their minds to any extent they might wish, besides its immediate ill effects in throwing unprepared into the bustle and battle of society the individual women who would have delighted to profit by it, has inflicted an indefinite portion of evil on the education of all; by introducing the notion, that any depth of knowledge is beyond the grasp of a woman's mind.[1]

She utterly denied the truth of the Edinburgh Reviewers' claim that men had a natural vigour which enabled them to educate themselves after having left school; they had Universities, where their higher studies were continued under direction:

This line of argument either excludes—very unjustifiably—from all consideration, that large class of young men who receive direct instruction from their superiors in universities long after the age of seventeen; or it asserts that a college education and self-instruction are identical. We think the usual opinion is that these are the opposite of each other; and confess that in this we are inclined to follow the multitude. Certainly, we think that the instruction which a youth receives at the university, though of course less compulsory than that which he received when a boy at school, is still of the same nature,—still to be classed with that instruction which young people receive from their elders. And where is the counterpart to this most valuable part of the education of young men to be found in the education of young women of the same class of society to which these young men usually belong? No counterpart to this is found in the education of any class of young women. When a young man leaves school, he is said to be prepared for college. When a girl leaves school, her education is said to be *finished*; and in that phrase one of the evil influences which pervade the education of girls may be seen.[2]

Here we see the demand for a university education for women formally presented, in the year 1843, some four years after the poem which was to be called *The Princess* had been planned. Clearly Tennyson was not indebted to this work for the idea of

[1] p. 177.   [2] p. 187.

the poem, a truth made the more certain by the fact that Mrs. Reid confined her aggressiveness to theory and principle and advocated no militant action to achieve her ends. She made it clear that none of the reforms she had advocated need cause an angry collision between the sexes, for women could achieve nothing without the help of men; she was confident that the justice of her cause would lead many men to aid it. 'What we wish, and what alone we are likely to see, is, that the sexes should go hand in hand in their endeavours to better the condition of women.'[1] Mrs. Reid's book was warmly received by *The Athenaeum* in the following year,[2] when a writer observed:

Curious—the change, in opinion and in feeling, which has gradually taken place relative to the true social position of one half of the human race! . . . It is not very long since there was a meeting held in one of the chief cities of the empire for providing more effectually the means of education for girls in the middle classes of society. In the discussion which followed, none pressed the measure, some sneered, some talked of 'pies and puddings' and so the matter was allowed to drop. The other day, a similar—no, not a similar, a very different—meeting is held at Liverpool: a member of parliament addresses his hearers on the propriety of giving a higher, a truer, a more useful education to the young women of the middle classes, and the people respond with cheers, and before they separate they lay the foundation of a school where 400 girls are to be trained for the best purposes and highest responsibilities of this life, which include, we presume, the best preparation for the life that is to come.

We learn from a later page that the meeting was held under the auspices of the Mechanics' Institute at Liverpool, presided over by Charles Dickens, who called it a 'new and striking chapter in the history of Education'.[3] (The connection of the

[1] p. 213.

[2] Issues for 2 March 1844 (no. 853), p. 189 and 9 March 1844 (no. 854), p. 215.

[3] No. 853, p. 189. Edgar Johnson, in his *Charles Dickens; his Tragedy and Triumph* (1953), p. 497, gives the following account of Dickens's speech: 'He spoke warmly of the decision to add a girls' school to the institution and extend education to "those who are our best teachers, and whose lessons are oftenest heeded in after life". All society, he contended, had one common goal of human improvement, transcending differences of rank and wealth. "True hearts are more worth than coronets," he quoted Tennyson, "And simple faith than Norman blood."

K   129

The Feminist Controversy in England

Mechanics' Institute with this reform is, as I attempted to show in an earlier chapter, not without significance for an understanding of the Prologue to *The Princess*.) This article shows how a new public sympathy was taking practical expression in a form which a very few years before would have provoked pungent comment. This circumstance has to be taken into account in considering the genesis of Tennyson's poem, the planning and execution of which spanned years in which something of a minor revolution occurred in the field of feminism.

The first steps in practical education for women took cognizance of the great need to improve the lot of working women who needed a general education; but beyond these stood the dream of a college for more advanced studies. The class of women who could most immediately benefit were, of course, the governesses, many of whom lacked the qualifications needed for their work. The problem was how to organize suitable instruction.

This was considered by both the Governesses' Benevolent Institution and the Hon. Amelia Matilda Murray, a Maid of Honour to the Queen, and a friend of Mrs. Jameson and Lady Byron. Charles Grenfell Nicolay, writing in *The English Journal of Education* on Queen's College, London, observed that Miss Murray, not without the Queen's knowledge and assent, had attempted to establish a College for women 'three or four years since', that is, in 1845 or 1846.[1]

The scheme was conceived on a scale of magnitude worthy of its courtly origin, but failed, partly on this very account, but more from its being in the main an exclusive thing, designed solely for

At these words the thirteen hundred people in the audience cheered, clapped, and stamped their feet in a way "thundering and awful".' Another novelist, Edward Bulwer, recommended the Leeds Mechanics' Institution to add a female class to the establishment, to 'endeavour as far as possible to fit women to be the worthy companions of intelligent men'. But the author of 'The New Timon' did not see fit to quote Tennyson. See *The Life of Edward Bulwer, First Lord Lytton, by his grandson* (1913), ii, p. 202.

[1] I met with this article in the form of a reprint dated 1849 in the possession of the Governesses' Benevolent Institution, to whose Secretary I am also indebted for permission to inspect private correspondence etc. in their possession. The article originally appeared in *The English Journal of Education*, n.s., iii (1849), pp. 90 and 174.

educating ladies as governesses, and admitting none but those resident to the advantages it held forth, except some few selected children of literary, scientific and professional men, and they supposed to be training for the same purpose. At any rate, whether from this cause, or because the time was not yet ripe, it failed; but the labours of the philanthropic projectress were not unrewarded having created a very general interest on the subject, and thus prepared the way for further efforts; for it may be recorded to her honour that all first concerned in projecting and founding Queen's College, had already been interested in behalf of Miss Murray's scheme.[1]

The Governesses' Benevolent Institution had the question of training governesses thrust upon them. They originally intended only to help women in straitened circumstances, but it soon became apparent that they could only determine who really was a governess by instituting a system of diplomas. This required examinations, and examinations presupposed teaching. In 1845 the question was discussed and investigated with considerable energy, though in fact it had been decided as early as 1843 to provide a general as opposed to a specialized education. In 1844 an approach was made to the Government. In 1846, Miss Murray transferred several donations she had received for her own project[2] to the Institution, for by then the idea of founding a College was fully established; unfortunately the Government was not enthusiastic about the idea, though the Queen had already granted her permission to the Institution to undertake the project. The heads of the Church had been approached in 1844, and the then Primate had been disposed to allow the Female College to be established under the auspices of the Church of England. His purpose was, however, turned aside by the doubts and scruples of an influential brother-prelate.[3] In June 1847, F. D. Maurice refused the

[1] ibid., p. 91.

[2] She sought to execute her scheme with the aid of the College of Preceptors, whose records unfortunately do not go back sufficiently far to provide more information concerning the scheme. The Governesses' Benevolent Institution's files contain a letter dated 24 March 1847 from Miss Murray warmly applauding their efforts. Mr. Nicolay was responsible for persuading Miss Murray to transfer her interest to the Institution.

[3] I am indebted to the Annual Reports of the Governesses' Benevolent Institution for these details.

office of Principal of the College, but later reconsidered his decision; he had been associated with the project since 1843, and despite his diffidence, he was, by virtue of an interest in women's education extending from his Cambridge days, a most suitable choice. Some have seen a connection between Maurice's interest in Queen's College and Tennyson's writing *The Princess*, to which Maurice warily referred in his lecture entitled *Queen's College, London; its Objects and Method,*[1] only three months after its publication. It is unlikely that Maurice contributed anything to the poem, since he only had the opportunity of seriously considering a practical reform in education in 1843, when Tennyson had already had the poem in mind for four years. Moreover, there seems to be no reliable evidence of any discussion on this subject between the two men, though that they were acquainted seems fairly certain.[2] I think it is necessary, in the absence of any contemporary evidence, to discount the suggestion that there was consultation between Maurice and Tennyson on the founding of Queen's College, Harley Street. The association with it of the poet's name would certainly have added lustre to the college, and indeed Mrs. Alex Tweedie, writing in the Preface to the Jubilee Book of Queen's College (1898), which she edited, observed that 'The plan of establishing a College for Women had been much discussed by Alfred Tennyson, Charles Kingsley, John Hullah, Mrs. Marcet, Mrs. S. C. Hall, etc.'[3] Certainly Charles Kingsley, John Hullah, Mrs. Marcet and Mrs. Carter Hall *were* associated with the Governesses' Benevolent Institution project;[4] but confidence in the assertion that Tennyson was too, is somewhat diminished when we read in one of the essays composing the Jubilee Book, which was based upon the Annual Reports of both the College and the Governesses' Benevolent Institution:

---

[1] 'Delivered in the Hanover Square Rooms 29 March 1848, by F. D. Maurice M.A. Chaplain of Lincoln's Inn.'

[2] From 1839, both Maurice and Tennyson were members of the Sterling Club.

[3] *The First College for Women: Memories and Records of Work Done, 1848–1898* (1898), p. vii.

[4] Hullah was a lecturer, Mrs. Marcet a Lady Visitor; Mrs. Carter Hall wrote at least one story in the interest of the Institution.

The Feminist Controversy in England

But to turn to the group of remarkable men who were associated with him [C. J. Nicolay] in his work—they were a band of college friends, many of them are mentioned in the recent 'Life of Lord Tennyson,'—Frederick Maurice, Richard Trench, Charles Kingsley, Francis Garden; a band of friends who, with Alfred Tennyson himself, in all probability, often talked over the question of women's higher education; the outcome of these talks, in the world of literature, was the publication of the 'Princess' in 1847; and the *practical outcome* was the founding of Queen's College in 1848.[1]

The errors in this statement are obvious; to mention only one, Charles Kingsley was not a member of the 'band of friends' about Tennyson at Cambridge; in fact he went up to Cambridge over seven years after Tennyson had returned to Somersby. Clearly it is possible that Tennyson may have become aware of the project about 1845 when he seems suddenly to have resumed his work upon the poem: equally well he may have heard of Miss Murray's scheme. There are, however, two decisive considerations to be borne in mind. First, the plan of the poem was fixed upon in 1839, and it seems, if we assume that the early MS fragment was written at that time, to have been intended to follow the some romantic narrative that was finally adopted. Secondly, whatever *we* think of Tennyson's concluding passage of hope and encouragement, Maurice himself looked upon *The Princess* as basically opposed to projects like his, or at least to large-scale attempts on such lines. I do not think that this was the poet's intention; but Maurice's response to the poem does not suggest that Tennyson and he worked together upon the scheme.

The launching of a practical attempt to provide a superior education for women might lead one to suppose that the old ideal was losing ground fast in the mid-eighteen-forties. In large measure this appears to be true. *Fraser's Magazine* contained an article in the June 1845 issue which began with a rousing call to action:

Before we throw out any hints on the subject of the present inquiry, we must request our readers to bear in mind, that we assume as facts the extension of womanly duties and the necessity

[1] p. 21: from an essay by Camilla Croudace, Lady Resident, 1898, entitled 'A Short History of Queen's College, London'.

of more active exertion than has hitherto been required from the sex. It would take too much time and space for us to state the causes from which we have drawn such inferences; but we need only point to our machinery and our distant colonies, to the eager rush made in every profession and calling of life, to be assured that the leisure of 'merry Englonde' is fast growing into 'all work and no play'. Women will share in the social revolution: indeed by every token we may know that, for the future, the bulk of English women, married and single, must bear their part in the *work* of life. With those, therefore, whose views of womanhood do not range beyond the vista of society, we have nothing in common; but of those who believe that woman is capable of being more than a toy or a slave we would ask, 'Have the means of improvement kept pace with the growing demands on the powers of women?' 'Is their education suited to their extended responsibilities?'[1]

As we have seen, conservative works continued to appear; but the weight of opinion was against such books, though ten years before the contrary would have been true. Evidence for this is forthcoming from a book published anonymously in 1844 by Anne Richelieu Lamb, called *Can Women Regenerate Society?*

Who can read without a shudder the reports of those who have lately made inquiry into the state of the morals and education of the lower classes of the people; has woman nothing to do with this? Ought she to sit with folded hands when she knows that such misery, such fearful degradation, exist in the heart of her country? Mothers are become poisoners of infants—fathers murderers of their children! and still we boast of our morality! Let woman be dumb about her influence so long as such a brutal state of things exists.[2]

The writer praises *Woman's Rights and Duties*, which was the first of the ladies' manuals—it was published in 1840—to substitute a section on political economy for the usual one on religion.[3] She likewise always considers economic facts first. Marriage has become, she tells us, such an affair of the purse

---

[1] 'An inquiry into the state of girls' fashionable schools', *Fraser's Magazine*, xxxi (January–June 1845), p. 703.

[2] p. 29. See pp. 31–3 for her awareness of the full effect of industrialism upon women. Cf. *Maud*, Part I, XII.

[3] p. 73.

that as a consequence normal conversation between the sexes has been spoiled by suspicion on one side that some other motive was present than a desire of rational pleasure: 'Young persons . . . cannot meet a few times, without some love affair being gossiped about, given out as a hint, that if they are not in love they ought to be so, or else it is very imprudent, and such other absurdity; until it has become absolutely dangerous for a Victoria shawl to say, 'How d'ye do?' to an Albert surtout.'[1] The book denounces the circumscription of women by nonsensical ideas of 'spheres' and 'influence' and lady-like incompetence: 'Since our population has become so vast, our competition so enormous, our difficulty of finding the means of livelihood so great, and every day becoming greater, we have at length begun to ask whether it is always convenient to keep women idle.'[2] Women, she says, have a duty to stop pretending that they can influence a society governed by principles and practices of which they are kept ignorant. At present they are mere pawns in a man's world. She draws a painful picture of a 'modern woman':

> Treated at one moment as a child, at another as a plaything, if fair as an angel—for a while! Then wearied of as the child, thrown away as the toy, and beauty vanished, stript of her angelic splendour, and forced to tread the miry paths of life in the way she best can. Such is woman now; trained from childhood to believe that for man, and for man alone, she must live, that marriage must be not only her highest, but her only aim on earth, as in it is comprised the whole of her destiny.[3]

The Princess Ida expresses this very well:

> Knaves are men,
> That lute and flute fantastic tenderness,
> And dress the victim to the offering up,
> And paint the gates of Hell with Paradise,
> And play the slave to gain the tyranny.

While women remain in a false position with regard to society they are condemned to untold miseries. The elaborate pretence that modern life is still as simple as it was when the old ideal was formulated is being revealed for what it is:

[1] p. 101. See also pp. 20, 22. [2] p. 176. [3] p. 13.

The Feminist Controversy in England

I would not willingly represent matters to be worse than they are, but when we peep for even a moment behind the veil which gaily floats over their surface, we see such fearful sights, such appalling pictures, that we start back affrighted, and can scarcely admit, even to ourselves, that we have gazed upon reality, or seen the false foundation upon which the edifice rests, and the hidden springs which make the actors move. Those who glance only at the superficies of things, or judge merely from outward appearances, can have no conception whatever of the guilt, the misery and the wretchedness, which lurk beneath the specious covering.[1]

What part of that misery was she makes plain. Like the Owenites she was not afraid of taking cognizance of the prevalence of prostitution in large cities.

Another writer, in the following year, gave praise to Mrs. Jameson for treating this topic, and denounced the belief that such things are inevitable, a necessary part of civilization. The author wrote:

So speaks the *citizen*. Man born of woman, the fa her of daughters, declares that he will and must buy the comforts and commercial advantages of his London, Vienna, Paris, New York, by conniving at the moral death, the damnation, so far as the action of society can insure it, of thousands of women for each splendid metropolis.[2]

The work from which this passage is taken, Margaret Fuller's *Women in the Nineteenth Century* (London, 1845), is of some importance for this study, for it might be said to record one of the sweet dreams of the New England Transcendentalists in which Dawson considered the woman question of the nineteenth century to have originated. Margaret Fuller originally contributed a short version of it to *The Dial*, the Transcendentalist journal lately transferred from her own editorship to that of Emerson. It was then called *The Great Lawsuit. Man versus Men: Woman versus Women*, and it appeared in the issue for July 1843.[3] That it in no way originated the feminist movement is, I think, sufficiently clear from the foregoing chapters; indeed Harriet Martineau's harsh description of the Discussion Circle at Boston, of one of whose deliberations it was the outcome, as a group of 'gorgeous pedants' sufficiently indicates the book's relationship to the situation in England in 1845. The book is a remarkable *mélange* of lofty literary criticism, especially of the Greek dramatists and Goethe and Schiller, and on the other hand, the reflections on feminism prompted by extensive reading and an acquaintance with the Abolition discussions of the day. That America was drawing inspiration from Europe on this question is also indicated by her reference to Swedenborg, Goethe and Fourier as prophets of the coming age;[1] these writers were of particular interest to the Transcendentalists, Fourier later inspiring the mode of governing their experimental community, the Brook Farm Association.[2]

With this mention of one of the first important American contributions to the discussion of feminism, published in 1845, I can sum up the developments since 1839. During these years an improved education for women came to be seen not merely to be desirable, as in the thirties, but wholly necessary. Conservatives still insisted that its purpose should be moral and directed to preserving the old ideal, which was itself in jeopardy from the type of education which had grown up as a symptom of its own inadequacy. Progressives, however, were bent on complete equality of opportunity; the situation had so far progressed that a practical beginning had been made. The major factor which prompted this development seems to have been the new social knowledge disseminated by Mrs. Jameson and Harriet Martineau in the late eighteen-thirties, but only driven home by the revelations of 1842.

It is pleasant to be able to take leave of this survey on a light note. Richard Monckton Milnes unwarily involved himself in the woman question by publishing in 1844 a volume of poems called *Palm Leaves*. Milnes had visited the Near East in the winter of 1842–3, and wishing to give his impressions without adding to the long catalogue of travel-books describing that fascinating region,[3] he decided to embody them in a

[1] pp. 114 ff.
[2] See William P. Trent, *A History of American Literature 1607–1865* (1903), pp. 306, 308.
[3] He lists the well-known ones. For a discussion, see Wallace C. Brown, 'The popularity of English travel books about the near-east', *PQ*, xv (1936), p. 70.

book of poems. He was sufficiently conscious of developments in contemporary feminism to join the list of subscribers to the Governesses' Benevolent Institution in 1844; and what he saw, or did not see, on his travels decided him to imitate Mrs. Jameson in defending a people normally charged with a callous indifference to women. Many of the works discussed in this study inveighed against the low condition of women in the East; Lady Morgan's *Ida of Athens* and Lawrence's *Empire of the Nairs* were typical. Aimé-Martin had shuddered at the thought of the life of women in the East; Princess Ida scorned the 'stunted squaws of east or west'. As we shall see, Caroline Norton had reason to sum up the state of English law in 1839 as 'in a degree the Turkish creed, whereby woman is merely regarded as the toy of an hour'; this, of course, was meant to shock the reader; and this was Junius Redivivus's intention when he had some years before called an English wife a member of a harem.[1] One of Milnes' poems essayed a rehabilitation of the oriental lady by picturing her alone, enjoying many of the privileges and pleasures of the English 'home', and quietly exercising her gentle influence in the same manner as her occidental sister. This poem was called 'The Hareem'.

> Thus in the ever-closed Hareem,
>   As in the open Western home,
> Sheds womanhood her starry gleam
>   Over our being's busy foam;
> Through latitudes of varying faith
>   Thus trace we still her mission sure,
> To lighten life, to sweeten death,
>   And all for others to endure.

Such sentiments as these, quite apart from their rather unflattering comparison, were a little out of date. But Milnes was in a serious mood, and took pains to disarm his readers. In the Preface to the volume he wrote:

I am not sure that the picture of ordinary life in the East, as given in the poem of the Hareem, will not appear novel and strange: for we have taken our notions of Eastern domesticity much more

---

[1] 'On the condition of women in England', *The Monthly Repository*, N.S., vii (1833), p. 217.

from the ballet than from reality, and have coloured them with so much ferocity and vice, that what is really commonplace becomes paradoxical. Polygamy is usually spoken of as the universal practice of the East, while a little inquiry will inform the traveller that it is a licence almost confined to the very wealthy . . . Occasionally, the abuse occurs of a young wife being brought into the family to supersede the old one, who becomes degraded almost to a servant; but this could hardly occur where the family of the first wife was of respectable rank in society, or where there had been any children, the character and position of the mother throughout the East being most scrupulously respected. The Woman there earns her dignity by maternity; the Sultana Vàlide is a greater personage than any European queen-mother; and the slave who bears a child to a Mohammedan father at once becomes free . . .[1]

Milnes' intrepidity in trying to suggest that woman's influence was the same the world over fortunately met its inevitable chastisement in a review by one able to extract the last drop of humour from the thought of Milnes' explorations of the harems he met with on his travels. Kinglake, then just at the zenith of his fame,[2] hit upon the idea of including the volume of poems in a list of books by Mrs. Jameson and Mrs. Ellis which he reviewed under the general title 'The Rights of Women'.[3] This served him well, for not only could he enjoy the joke of putting Milnes among very strange company, but he was also able to extend the light-hearted tone (suitable to rectifying any public misapprehension Milnes might have created) to the rarified notions of Mrs. Ellis.[4] The result is an article as witty as Sydney Smith's in the *Edinburgh Review*. How, asks Kinglake, did Milnes walk the 'deeply-shaded gardens where Beauty and Mystery dwell'? Remembering one of his nicknames ('the cool of the evening'), we can enjoy Milnes' discomfiture at the following:

One contrivance, they say, is this; to put on the attire of a woman, and gain admission upon pretence of selling choice trifles

[1] *Palm Leaves*, Preface, p. xvi.

[2] See James Pope-Hennessy, *Monckton Milnes. The years of promise, 1809–1851* (1949), p. 229.

[3] *The Quarterly Review*, lxxv (December 1844–March 1845), p. 94.

[4] The works of Mrs. Jameson also quoted were *The Characteristics of Women* and *The Romance of Biography*, which do much less than justice to her achievement.

The Feminist Controversy in England

from Paris and London, and especially toilet luxuries: did **Mr.**
Milnes thus disguised, make his way to the women's apartments,
entreating them 'just to try his only true and genuine Kalydor for
the People', or his pots of modest 'blushing Paste *à la jeune Angle-*
terre', and imploring them too to 'beware of the unprincipled persons who imitate his inimitable and refreshing Essence *à la fraicheur*
du soir?[1]

Kinglake's high spirits made short work of Mrs. Ellis's well-
meant, but fatiguing advice:

This subject of 'Woman' is so splendid, so terrible, so enchanting, so vast—and, in short (to use the language of the polka
dancers), so 'Catholic' that perhaps no imaginable treatment of it
would ever seem quite satisfactory. Sometimes, for whole pages
together, we find so much virtue inculcated, that we almost give
ourselves credit for having perused some sermons, and long, by
way of relief to find our authoress stooping to practical views . . .
We long, and not in vain—for presently the descent takes place;
but it is effected by the writer with such admirable gravity of
countenance, that the gravity of the reader becomes impossible.
Thus we are told that, 'in the character of a noble, enlightened, and
truly good man, there is a power and a sublimity so nearly approaching what we believe to be the nature and capacity of angels,
that as no feeling can exceed, so no language can describe', but
presently, and without at all quitting her solemn, didactic style,
the writer speaks of 'the complacency and satisfaction which most
men evince when finding themselves placed at table before a
favourite dish'. In touches such as these there is something of a
Cervantes-like humour, delightfully improved upon by drawing
the elements of sublimity and bathos from the same person. Most
pleasant it is to see the bright 'angel' fold up his celestial wings, lay
a napkin under his chin, and sit down Sancho Panza confessed![2]

We shall see later that Tennyson, like Milnes, shows in his
poem a taste for the oriental, diluted in its effect by being
mingled with other strains; but the fascination of *The Princess*
lay in its portrait of a new pattern of woman, admirably described by Kinglake in the concluding paragraph of his article:

Books can instruct, and books can amuse, and books can **exalt**
and purify; beauty of face and beauty of form will come with

---

[1] p. 100. See Nowell C. Smith, *Letters of Sydney Smith* (1953), ii, p. 755.
[2] p. 112.

bought pictures and statues, and for the government of a household hired menials will suffice; but fondness and hate, daring hope, lively fear, the lust for glory, and the scorn of base deeds, sweet charity, faithfulness, pride, and chief over all, the impetuous will, lending might and power to feeling—these are the rib of the man, and from these, deep-veiled in the mystery of her very loveliness, his true companion sprang. A being thus ardent will often go wrong in her strenuous course—will often alarm—sometimes provoke— will now and then work mischief, and even perhaps grievous harm, but she will be our own Eve after all—the sweet-speaking tempter, whom Heaven created to be the joy and the trouble of this 'pleasing anxious' existence—to shame us away from the hiding-places of a slothful neutrality, and lead us abroad in the world, men militant here on earth, enduring quiet, content with strife, and looking for peace hereafter.

CHAPTER VII

John Mitchell Kemble, Caroline Norton and the Idea of a University

THE fresh attitude to the woman question which developed so suddenly in the eighteen-forties is very fairly summed up in Mrs. Jameson's remark that people were all at once obliged to see woman as the *labourer*. This idea was soon given literary expression in Clough's *Bothie* (1848). The poem tells of the heart-searchings of a young man, Philip Hewson, who holds the view that the beauty of women is not a purely aesthetic matter, but is connected with their usefulness to society. This relating of beauty to utility earns him the affectionate title of 'the Pugin of women' from his Oxford friends. He addresses the accomplished women of his time thus:

—Ye unhappy statuettes, and miserable trinkets,
Poor alabaster chimney-piece ornaments under glass cases,
Come, in God's name, come down! the very French clock by you
Puts you to shame with ticking; the fire-irons deride you.
You, young girl, who have had such advantages, learnt so quickly,
Can you not teach? O yes, and she likes Sunday-school extremely,
Only it's soon in the morning. Away! if to teach be your calling,
It is no play, but a business: off! go teach and be paid for it.
Lady Sophia's so good to the sick, so firm and so gentle.
Is there a nobler sphere than of hospital nurse and matron?
Hast thou for cooking a turn, little Lady Clarissa? in with them,
In with your fingers! their beauty it spoils, but your own it
        enhances,
For it is beautiful only to do the thing we are meant for.

Eventually he marries a poor Highland girl and sets off with her to a settler's life in New Zealand.

Mrs. Browning's *Aurora Leigh* (1856) tells the story of the scion of a noble house, Romney Leigh, who likewise seeks to marry a woman of lower station than his own; but this time

142

the events are seen through the eyes of his cousin Aurora who had earlier refused him. In this poem we are persuaded to reject a notion implicit in Clough's, namely, that a woman should see in marriage the means of furthering the social ideals of her husband. (The poem draws the moral implicit in the Rivers episode in *Jane Eyre*.) Aurora cannot accept Romney's belief that love is to be subordinated to social service, and that a woman's own choice of life-work is to be put aside on that account. Moreover, as a poet, she puts more trust in spiritual than in social reform; and she is justified in that her book of poems succeeds, while Romney's 'phalanstery' at Leigh Hall, 'Christianised from Fourier's own', is burnt down by an ungrateful mob.

It is of interest that both these poems show an awareness of a link between French social theories and the woman question which is their common theme. Philip Hewson is judged to be tinged with this 'confounded égalité, French manufacture', while Romney Leigh drew his social theories from the writings of Fourier, Proudhon, Considérant, Louis Blanc and others.

The Princess does not directly treat the question of woman's work at all, but deals with the more fundamental issue of the marriage relationship after women have been allowed to exploit their intellectual capacity. We may therefore say that it is to some extent less topical (though this is not to say that it is inferior). The reason for this is that the plan formed in 1839 —and if we take the MS fragment to be of about that date, we can see that the story selected then was unchanged in 1845 when composition was actively pushed forward—better fitted the attitude prevalent at that date. What that attitude was I attempted to describe in Chapter V. Briefly, it may be said that although feminism had then been brought prominently before the public eye, and had earned some sympathy, there was still a determined opposition to an abandonment of the old ideal. The tone of the earlier part of the poem is set by the story, which strongly recalls a fairy tale, and we inevitably receive the impression that Ida's aspirations are to be mocked as are those of the young aspirants in *Love's Labour's Lost*. But everyone notices the change which comes over the story near its end; the fairy-tale quality disappears, and the discussion between Ida and the Prince becomes serious. This change of sympathy was acknowledged by Tennyson himself, and the Prologue and Conclusion were written later (as the MS establishes) partly to explain the change away. The story-tellers and their audience, he says, had different views on the way the subject should be treated. The men wanted a 'sort of mock-heroic gigantesque', but the women of the party opposed this, and drove them in the end to 'quite a serious close'.

> And I, betwixt them both, to please them both,
> And yet to give the story as it rose,
> I moved as in a strange diagonal,
> And maybe neither pleased myself nor them.

The true reason for this unsatisfactory state of affairs is probably that the poet was given cause to change his own approach to the theme by the events of the eighteen-forties which I have described in Chapter VI, though other factors still to be discussed have also to be taken into account. These events all occurred during the period of the poem's gestation.

Two questions now arise. What could have led Tennyson to adopt his original point of view, to seek to ridicule, though in genial terms perhaps, the idea of a college for women; and what definite proposal that a woman's college should be founded was made in or just before 1839? Hitherto nothing has been mentioned of a definite suggestion before Mrs. Hugo Reid's in 1843. Moreover, Tennyson's poems had not given any strong indication of hostility to women's aspirations before this, but rather the reverse. It is this which might lead one to suspect that he had been influenced by events occurring in or just before 1839 to adopt a viewpoint in some measure opposed to his previous inclinations, and which he was not long able to sustain.

Clearly, the first matter to be decided is when and where a suggestion for a women's college was made which could have come to Tennyson's notice at the right time. In the ordinary way such an idea would in all probability at this date have seemed so bizarre that it would have passed practically unnoticed, as did Mrs. Grimstone's recommendation a few years

before. Consequently we may infer that whatever the suggestion was, it must have received a quite unusual amount of
publicity, and it is this which I think makes identification
more easy.

In the issue of *The Metropolitan Magazine* for May 1838,[1]
there appeared an unsigned article called 'An Outline of the
Grievances of Women'. This article had been extensively advertised in advance by the publishers, Saunders and Otley, so
that many more copies than usual of the magazine were sold.
But on the whole, it was not a particularly arresting piece of
journalism. Its theme was a bold enough re-statement of much
that had already been said by progressives. As its motto, it
bore the words 'Equal rights, equal privileges, and equal laws'.

It began with the three leading ideas of the reform movement. Women are before the laws no better than slaves, and
this, in view of the British attitude towards American slavery,
is an anachronism. Knowledge, not force, is now the source of
power. The barriers between race, creed and class are all falling, and now is the time to act:

> I fearlessly ask if the women of this country are inferior to the
> men either in patriotism, in honour, or in honesty? Are they in-
> ferior in moral courage, in fidelity, or in political consistency? 'Per-
> haps not; but they are inferior in ability and in knowledge.' With
> sorrow I confess that at present they are deficient in knowledge,
> but that they are so in ability, I deny. Have they ever been tried?
> On the contrary, have they not been systematically kept in igno-
> rance—and has not every imaginable means been resorted to in
> order to perpetuate that ignorance? I say it, and I say it boldly,
> that there is no post of trust, no important office, for which women
> are not naturally as well qualified as men. Every employment
> should therefore be open to them—no favour should be shown, and
> if they fail, let them incur the penalty of their incompetence.[2]

Since the Reform Act, women of ability, property and strong
political views have had to suffer the humiliation of witnessing their most incompetent tenants, often mere servants and
road-makers, entitled to a set of privileges in representation
denied to themselves. The argument that women are represented by their male relatives is a plausible deception, for

[1] xxii (May–August 1838), p. 16.   [2] p. 17.

some women have none; and some sorts of legislation concerning the married state must determine questions over which the sexes are at variance. That women have *influence* is equally a vain argument against denying them rights: often the greatest influence is exercised by the least admirable women, while political influence is often exercised with a complete irresponsibility. The remedy for this painful situation lies in education and in combination. An intellectual education would not be wasted upon women because of their lack of steadiness, since young girls often outstrip boys in the same scholastic pursuits. Women really differ between themselves as much as men, and seem to be so much alike only because at present they are spoiled by a foolish upbringing.

Here we see a thorough-going claim to something practical —education and combination, words which at this date were familiar, indeed too familiar. The prickly problems of state-aided education and trade unionism were at this time the subject of constant discussion and heart-burning.[1] The Saint-Simonian doctrine that the interests of women and workpeople were the same was proving unpleasantly true to fact.

The writer (who is only known to be a woman) then gives closer attention to girls' education, and denounces the over-taxing of memories at the expense of the reasoning powers. She seems to foresee something of the syllabus of Tennyson's imaginary women's college. The mathematical and physical sciences, metaphysics, astronomy and mechanics are the things she has in mind. She makes no cavil over the womanliness or otherwise of such inquiries. 'The best-ascertained facts in science are unknown to the greatest proportion of women of leisure; and I imagine that few young ladies would not be puzzled to solve the simplest problem in astronomy or mechanics.'[2]

A reader thus far might expect that a proposal to educate women on such lines, involving as it would the establishment

---

[1] The collision between the Unions and the Government signalized by the Tolpuddle Martyrs episode occurred in 1834, remission of the sentence occurring in 1836. Lord Brougham proposed a scheme of national education in 1837. The grant in aid of education established in 1834 was raised to £30,000 in 1839.

[2] p. 22.

of a new style of University, would go the way of all such notions—be forgotten or put on one side with a good deal of male scorn. But its connection with a parallel proposal to organize large-scale agitation to cut the ground from under the feet of male opponents gives a touch of revolutionary fire much more exciting than the well-meant but vain exhortations of other writers. She goes on to recommend that women should form associations to realize their ambition to have a women's college and like objects. These associations would turn every possible occurrence to account, and thrust feminist doctrine into publications of all sorts. It had been said at the time when it was proposed to have a gallery for ladies in the new House of Commons that no petition from the ladies themselves supporting the measure had been presented. Very well, let women so organize themselves throughout the country as to be able to collect signatures for petitions to the House quickly—and overwhelmingly. A woman's party consisting of half the nation would be irresistible.

Those who now laugh at the idea of female emancipation, would find their mirth suddenly checked when they saw associations of enlightened and determined women springing up in every town and village, and numbering thousands and tens of thousands amongst their numbers. Even those most opposed to our views would be unable to close their eyes to the fact that when women systematically begin to investigate their grievances, a great social revolution is at hand, and the tyranny of sex is nearly over.[1]

Such was the well-publicised article which greeted the readers old and new of *The Metropolitan Magazine* in May 1838. To many, its ardour and succinctness must have come as a revelation, even though a great deal in it was not in any way new. It soon received notice in another journal, *The British and Foreign Review, or European Quarterly Journal*. In the issue for July of the same year, an article was published in which the writer observed that 'Our notice was first attracted to it by a flaming puff preambulatory, inserted for several days in the public journals; to wit,—that the article was from the pen of one of the most talented and amiable of her sex, who, from her own experience, could do full justice to the subject'.[2] This comment

[1] p. 26.   [2] vii (July–October 1838), p. 394.

supplies the clue to the success of the article, and the increased sale of the magazine. Most people would certainly have expected revelations from the most celebrated of the *mal mariées* of the time, for she was certainly considered talented and amiable. This was the Hon. Mrs. Caroline Norton.

The details of Caroline Norton's unhappy marriage to George Chapple Norton in 1827 which culminated in her husband's bringing an action against the Prime Minister, Lord Melbourne, in June 1836, are well known and need not be rehearsed here. The case naturally caused a sensation, and may well have done a good deal towards drawing attention to the injustice of the divorce laws of the time, which did not allow a woman to defend herself in court against the allegation of misconduct with the defendant, who as a result might, of course, be in collusion with a plaintiff desirous of ridding himself of a wife at all costs. In any case, Caroline Norton herself certainly spared no effort afterwards to disabuse the public's mind. Her social position and reputation as a poetess had ensured her literary success in the Annuals, and consequently in the eyes of an extensive public. When she found herself barred from access to her children on living apart from her husband, she bravely took a part in an attempt to reform the law governing the custody of infants by supporting in 1837 a private member's bill in the name of Serjeant Talfourd (who had acted with Sir John Campbell in the defence of Melbourne in 1836). This Bill sought to give the courts powers in certain circumstances to award the custody of infant children to their mothers; at this time the father's right was unchallengeable. The combination of talent and well-advertised grievance[1] in

---

[1] She wrote to some of the people I have mentioned as being concerned with feminist matters. On 11 January 1837, she wrote to William Johnson Fox, Tennyson's earlier reviewer, asking his advice about a pamphlet she proposed issuing on the custody of infants. See *The Life of W. J. Fox*, ed. Richard Garnett (1910), p. 187.

She wrote to Edward Bulwer on 2 March 1838, seeking his support for Talfourd's Bill (he was at this time an M.P.) on the grounds of his being known to hold radical opinions, and also because he had permitted his own children to remain with Mrs. Bulwer on their separation two years earlier. For Bulwer's interest in feminism, see above, p. 52, n. 7. She also wrote to Charles Buller. See *The Life of Edward Bulwer, First Lord Lytton, by his grandson* (1913), ii, pp. 517–20.

Caroline Norton would, in 1838, have certainly led many people to think that the article in *The Metropolitan Magazine* was very probably by her. Talfourd's Bill was withdrawn in the course of the session in 1837, but was reintroduced in 1838, when it passed the Commons but was thrown out by the Lords in August. Next year, 1839, it passed both Houses, and although the concessions it made were really almost pitifully slight, it marked the first official recognition of the new view of the rights of women[1]—the claim of women whose marriages had foundered to have their cases for the custody of their infant children at least considered, instead of being denied even a hearing. In 1839, the law of England recognized that children were not the property of their fathers in all circumstances, but that women sometimes had a higher claim than men.

The article in *The British and Foreign Review* which reviews 'An Outline of the Grievances of Women' seems to suppose Caroline Norton wrote it, though it makes the suggestion in a very curious and apparently malicious way. The contents page placed at the beginning of the number as a whole gives the publications to be reviewed as the Custody of Infants Bill, two of Serjeant Talfourd's speeches (14 December 1837 and 14 February 1838) as reported in *The Times*: and finally:

Statement of the Wrongs of Women by the Honourable Mrs. C. Norton.

When we come to the article itself, expecting to find this list repeated at the head, we find first that an additional speech of Serjeant Talfourd is included—one for 9 May 1838—and also a pamphlet *The Separation of Mother and Child by the Law of 'Custody of Infants' considered.*[2] No mention whatever is made of Caroline Norton's so-called *Statement of the Wrongs of Women*, but instead the article itself contains (in a Postscript) a review of the *Metropolitan Magazine* article already discussed, though no mention of this article had appeared in

---

[1] Such was the view of Harriet Martineau: see *A History of the Thirty Years' Peace*, iv, p. 10, where the Bill is discussed in detail.

[2] It was first distributed, not sold, in 1837. See *Some Unrecorded Letters of Caroline Norton, in the Altschul Collection of Yale University Library*, ed. Bertha Coolidge (Boston, 1934), p. 6.

either of the lists of publications under review. If we wish, we can charitably assume that the editor had intervened, extremely inefficiently, before the review was printed, and that Caroline Norton was not meant to be considered as the author of the *Metropolitan Magazine* article; but it is extremely difficult to resist the conclusion that his intention was to make clear Caroline Norton's authorship without actually being held responsible for any such inference.

The extreme topicality of the article will be understood when it is remembered that it appeared in July 1838, after the Custody of Infants Bill had passed the Commons in May, and before it was defeated in the Lords in August. It was obviously intended to influence the public as much as possible on the subject of the Bill while there was yet time: the *Metropolitan Magazine* article, which many could excusably believe to have been written by Caroline Norton, came opportunely to hand to receive a *coup de grâce*. But before this section of the *British and Foreign Review* article is discussed, something must be said about the main part. It occupies no less than one hundred and twenty-five pages, amounting to about 55,000 words, and gives no less than eleven objections to the Bill. The tone of the article is not, however, dispassionate: there is a note of anger running through the writing, and emphasis is attained by the frequent use of italics:

> Undoubtedly, *at present*, and this mainly because *at present* the law affixes to a mother's desertion of her little ones the merited punishment and disgrace of non-access, these are looked on by society with a different eye,—just and well that it is so!—and except some few, who either on account of their husband's *notorious* bad treatment of them, or by their own distinguished talents, wealth, personal attractions or political connexions, still manage to keep up an equivocal position in society, the most of them are branded in public opinion, as mothers, who can lightly desert their offspring, ought to be.[1]

Serjeant Talfourd is not met on the grounds of his explicit arguments in favour of allowing innocent wives separated from their husbands access to their children, but on the assumption that he has dark designs of favouring other women

[1] p. 286.

less pure: the conclusion regarding his own moral position is not left undrawn.

It would be tedious to rehearse the detailed examination of the Bill: suffice it to say that it is both prolix and excited, and adopts an extremely reactionary position. It makes very large deductions from small premisses. Indeed, it is apparent that the writer judged the Bill on grounds which were arrived at only as a result of long reflection upon the whole question of a reform in the social status of women. A footnote[1] indicates, moreover, that the heat was not generated by encountering the combustible *Metropolitan Magazine* article: the review was obviously almost finished, if not wholly so, before the latter was met with. It is very probable that the writer had wished for an opportunity of denouncing the whole development towards emancipation. He sees Serjeant Talfourd as subscribing to '*St. Simon*, rather than St. Paul', and according to him, the Pauline view of woman's subalternity had in recent times been much contested and denied, 'openly in France, more secretly in England'. The view that the two sexes are equal is so fundamentally opposed to English traditions that an

entirely different system of legislation and society must necessarily spring from it: and this also is equally certain, for it has been proved by experience; that this last doctrine, pushed to its furthest limit, as the Saint-Simonians tried to push it, must inevitably end in domestic anarchy, and the destruction of the family. Indeed, Mr. Fourier, who, strange writer though he be, is yet a far more consistent logician than Mr. de St. Simon, openly avows his intention, as does Mr. Owen, to destroy the family as at present constituted.[2]

Mr. Serjeant Talfourd must surely see that his advocacy of equal rights for women will tend in the same direction, since common experience shows the inferiority of women to be natural, and in accordance with Christian teaching:

Why do we dwell so earnestly on this? Because it is the root of the whole matter; because if we were once to admit, and establish by law, the speculative doctrine of the equality of the sexes, of the

[1] p. 332. [2] ibid.

151

J. M. Kemble, Caroline Norton

'co-equal rights of parents', the most dangerous and alarming practical consequences would speedily follow. We say there is strong reason for every man who is asleep to be alarmed from his slumber at this time. Are there no symptoms of danger, no signs of *alarming* changes among us? Is not this speculative falsehood, which we here reprobate, becoming more and more the creed of hundreds and thousands of persons in this country? If any one doubts this, let him broach the question in any place where such a subject could be admitted as discussible, and he will soon see how many partizans that gallant doctrine of the sexual equality can number. Let him look at the general tone of the literature most generally read and circulated, and read himself with his own eyes whether the propagation of this doctrine, indirectly and directly, is not becoming more and more frequent so as almost to pass without remark! But we ask of those purblind, short-sighted legislators, who are so ready to revile and destroy the fundamental principle of the old law of England, as a hideous tyranny, whether they are aware that, at this moment, in the very centre of London, exists a society, consisting principally of the working classes, numbering thousands of members, and having agents and booksellers and branch societies in almost all the great towns of England, whose professed object is entirely to revolutionize the whole social system? While Lords and Commons are disputing about insignificant forms and small amendments,—legislating for their own selfish interests,—these men are meditating, nay, already preparing, nothing less than the destruction of all Christian society,—propagating the belief of the necessity of a complete social sub-radical change; and what is more, *one of the chief doctrines that they most zealously propagate in order to effect this change* is this very one of THE EQUALITY OF THE SEXES. In France, their co-revolutionaries have gone still further, and scruple not openly to demand the admission of the doctrine to its fullest extent, and to talk of the necessity of a *female Messiah*!!! Great indeed must be the exultation of these female emancipators to hear of the success of the revolutionary Custody of Infants' Bill in the Commons, through the legislative talents of Mr. Serjeant Talfourd.[1]

It is not difficult to identify the 'society . . . having agents and booksellers and branch societies in almost all the great towns of England . . .' The association of the Owenists, Saint-Simonians and Fourierists in the reviewer's mind shows how

[1] p. 353.

152

well-publicized the doctrines of the social reformers were. The writer is careful to give full details of Caroline Norton's domestic misfortunes and her connection with the Bill, and, while seeking to defend the journal as far as possible in advance by saying that it usually refrains from dealing in personalities, uses a good deal of space in heaping opprobrium upon her character; he concludes the almost interminable review (he regrets that it is not longer) with a sidelong attack upon a Married Women's Property Bill and a vigorous exhortation to true-born Englishmen to resist such legislation.

We then come to the Postscript dealing with the article in *The Metropolitan Magazine*. The writer begins by utterly deriding the parallel made between the disappearance in the nineteenth century of discrimination against religious sects and the elevation of the status of women which is to be achieved by agitation. Women are naturally inferior; no example of a woman of genius is known; any attempt to reform on the basis of equality would lead to anarchy:

> What! could not she about whose talents so much has been said by her publishers, as if she were to be turned out a new Bradamante, armed or denuded, *cap à pied*, to run a joust or wrestle with any man,—nay, with the whole male sex one after another, an they choose, in proof of the rights and capacity of women;—could not this bold Bradamante of the nineteenth century, who 'fearlessly denies' that her sex are at all inferior in ability,—and doubtless, therefore, as their self-constituted champion, and foremost woman belligerent, has no mean opinion of her own abilities; could not she, with all her talents, perceive, what is perceptible to the most ordinary mind possessing common sense, the absurdity of reasoning on things entirely disparate, as if they were homogeneous?[1]

She overlooks the fact that male privileges co-exist with liabilities and that no one prevents women from obtaining whatever education they desire:

> If they be 'retained in profound ignorance', who is it that so retains them, unless it be themselves? We know of no places devoted to education from which they are excluded, except the dissecting room and its adjuncts: for if women cannot go to the universities, they lose little by that; since there is nothing useful

[1] p. 395.

taught there which might not just as well be taught, if desirable, at any well-regulated female-school. Nay, should women desire, as this publicity-courting lady seems to do, to have a female university; to confer degrees in *Arts*, Medicine, etc.;—why do they not institute one? Should they find at first any difficulty in obtaining a charter, they might console themselves by reflecting, that other male institutions of this nature have also been compelled to wait long enough for theirs![1]

It will be seen that the somewhat nebulous aspirations of the writer of the article in *The Metropolitan Magazine* for an intellectual education have here been given distinct shape. The reviewer takes her literally, and specifies a *female university*; and, be it noted, makes two points which show a realistic approach to the question: he believes men's university education to be of no very high standard: and a new university would in all probability meet stiff opposition when it sought the grant of a charter.

Paragraph by paragraph the article in *The Metropolitan Magazine* is anatomized and held up to ridicule. The writer is termed 'this sage and well-disciplined would-be Semiramis', a 'she-Spartacus', 'the *Tous-Sainte l'Ouverture*', 'the real personification, in its utmost significance, of the Saint Simonian *Femme Libre*'. Her article is called 'a female manifesto against the whole human race of male tyrants—of war to the bodkin'. It is deduced that its real purpose is to propose to abolish marriage—'Marriage henceforth to be a state of perfect liberty for women to do whatever they please! Avatar of the *Femme Libre* by act of parliament!' Her claim that women are not justly represented by men is handled thus:

We begin to fear that, after all, this fair lady is also one of the ungrateful ones. What! when but so short a time since Serjeant Talfourd brought forward a Bill to give to women, in the most important of all cases, an equality of power with men . . . After this signal triumph over the wisdom of ancestors, and the vulgar old prejudices of common sense, we must say that the fair lady is somewhat *exigeante* and ungrateful to complain 'that women are not represented by men!' Alas! after all his late exertions in the cause of female emancipation, has the honourable and eloquent

[1] p. 396.

member received from his fair client no dearer guerdon of thanks,
—no sweeter reward than that?[1]

The reviewer here clearly shows that he believed this article
to have been written by Caroline Norton. Other dark hints
occur in the article. Towards her he uses the most virulent
language, and the cruellest innuendos, to be justified only by
the worst possible interpretations of her words. To adopt her
views, he suggests, would set all women in opposition to men,
she being the she-misanthrope-in-chief:

The *family*, the foundation of all society, would be at once, and
completely destroyed; and this indeed is the avowed object, though
not as yet quite openly, of this writer, yet of many of those who, in
France and elsewhere have advocated the doctrine of female
emancipation.[2]

The marriage ceremony would become an act of perjury.
'However, if report be true, that would matter little to the
advocates of female emancipation, and the *Femme Libre*! Lust
may exist where love does not.'[3] He for his part desires to see
marriages increase and multiply instead of diminishing, believing that marriage is the highest and noblest estate possible for a race of social and human beings. We then see his
mind turn, by that association of ideas which it has been one
of my aims to point out, to the Socialist theories concerning
the rightful status of women. He suggests that an *exposé* of
the lives and esoteric doctrines of some of the more talented
propagators of Socialism would be a warning to his readers:

Miss Martineau and other 'talented' female writers have advocated a community of goods; and some people have been taken by
their eloquence! This 'talented' writer (together with other female
emancipators, and amongst the rest, Miss M. again) has not illogi-
cally coupled together the institutions of property and marriage.
But though the conclusion aimed at be evident, we apprehend that
if this *exposé* were published, few readers, however much charmed
by such 'talented' eloquence, would be willing to admit all the
consequences, and come to the conclusion of a community of
women . . .

Without going then a hundred miles from London, or raking up

[1] p. 401.   [2] p. 405.   [3] p. 407.

the vices of past centuries we think we should be forced to mention to them a few facts about the propagandists of this female emancipation, that would astonish our uninitiated posterity . . . facts which to employ for our purpose a verse somewhat altered from Milton,—

'Would make old Guy of Warwick stare and gasp!'

They would then understand, either from the facts that have been *laid bare* in criminal trials, or from the published confessions of renegade St.-Simonians, and other such secret worshippers of the 'dark-veil'd Cotytto', both in France and *moral* England, what is meant by female emancipation, opportunities, resistance etc., with the whole doctrine of agitation, both active and passive . . .

The article we have exposed above is nothing more nor less than a *rifaccimento* of the 7th section of the third chapter of Miss Martineau's *Society in America*; from that section, entitled 'Political Non-existence of Women', the authoress of the article, whoever she be, seems to have derived all her arguments—minus indeed some absurdities of ratiocination, which are peculiar to Miss Martineau. Next to Mary Wollstonecraft, and Frances Wright from America, we believe Miss Martineau to be the propagandist of sexual equality most notorious in our days, and in this country. Other renowned agitatrices are the Hon. Mrs. Caroline Norton, who is understood to have circulated a book on this subject; and Lady C. Bury, of whom still less need be said, if, as our contemporaries the Edinburgh and Quarterly Reviews have publicly accused her, she be indeed that *Lady of Honour*, authoress of the foulest and most infamous publication of *treachery* that has ever yet appeared in England![1]

The interest of this article is threefold. It reveals how strong a feeling could be evoked in 1838 by the still inflammable subject of higher education for women, at least in the mind of a reviewer of the old school of hard-hitting *argumentum ad hominem*. (One can almost sympathize with the at first sight bewildering attitude of Lord Brougham to the Custody of Infants Bill when he advocated in the House of Lords that it should be rejected because the woman question was so complex and full of snares that it was useless to try to introduce a reform of the kind under discussion.) Secondly it shows how complete could be the connection in the contemporary mind

[1] pp. 408–10.

between the feminist ideas of Socialists like Saint-Simon, Fourier and Owen and those of literary women of totally different temperaments. Feminism attracted to its adherents a reputation for subversiveness in regard to the received notions about property and the distinctions between the classes. In a few years, knowledge of the life of women in the industrial north of England was to make people realize that Harriet Martineau, though no Socialist, was right to view the question on lines superficially resembling those of the Socialists. Finally there is a special interest in the choice of *eidolon* to represent the authoress of the article in *The Metropolitan Magazine*: 'a new Bradamante, armed or denuded, *cap à pied*, to run a joust or wrestle with any man'. The writer of the article was pleased with the image, for he used it again; he refers to her as 'this bold Bradamante of the nineteenth century, who "fearlessly denies" that her sex are at all inferior in ability,—and doubtless therefore, as their self-constituted champion, and foremost woman belligerent, has no mean opinion of her own abilities'. The choice of Bradamante is perfectly natural, since after all she was in Ariosto a female warrior who engaged, in the usual manner of mediaeval warfare, in martial exploits: her English equivalent was Spenser's Britomart, who was modelled upon her. Now it is interesting to note that Britomart has been seen as a model for Tennyson's princess. I do not myself think that there is any significant parallel with the heroine of Tennyson's poem at all, as will be seen from later chapters; but the Bradamante type of heroine is admired by Lilia and the poet-speaker when, in the Prologue, they are both described as being struck by the nobility of that lady whose defence of her castle is related so stirringly in an old chronicle,

> one that arm'd
> Her own fair head, and sallying thro' the gate,
> Had beat her foes with slaughter from her walls.

The fine passage immediately following, which describes her action in more detail, beginning

> 'O miracle of women', said the book,

was added only in the fifth edition in 1853. Nevertheless, and despite the fact that the Prologue was composed after the main part of the poem was well advanced, the poet clearly had to use some such incident in order to justify the mediaeval setting he gave to the main part of the poem, most notably in the scene of the tournament. He must, in other words, have had in his mind an image of the militant heroine of romance from the beginning. Though he did not care to make his princess resemble such a heroine, he supplied the explicit allusion when he came to write the Prologue.

I do not suggest that the poet borrowed the Bradamante figure from the article in the *British and Foreign Review*, though, as will become clear, I do not rule out the possibility. We may take it as a commonplace which might have occurred to anyone. But Tennyson's mediaeval heroine is the genuine female knight of whom Ida is the nineteenth-century successor, at least in respect of her courage in defying men by setting up a college for women. And the reviewer, it must be remembered, saw fit to make exactly the same parallel when he came upon a real-life instance of a woman bent on the same end— setting up a college on a basis of misanthropy. He meant, obviously, no compliment in drawing the parallel. He saw the proposal as nonsense, and he dubbed the militant author of the offending article Bradamante primarily to suggest that she was living not in the real world of practical bargaining for charters for new colleges, but in a world of romance, enchanting to the view but so ideal as to come perilously near the out and out comic (as in Ariosto). It is this attitude which we detect in the early part of *The Princess*. That Tennyson chose a romantic story to illustrate his theme in 1839 seems to me to bring him very close in approach to the reviewer. He clearly could not use an actual romantic tale, but I think that he found in certain fairy stories suggestions for a plot which represented remarkably well the situation as he saw it when he first considered treating the subject.

There is something to be said about the reception of the review, for this, I think, will show that although such practical proposals as setting up a woman's college by militant action would not in the ordinary way have caused much stir at this date, the handling of the suggestion in the *British and Foreign Review* was such as to give it special prominence. As might be expected, Caroline Norton herself was stung into a reply. She first had published in Fonblanque's *Examiner* for 26 August 1838,[1] a letter which simply denied authorship of 'A Statement of the Wrongs of Women'. (She made, unfortunately, no attempt to rectify the confusion in the title of the *Metropolitan Magazine* article.) She went on to say that she had not written any other work advocating sexual equality. She insisted that her pamphlet (*The Separation of Mother and Child by the Law of 'Custody of Infants' considered*) and her novel *The Wife*[2] contained nothing whatever subversive to the doctrine of female subordination. Finally, she denied any acquaintance with Serjeant Talfourd prior to his championing the Custody of Infants Bill. This letter she signed with her own name. Again, Harriet Martineau, who as we have seen had been dealt a swashing blow in passing, retorted in the *London and Westminster Review* for April 1839.[3] Ostensibly reviewing some pamphlets on her topic—'Abuse of Women'—she stigmatized all reviewers who attack women with personal animus as 'Crokerites':

> When a woman who has had her name blighted by slander, and her honour implicated by imbecility—has obtained a verdict of acquittal from a jury of her countrymen, and her husband himself has declared her innocence—if a set of men are found who, under the shelter of the anonymous, and laws which give no redress for the foulest wrong which words can inflict upon a human being— the sullying of the fair name of a woman—still brutally denounce her as guilty, they, whatever may be the vehicle they use—are a set of Crokerites.[4]

She then reviews articles attacking Queen Victoria (shown in a caricature patting the lions which trample Shakespeare— 'Britannia patronizing the Drama'), Caroline Norton, Lady Morgan, Mrs. Austin, Maria Edgeworth, Mrs. Jameson and herself. (It may well be that it was this sort of thing which cast the shadows upon Mrs. Jameson, causing her at about

---

[1] It was reprinted in most of the morning papers.

[2] She called the theories of 'equal rights' wild and stupid. See Jane Gray Perkins, *The Life of Mrs. Norton* (1909), p. 149.

[3] Written under the initials J.R., xxxii (December 1838–April 1839), p. 454.

[4] p. 459.

this time to shrink from publicly expressing opinions like those contained in *Winter Studies and Summer Rambles in Canada—* at least until 1843.) She then refers to the review of the article in *The Metropolitan Magazine* in the *British and Foreign Review,* 'a periodical said to be the property of Mr. Beaumont, the late member for Northumberland'; refutes the statement that Caroline Norton sponsored the Custody of Infants Bill introduced by Serjeant Talfourd; draws attention to the seemingly sharp practice of implying that she wrote the article; and publishes the fact that Saunders and Otley, the proprietors of *The Metropolitan Magazine,* have issued a statement declaring her to be entirely unconnected with its authorship. She gives specimens of the vituperation employed thus groundlessly by the author of the article, and enters him on the list of 'Crokerites'.

In 1839, Caroline Norton herself returned to the charge, this time pseudonymously. She published *A Plain Letter to the Lord Chancellor on the Infant Custody Bill,* under the name of Pearce Stevenson, reviewing the whole question of the iniquity of a law which denied an innocent woman access to her children while permitting a husband guilty of the grossest immorality to assign the charge of them to a mistress: she also took the opportunity of denying once again the truth of the innuendoes in the *British and Foreign Review*:

> The author of the article in The British and Foreign Review has earnestly endeavoured (as a *second* chance of creating a prejudice) to connect the ill-advised public attempts on the part of a few women, to assert their 'equality' with men; and the strange and laughable political meetings (sanctioned by a *chair woman*), which have taken place in one or two instances, with the effort to remedy the injustice of the law of Custody: and in order to perfect the chain of his argument, it is impudently, most impudently asserted, in the title page of the review, that an anonymous article, entitled 'An Outline of the Wrongs of Women', (which article this author proceeds to criticise in the grossest and most bitter terms) is the production of Mrs. Norton.[1]

To support her disclaimer she gives the text of the letter from Saunders and Otley certifying that she was not the author of

[1] p. 91.

the article called 'An Outline of the Grievances of Women'. (The perpetual discrepancies over the title of the article are made even more confusing when Caroline Norton misquotes it.) From the same work we learn an interesting fact—that the review to which she and others took objection had been permitted to appear before the public by Tennyson's old friend from the Cambridge days, John Mitchell Kemble, who was editor of the *British and Foreign Review*. The fact is the more startling since Kemble's sisters, Adelaide and Frances (Fanny Kemble) were her friends. We also learn that the review was a redaction of a pamphlet written against the Custody of Infants Bill for circulation among the Lords before it came before them in the Upper House. This (anonymous) pamphlet was censured in *The Examiner* for 15 July 1838 quite independently of Caroline Norton's remonstrance in that paper against the article in the *British and Foreign Review*.

In the issue for February 1839 of *Fraser's Magazine*, Caroline Norton's *Plain Letter* was sympathetically reviewed,[1] and the writer of the pamphlet which became the article in the *British and Foreign Review* was denounced.

That pamphlet was written, we presume, by a barrister, whose name we have been unable to ascertain, or it should have been given to the world, to have been held up to the scorn of every woman, and the contempt of every man who has the remotest pretensions to the feelings of a gentleman. We have learned that he is one of the heartless things who has availed himself of the practice of the Court of Iniquity, (not Equity), and severed his wife from her little infant, and then vents his collected venom on the whole female sex: which not being sufficiently concentrated to gratify his malignant spleen, he selects the Hon. Mrs. Norton as his victim.[2]

The article refers to the absolute denial by Saunders and Otley that Caroline Norton was the author of the article in *The Metropolitan Magazine*, and then continues:

It may not be, as our author [Pearce Stevenson, i.e. Mrs. Norton] keenly observes, 'of any importance to the public, that Kemble's son should make his editorship of a magazine an instrument for flinging mud at Sheridan's daughter'. But Mr. Kemble holds a public position; and it was his duty, as an editor, not to have permitted

[1] xix (January–June 1839), p. 205.   [2] p. 210.

such unmanly and shameless slanders to have been launched from his periodical against any woman.[1]

The conjectures of *Fraser's* on the authorship of the review may be founded on nothing more than guess-work and rumour, though the writer of the article in *The Examiner* also hinted his awareness of the quarter from which it proceeded and the motive for its composition. That the writer (or writers) of it had some legal knowledge is obvious; but it is hardly more obvious than that he (or they) had special familiarity with the early history of the customs on which the law governing the family was based, some awareness of the present state of university institutions, and an unusual familiarity with the doings of the French and English Socialists. Caroline Norton, for her part, had no doubt who the writer of it was. It was the editor, J. M. Kemble, himself. In a letter to Lord Conyngham enclosing a copy of her pamphlet (mentioning that it had been written by her friend 'Mr. Stevenson') she remonstrated against the appointment of J. M. Kemble to his father's place as Censor of Plays; she had, incidentally, previously written to recommend Sheridan Knowles for the place:[2]

> It is monstrous and incredible to me that *this* Government should undertake and reward a man with a place and life annuity for *writing me down* in a style so blackguard and coarse that even his *friends* apologise for it—or that a person should be selected as *censor* of the Drama, and the language of plays, who openly calls me in print a 'she devil'; a 'she beast',—says the cause of my accepting a husband could only be that '*lust may exist, where love does not*', and reviles me through 120 pages of print.[3]

These are the very expressions used in the article, and her feelings can be understood. She also wrote to Murray, her publisher, some time later:

> You have been very kind in sending me books. I send you a very interesting one, in my opinion, though I fear not one of general interest. It is a letter to the Lord Chancellor on the subject of the Infant Custody Bill; and in the course of which (in answer to a

---

[1] p. 211. For 'daughter' the paragraph should have read 'grand daughter'.

[2] Bertha Coolidge, op. cit., p. 7.   [3] ibid., p. 8.

direct and most bitter personal attack made on me by Mr. John Kemble) the facts of my case are briefly given.

I hope you will read the letter and let me know your opinion upon it. Mr. Kemble's attack wrung from me a contradiction last summer, which first appeared in *The Examiner* (signed with my name) and afterwards was copied into other papers. It is so easy to crush a woman, especially one whose reputation has been already slandered, that I do not think his triumph is very great, in having created a prejudice by inventing a gross falsehood; attributing to me that which I never wrote, and then abusing me in very foul and gross language as the author.[1]

She asks him at least to notice the pamphlet, but to refrain from alluding to her name.

It may seem strange that Mrs. Norton should not have exposed Kemble's actual authorship in her own pseudonymous work; the explanation could be that such a course was not open to her because a woman could not seek such redress separately from her husband.[2] Any attempt to denounce the writer might consequently have led her into further marital difficulty.

Caroline Norton mentioned in the letter to Lord Conyngham quoted earlier that even Kemble's friends apologized to her for the article appearing in the *British and Foreign Review*. Certain ly W. B. Donne—another of the Apostles—was uneasy about it, and remonstrated with him. But Kemble was unrepentant:

I am a little disturbed by the tone in which you speak of the 'Custody of Infants'. What in the name of the Devil and all his angels has so insignificant a person as Mrs. Norton to do with so mighty a question? Both Norton and his wife are blackguards alike: there was and is no part⟨i⟩zanship in the case: but *she* was the prime mover of Serjeant Talfourd's Bill; was the person who had persuaded Members of P. to vote for it; had written pamphlets, novels and poems in favour of it, and it was called in London 'Mrs. N's Bill'. Hence & hence only was her name introduced into the Article. She was not *convicted*, but she was not innocent: and when we meet I will give you a few details respecting her which will open your eyes. Had Milton lived, Milton would have been on our side: and so is all the soundest portion of the Country. As for the nervous, if you will angry, eloquence of the papers, it was required by the subject. You cannot make sugared phrases and baisez mains

---

[1] Jane Gray Perkins, op. cit., pp. 150 ff.   [2] ibid., p. 149.

when the groundstone and very kedge anchor of society is about to be moved. *We killed the Bill:* killed it, and hung it up in terrorem. Not a word could Brougham, the most eloquent man of modern times, say that was not already in the Article: not an argument could Wynford, a judge preeminent for his acuteness as a Lawyer, discover that had not already been laid down. It is the most complete, the most powerful, and I think considering the nature of the subject, the most honourable paper that has appeared in any Review, in our days. It, and it alone, (or rather the first half of it, circulated as a pamphlet among the Peers) killed the Bill, sent up by the Commons, introduced by Lord Lyndhurst, supported by Lord Melbourne, voted for by all who have enjoyed or ⟨who⟩ hope to enjoy the favours of our would be Aspasia of Modern times, a⟨nd⟩ by all the hangers on of our most profligate Premier. It is a Bill moreove⟨r⟩ which had been put off six times in order that Lds M & L might *pack* their house. No No! Willie, in God's name let *us* hold fast the faith and morals that Milton held! For it is in us, in our class, in our earnest, wise and therefore powerful coequals in age and standing and station, that the hopes of this poor country rest; and to us it is given to arrest that vile sectarian sentimentalism which is flooding the land. Daily and hourly is the fatal doctrine gaining ground that forms are the one thing needful: morals are daily and hourly waning and fading: we shall live to see politics severed from ethics: and when we do, we may put on our crape and weepers for our country. Speculation instead of honest mercantile adventure; sentiment instead of morals, expediency instead of principle; the force of the numerical masses instead of the power of law & the right of institutions; radical democracy sheltered under the letter & the form that kill, instead of a high souled Republicanism based on the spirit that enlivens, the moral dignity and household virtue of the citizens: This, this is the course of England now! And is this what we who have not read history in vain, [are] to suffer tamely? God forbid![1]

Donne appears to have been convinced by this letter, which was written on 24 September 1838. But Kemble was not inclined to let him off lightly. On 8 October he wrote again:

. . . Sixth, I don't believe a single word of your excuse about the Custody of infants' Bill. You wrote to try my mettle, quotha!

---

[1] My thanks are due to Mrs. Barham Johnson for allowing me to print extracts from these letters of J. M. Kemble, the copyright of which belongs to her.

Marry! like the villains in the Old Plays, who never attempt their friends' wives but with the charitable purpose of trying their virtue! Now in truth Willie, you had read the article in a lazy, lounging, armchair humour, with a good fire or warm sun to make you feel comfortable; and in the full conviction that your own wife was an excellent one, you quite 'didn't care a damn' whether others were so lucky or not. But the Censor Morum thought otherwise, however convinced he might be that *his* wife also was a pearl beyond price: and he laid it on the thicker because he felt and knew that the Antichrist of the Women of our day is 'Intellectual Developement', that is the half education of the Understanding, which is preeminently the distinctive and characteristic of men [*sic*]. I identify myself entirely with the author; adopt and defend every one of his views, in that much of the article was written in my own study, and the result of moral and metaphysical investigations in which I took a share which I shall never regret. I start from the proposition that there is a Sex in souls just as much as in bodies: that the perfect humanity results from the spiritual and corporeal union; the reconstruction of the Androgyne in soul and body. That this union can only be thro' that diversity of the sex in souls and bodies: and that to make our Women *men* is as great an inconsistency as to make our Men *women*! Tell it not in Gath! or far rather proclaim it at Market crosses! Proclaim that women, next to the angels, are the most Godlike of God's creations, are not to be stunted by being forced into the uncongenial realm of the *Understanding*! But God help them and us, Perversity is one of their angelic qualities, and for one woman that recognises her own glorious and most excellent prerogative, there are ten who would fain unsex themselves to make addled *men*, a thing as vile as addled eggs—neither fish nor flesh nor good red herring! Moreover the means adopted were such as my soul hateth; an appeal to all that is sickly, sentimental and unmanly. To close my mouth for ever on this subject, we have written as Milton would have written had he lived, and as Selden would have thought; moreover as Paul taught; and our adversary is the Weak, the Prurient and the Revolutionary Anarch of our day, under whatever name he may happen to be known! For at the root of all the antisocial and miserable doctrines of our day lies that most accursed heresy of Sexual Equality, the Miss-Martineauism of the Westminster, the Femme Libre of the St. Simonian sty. Let me intreat you by our old friendship to give this subject a new and earnest consideration! Not as if it were an indifferent matter, but as involving the whole social polity of the

165

present life, and the profoundest questions of religion: remember that God himself has placed his greatest glory in being GOD *THE FATHER*; that the very existence of this world and this human nature of ours subserve the sole purpose of *his* paternity! Above all, remember that this battle is to be fought again, and that on its decision depends half the futurity of this country. These are considerations which ought to be of weight with us as citizens, even as those loftier ones interest us as members of the Spiritual Community of *Xns*!

The second of these letters confirms what the evidence of Kemble's other writings would suggest[1]—that Kemble had a hand in the composition of the article denouncing, among other things, the setting-up of a university for women. Now it is surely significant that one of Tennyson's friends drew

[1] Kemble placed great reliance upon ancient precedent. In an anonymous pamphlet, for example, he drew upon his knowledge of old English records to show that church-rates were not paid in Anglo-Saxon times, and thus did not have any special sanctity. (*A Few Historical Remarks upon the Supposed Antiquity of Church Rates and Three-fold Division of Tithes* (1837), by a Lay Member of the Church of England.) As their abolition was being proposed by the Government, his intervention brought him into official favour, a circumstance which may well explain why his appointment as Censor of Plays was proceeded with despite Caroline Norton's protests. See [The Rev.] W. H. Hale, *The Antiquity of the Church-Rate System considered* (1837).

His general grounds for opposing the Custody of Infants Bill also rested upon the oldest English practices—as did those of the writer of the article in *The British and Foreign Review*, who condemned it as an act calculated to 'revile and destroy the fundamental principle of the old law of England', and as a 'signal triumph over the wisdom of ancestors'. At the time the July 1838 number appeared, Kemble was engaged upon Book III of his book *The Saxons in England*, which did not appear, however, until 1849. This Book was concerned with Marriage, Divorce and the Family, which were in a sense the subjects of the article. (See Donne, p. 46.) Unfortunately this particular Book did not appear, but its contents were touched upon in chapter VIII of Book I of the version which eventually came to be published in 1849. Kemble discusses there the question of the status, serf or free, of children born in Anglo-Saxon times of a free mother and an unfree father, or vice versa. The question interests him enough to cause him to trace the subsequent history of the English legal view of the matter. Fortescue, he tells us, confirmed the law of Henry I by deciding that 'the English Law adjudges an offspring always to follow the father's condition, and never the mother's: so that a free man may father only a free child from a woman either serf or free, while a serf can beget in marriage only a child accounted a serf'. But Glanville had appeared to demur, and Kemble actually goes so far as gratuitously to pronounce his own opinion upon the subject:

166

together—not long before the poet formed a plan for a poem on the topic—most of the revolutionary views on feminism of Socialists and non-Socialists which I have sketched in previous chapters, even if only to condemn them. The poem itself seems to refer obliquely to the Owenists in the Prologue, and to the French Socialists in the Conclusion; in addition the attitude to the idea of a university in all but the latter part of the poem approximates to Kemble's, though the tone is much lighter. Even his derisive reference to a Bradamante of the nineteenth century is expanded by way of the reference to a mediaeval heroine in the Prologue, and also perhaps by treating the theme as a romantic story.

Whether Tennyson received a copy of the article from

> To the English principle I am bound to give my adhesion, inasmuch as the natural and original social law can recognise none but the father, either in the generation or in the subsequent rule, of the family: whatever the alleviation the practices of chivalry, the worship of the Virgin mother, and the Christian doctrine of the equality of man and woman before God, may have introduced, the original feeling is on the father's side, and the foundations of our law are based upon the all-sufficiency of his right. A woman is in the mund or keeping of a man; society exists for men only, that is, for women merely as far as they are represented by a man. (*The Saxons in England*, i, p. 205.)

The passage shows perfectly why the advocacy of the Custody of Infants Bill could extort from J. M. Kemble so violent a chastisement, although to us it appears to be a pitifully small concession to the independent rights of women. To a mind revering England's oldest institutions, however, the invasion of a father's privileges would seem to strike at the very heart of all law and stability; and belief in this would, in turn, very naturally excite the most heartfelt detestation of those who openly joined their pleas for the emancipation of women with denunciations of the traditional views of property and the labouring classes. It will be remembered that the review took the originally rather nebulous aspirations towards university education for women in the *Metropolitan Magazine* article and gave them firmer shape by talking of the practical difficulties. It is interesting to find in his writings clear evidence of Kemble's great interest in the contemporary position of the Universities. He contributed two articles to his own Review, one on Oxford, the other on Cambridge, recommending their reform. Indeed, after his pamphlet on Church-rates, he was seen to be a possible member of a proposed Commission of Inquiry into the state of the Universities. (Hale, op. cit., p. 4.)

For the tone of the review, which as we have seen, gave great offence, Kemble was naturally responsible as editor. Whether he was sole *author* is difficult to say, but it is not to be overlooked that Kemble was well known for the virulence of his expression when dealing with subjects near his heart. (See, e.g., *Record*, i, p. 199, Trench, i, p. 141.)

J. M. Kemble, Caroline Norton

Kemble is unknown, though the habit of circulating their compositions was well-established among the Apostles set. But it is possible that he was made aware of the views of Kemble on the subject by another means. In 1837 Tennyson moved with his family from Somersby to High Beech, Epping, near London, and was thus able to meet old friends again, including Kemble.[1] During 1839, the year in which he discussed the plan for *The Princess* with Emily Sellwood, he wrote to her of his doings in London. Only fragments of the correspondence survive, but one of them supplies a clue:

> There is no one here but John Kemble with whom I dined twice: he is full of burning indignation against the Russian policy and what he calls the moral barbarism of France: likewise he is striving against what he calls the 'mechanic influence of the age and its tendency to crush and overpower the spiritual in man . . .'[2]

Kemble's indignation against the Russian policy was the subject of a slashing review in the *British and Foreign Review* (written by Kemble himself).[3] We can only guess at what was meant by 'the moral barbarism of France', but it seems likely on the evidence of the article which has been discussed that he had in mind the doctrine of the 'Femme libre' and liberal opinions on the relations of the sexes. To him these were no less than moral barbarism, since they undermined, in his view, the hard-won social stability rooted in the laws and age-old traditions on which the accepted concept of the family rested. Politically, Kemble was not a Tory; but all his prejudices were aroused by the suggestion that there was something fundamentally wrong with society. Reform there should be; but to believe that women could radically alter their status seemed

---

[1] *Memoir*, i, p. 150. He removed to Tunbridge Wells in 1839.

[2] *Memoir*, i, p. 169.

[3] His indictment of Nicholas I in 'The Present Government of Russia' in *The British and Foreign Review* (ix, pp. 543–91) drew an amusing comment from Edward Fitzgerald: 'Without losing one single instant, rush off to some Divan, Club or Bookseller's, and forcibly read the last sentence of an article called "the emperor Nicholas" in the British and Foreign Review. It must annihilate the person in question: he will either die, kill himself, or abdicate. It made *me* tremble.' (Quoted from Bruce Dickins, 'J. M. Kemble and Old English Scholarship', in the Proceedings of the British Academy, 1938, p. 14.)

to him both absurd and dangerous. He could not even approve of occasionally allowing an infant child to remain in the custody of a mother separated from her husband.

It is less difficult to decide what he intended in his reference to the 'mechanic influence of the age'. He was almost certainly talking in the vein of the letters to Donne quoted earlier, which show that he thought that the fundamental social institutions had a religious sanction. Socialist writings opposed this attitude bitterly, and supported the view that institutions were to be evaluated by their efficiency. It was for this reason that Kemble so mistrusted the Owenists; they had no wish to judge the future by the past, but to break with it. For them the time had come to apply positively to society the methods of scientific evaluation.

Both these topics were closely related in Kemble's mind to feminist arguments for a new attitude to the rights of fathers in their children and higher education for women. Bearing in mind the furore which his article on these subjects had provoked, it would be most unlikely that he would not have talked of them to Tennyson too. To assume that he did explains much that otherwise is difficult to explain. Kemble gave a sense of immediacy to the suggestion for a women's university which the temper of the time does not suggest would otherwise have been entertained; and his attitude to it is in part reflected by Tennyson in *The Princess* when his earlier work would lead one to think that he would have taken a different view if not influenced by someone whose opinions he adopted without sufficient reflection.

CHAPTER VIII

The Choice of Theme and Heroine

The *Princess* is a poetic romance, or even a fairy tale, supposedly related by seven young men for the entertainment of a house-party looking for an afternoon's diversion. In fact they were playing a game which Tennyson himself had played at Cambridge.[1] Taking up a topic of conversation—the aspiration that women should be allowed to enjoy a university education—they one after another fitted to it a story made up as they went along. (Tennyson appears to have invented the Prologue supplying these details to fit a story already planned and well-advanced in composition.)[2] This story is about a Princess who founds a university for women, and in order to preserve it from the encroachments of men imposes a death-penalty upon any male intruder. But a Prince from another realm and his companions enter in disguise, and eventually the Princess is forced by circumstances to admit her failure to preserve the sanctity of her academy. Nevertheless, she is still unwilling to marry the Prince:

> She still were loth to yield herself to one
> That wholly scorn'd to help their equal rights
> Against the sons of men and barbarous laws.

But finally she yields on learning that the Prince wholly shares her views. Together they will seek to free woman from the toils which enmesh her:

> Will clear away the parasitic forms
> That seem to keep her up but drag her down—
> Will leave her space to burgeon out of all
> Within her—let her make herself her own

[1] *Memoir*, i, p. 253.

[2] Tennyson was proud of the ingenuity of the Prologue: 'It may be remarked that there is scarcely anything in the story which is not prophetically glanced at in the prologue.' *Memoir*, i, p. 251.

The Choice of Theme and Heroine

To give or keep, to live and learn and be
All that not harms distinctive womanhood.

Obviously if women are to achieve this, not merely live but learn, there *must* be women's universities, and although Tennyson does not perhaps make it sufficiently explicit, it was not finally the university at all that was meant to be burlesqued by the poem. It is not difficult to see that what was objectionable in the university was its harsh decree that no man was to enter on pain of death, and its deliberate attempt to instil misanthropic doctrines. And it is this, too, which makes the story so like a fairy tale. Here, we say, Tennyson takes leave of the facts altogether. But this is not so. In a footnote to the article in the *British and Foreign Review* special mention was made of the sort of consequence which would follow exhortations to women to form irresistible combinations in order to gain their ends. As reported in the *Globe* newspaper for 20 February 1838, a public meeting was held under the chairmanship of a woman who was alleged to have recommended direct action by women to force through the repeal of an Act of Parliament. Caroline Norton particularly objected to being connected with such activities—she reveals that there was more than one such meeting, and that they were concerned with the law of Custody of Infants. But this is not all. At the meeting to which the article referred, the woman in the chair exhorted her audience 'to resist the enforcement of the cruel law *unto the death*'.[1] We may think it strange that the poet could have taken such a threat seriously; but perhaps after all it was in this that he came nearest to prophecy, for we all know that with the passing of time, women really did adopt militant courses to acquire their rights, albeit of suffrage rather than of education.

Later I hope to show that the death penalty imposed by the Princess upon male intruders is the real link between the theme and the story by which it is illustrated, but it may be well first to dispose of a few misunderstandings which have arisen from assuming that the poet was condemning the university altogether and without reserve. Hugh I'Anson Fausset,

---

[1] loc. cit., p. 354.

The Choice of Theme and Heroine

in his *Tennyson, a Modern Portrait* (1923), dismissed the poem because he believed it to lack emotional or intellectual sincerity, and made these observations about it:

> The public yearned for a poet who would provide it with all the self-satisfaction of Liberal sensations, but relieve it of the self-sacrifice entailed in Liberal duties.[1]
>
> His virtuous intention was vague enough to be vicious.[2]
>
> The supposed moral of the poem was that woman was not created for the uses of man or merely to satisfy the cravings of appetite or of philoprogenitiveness, but that she had a spiritual and intellectual significance of her own, and that only when she was recognised as the free complement of man could any true love exist between the sexes, or any true marriage be consummated . . . But the moral was completely submerged by its setting. The pill, to speak commonly, was so coated with sugar as to lose its value as a pill.[3]

Apparently dissatisfied with this account of the moral of the poem, he wrote again: 'Primarily, then, "The Princess" represents the manufactured rebellion of a number of very normal young ladies from a marriage contract which they would by nature have been the first to embrace, and their artificial reconversion to it through an aggravation of compassionate maternity.'[4] This reading of the poem is debatable. The rebellion against the marriage contract was in fact made by the Princess alone, and I think that the evidence of contemporary feminist writings shows that it was very far from manufactured. With the Princess it sprang from a desire to obtain access for her sex to the truths of science and art, and she was far from alone in this. It is true that 'very normal young ladies' would not subscribe to her views, but then the Princess was a conscious rebel, and was capable of exactly the kind of hostility to men that Tennyson had in mind. Consequently he tried to show that the posture of defiance into which an ambitious but frustrated woman might put herself could prove not only a matter for mockery but lead to tragic results as well. But this does not prove him hostile to allowing women a proper education, or hypocritical, or glib. The poem does not concern the university alone, nor marriage alone, but both; it

[1] p. 127. [2] p. 130. [3] pp. 130 1. [4] p. 133.

172

tries to illustrate the importance of conceding women what they want before they are driven to an aversion for the marriage relationship altogether.[1] Mr. Fausset's remark that a reconversion to the marriage contract was effected by 'an aggravation of compassionate maternity' is also only partly true. He is referring to the effect upon the Princess of witnessing the distress of her unfaithful friend Psyche when her child was taken away from her, and of the stirring of the Princess's own feelings when she holds the child. Tennyson told Dawson that the child is the link through the parts of the work, as could be seen from the intercalary songs inserted in 1850, which were meant to aid interpretation of the poem.[2] These songs differ from the five splendid ones in the body of the story which were present in the first edition, in being in rhymed instead of blank verse; they are also, in my opinion, markedly inferior.[3] It is difficult to agree with Tennyson that the later songs bring out the importance of the child in the story, since only two of them directly treat the influence of a child upon a woman. But this apart, it is still clear that the poet intended to make the Princess's awakened maternal feelings contribute to her abandonment of her scheme, even if not of her belief that her sex was unjustly treated. This may seem to many readers today a rather sentimental episode, though on reflection there is nothing in the idea which is false to the facts; the mode of presentation is perhaps not the best available. The novel, which affords better opportunities for careful preparation, could have given a better chance of avoiding the snares.

To say this is not to agree with Mr. Fausset's remark, which implies that Tennyson was 'emotionally insincere' in having introduced the episode to sway his readers to a conventional point of view. For in including it, Tennyson was not necessarily adopting the opinions of those (frequently reactionary) writers

[1] When Miss Emily Davies presented a memorial to the Schools Inquiry Commission (1865–7) drawing attention to the great need for a place of education for adult women students, she sought the signatures of the most eminent men of her time. Among the 200 she obtained was that of Tennyson. See C. S. Bremner, *Education of Girls and Women in Great Britain* (1897), p. 130.

[2] *Memoir*, i, p. 254.

[3] The blank verse lyric 'O swallow, swallow' in Part IV was originally composed in rhyme. See *Memoir*, ii, p. 74.

The Choice of Theme and Heroine

who insisted always on regarding women as *mères de famille*. If, as I have suggested, he was brought to consider the poem in the first place as a result of conversations with Kemble, it is not to be forgotten what had prompted Kemble to his tirade in the beginning. The wrangle over the Custody of Infants Bill brought to public attention the fact that an ambitious woman, an author who was intrepid enough to enter the lists of controversy despite the well-known risks existing at that time, could feel very sincerely indeed the 'aggravation of compassionate maternity'. Caroline Norton's efforts to acquire possession of her children by nothing less than an attempt to change the law of England must have drawn the attention of many to the strength of feeling that an 'advanced' woman could show; and Tennyson may very well have meant to illustrate not so much a sentimental line of thought as a fact very relevant to the discussion of his theme.

By this I do not mean to suggest that Caroline Norton was the model for the Princess in the poem. Tennyson did not meet her before 26 January 1845, when she came specially to a dinner party given by Rogers to see him. Tennyson, it seems, very much disliked her, and showed the fact;[1] this is confirmed by a letter from Frederick Tennyson written some time before 1857 (when he left Florence, whence the letter was sent):

While we were located at Villa Brichieri, up drove one fine day the famous Caroline [Norton] . . . who not to speak of her personal attractions, is really, I should say, a woman of genius, if only judged by her novel, *Stuart of Dunleath*, which is full of deep pathos to me. I asked Brin [her son Brinsley] one day what his mother thought of me. He stammers very much, and he said, 'She th-th-th-thinks very well of you, but I don't think she likes your family'. 'Good heavens! here's news', I said. Well, afterwards she told me of having met Alfred at Rogers', and of having heard that he had taken a dislike to her. 'Why, Mrs. Norton', I said, 'that must be nearly thirty years ago, and do you harbour vindictive feelings so long?' 'Oh!' she said, 'why, I'm not thirty!'[2]

[1] Henry Crabbe Robinson wrote: 'Tennyson did not hesitate to say that he shuddered sitting by her side, a strange remark from a young man.' See *Henry Crabbe Robinson on books and their authors*, ed. Edith J. Morley (1938), ii, p. 650; but see also p. 797.

[2] *Tennyson and his Friends*, ed. Hallam, Lord Tennyson (1911), p. 41.

The Choice of Theme and Heroine

Perhaps Alfred felt remorse on reading this, for in 1859, we hear of Mrs. Norton and her son Brinsley visiting Farringford.[1]

There is in fact a rival for the honour of standing as model for the Princess in the person of Lucie Duff Gordon, *née* Austin, some twelve years younger than the poet. As a child, Lucie Austin had constantly encountered brilliant members of the Whip Opposition and Radicals, Macaulay, Roebuck, Charles Buller, J. S. Mill and Sterling among them: she played in Bentham's garden next door. She met Caroline Norton in 1838 at just about the time the article in the *British and Foreign Review* appeared, and remained her close friend.[2] She married Alexander Duff Gordon in 1840 and resided at 8 Queen Square, Westminster, where Tennyson came to read his poems. He remarked on one occasion, 'I never loved a dear gazelle, but some damned brute, that's you, Gordon, had married her first.'[3] It seems that the 'books Lucie translated were always on the serious side, and her contemporaries considered this society young woman in her early twenties as very much of a highbrow'. This, it appears, was Tennyson's impression, who said that he was thinking of her when he wrote *The Princess*.[4] Mr. Waterfield, Lucie's latest biographer, adds, however, 'He probably had others in mind, too, but there are clear points of resemblance between the proud, erudite Princess and Lucie . . . [though] she would never have wanted to reform women in the Tennysonian University, and she would certainly not have wished to exclude all men, for she much preferred their society to that of women.'[5] This, of course, is an important reservation; and one feels that the character of the Princess must inevitably have been first suggested by the role she had to play in the narrative. This obviously combines two elements. She has to represent militant feminism on the one hand, and a dangerous aversion to men (combined with beauty to attract them) on the other. Neither of these qualities is supplied

[1] Sir Charles Tennyson, *Alfred Tennyson* (1949), p. 315.
[2] Gordon Waterfield, *Lucie Duff Gordon* (1937), p. 91.   [3] ibid., p. 96.
[4] ibid., p. 103 and Janet Ross, *The Fourth Generation* (1912), p. 16. Mr. Waterfield has kindly informed me that the statement is not based upon any of the unpublished letters he was using for his biography of his great-grandmother. But Janet Ross was Lucie's daughter, and the remark attributed to Tennyson may therefore be taken as correct.
[5] Waterfield, op. cit., p. 103.

The Choice of Theme and Heroine

by Lucie Duff Gordon. Later, however, I shall suggest that the source of the second element, that of a misanthropic beauty, is a tale, or rather two tales, drawn from collections resembling the *Arabian Nights*, whose heroines combine the haughty manner of an imperious royal lady, with the arresting beauty appropriate to romantic fictions. Lucie Duff Gordon may have served as model for the Princess in Tennyson's poem in the latter respect (though in any case, the poet was sparing of visual detail); Kinglake's description of her will serve to illustrate this possibility:

> The classical form of her features, the noble poise of her head and neck, her stately height, her uncoloured yet pure complexion, caused some of the beholders to call her beauty statuesque, and others to call it majestic, some pronouncing it to be even imperious. But she was so intellectual, so keen, so autocratic, sometimes even so impassioned in speech, that nobody feeling her powers, could well go on fully comparing her to a mere queen or empress.[1]

On the whole, it matters little whether it was Caroline Norton or Lucie Duff Gordon who was the 'model' for the Princess, since it is obvious that Tennyson was primarily concerned to write a poem with a theme, and chose a story to illustrate it which was to make his poem hover between realism and fantasy. This means that we should always measure the 'sincerity' of the poet's attitude with some tact, and in any case by reference to the hard facts of contemporary feminism. This should make us careful not to say that episodes are not true to the facts without first ascertaining what the facts really were. Again, since the story itself is a fantasy, we must be chary of seeking real-life models for the characters. A similar situation is encountered in Spenser's *The Faerie Queene*; here too, we can be bewildered at observing a serious theme treated by way of comic episodes, and by being told of resemblances between the fictitious personages and historical persons. Most works of art quickly indicate the level at which they are to be read, but 'medleys', or works that can be read in different ways, require an agility in the reader if he is to take the point which the poet intends that he should, no more and no less.

[1] ibid., p. 104.

CHAPTER IX

Anticipations

I. RECOLLECTIONS OF THE 'ARABIAN NIGHTS'

TENNYSON had long been interested in romantic stories, and indeed had continually to repress an impulse to write them; but even so their stock situations constantly recur in his work. Of his position in 1838 he remarked: 'I felt certain of one point then . . . if I meant to make any mark at all, it must be by shortness, for the men before me had been so diffuse, and most of the big things except "King Arthur" had been done.'[1] As a boy he was much interested in the poems of Scott and Byron, and he tells how, from about twelve years old, he wrote

an epic of six thousand lines à la Walter Scott,—full of battles, dealing too with sea and mountain scenery,—with Scott's regularity of octo-syllables and his occasional varieties. Though the performance was very likely worth nothing I never felt myself more truly inspired. I wrote as much as seventy lines at one time, and used to go shouting them about the fields in the dark.[2]

The song beginning 'Home they brought her warrior dead' between Parts V and VI of *The Princess* greatly resembles part of Scott's *Lay of the Last Minstrel*, Canto 1.[3]

He bent his faculty for story-telling to entertaining his brothers and sisters, 'who listened open-eared and open-mouthed to legends of knights and heroes among untravelled forests rescuing distressed damsels, or on gigantic mountains fighting with dragons, or to his tales about Indians, or demons, or witches'.[4]

The epigraphs of *Poems by Two Brothers* give interesting

---

[1] *Memoir*, i, p. 166.   [2] ibid., p. 12.
[3] But see R. H. Shepherd, *Tennysoniana* (2nd edn., 1889), p. 105 n.
[4] *Memoir*, i, p. 5.

evidence of the kind of reading enjoyed by the Tennyson children,[1] and as a result of the analysis made by Professor W. D. Paden of Alfred's contributions to the volume in the light of some of the books he seems to have read,[2] we can see that the poet's early mind was well-provided with stimulating material, not in itself narrative, admittedly, but rich in romantic qualities. It is impossible not to be impressed by the attack, the largeness of the intelligence behind this boyhood writing now that we can see more clearly how much of it is derivative.

The modern view of Tennyson is directed less to the later poetry which brought him the adulation of his enormous public, and depreciation after his death, than to the poems which were written before his greatest success measured in terms of sales and popularity. He has been defended as a devotee of poetry who would not surrender his allegiance to his art for an income,[3] and as a poet who really opposed the Victorian optimism he was expected to celebrate.[4] There is also a greater interest in the psychological implications of his work,[5] but of course it is often possible to draw inferences which while consistent, may very well be unjustified. But whatever may be deduced about the poet's inner life from his contributions to *Poems by Two Brothers*, for instance, we can see one thing quite clearly—that like many of his contemporaries he was deeply interested in the literature dealing with the Near East. The poems, both descriptive and narrative, are often set in scenes of voluptuous beauty: an example is a poem called 'Persia':

> Land of bright eye and lofty brow!
> Whose every gale is balmy breath
> Of incense from some sunny flower,
> Which on tall hill or valley low
> In clustering maze or circling wreath,

[1] *Tennyson and his Friends*, p. 34.

[2] *Tennyson in Egypt*, University of Kansas Publications—Humanistic Studies, xxvii (Lawrence, Kansas, 1942).

[3] Sir Arthur Quiller-Couch, 'Tennyson (After Fifty Years)', *The Poetry Review*, xxxiii (1942), p. 269.

[4] Harold Nicolson, 'Tennyson: Fifty Years After', ibid., p. 333.

[5] Prof. Paden's book expressly set out to make a study of the imagery of Tennyson's early poetry to see what psychological deductions could be made.

Sheds perfume; or in blooming bower
Of Shiraz or of Ispahan,
In bower untrod by foot of man,
Clasps round the green and fragrant stem
Of lotos, fair and fresh and blue . . .

Tennyson's love of such luxurious scenes is shown in poems published later. The most important of these is 'Recollections of the Arabian Nights', which Arthur Hallam singled out for special praise in his notable review in *The Englishman's Magazine*. In it Tennyson used the poetic method in which he particularly excelled, that of relying almost exclusively upon description for his effect, which is always charged with feeling.[1] Landscape-painting in words is here not intended to contribute to any paraphrasable meaning: the reader's response is controlled solely by the juxtaposing of images, which are selected, one feels sure, not mechanically from a source, but with a view to producing a certain, predetermined response. In other words the poet has moved beyond the method used in *Poems by Two Brothers*. There he often makes a point of parading the width of his reading by mentioning the sources of his subject-matter. The poem 'Egypt', for example, has a footnote indicating reliance upon Savary's *Lettres sur l'Égypte*. 'Recollections of the Arabian Nights' achieves a far profounder unity of effect. The aim, as the title suggests, is to communicate in a lyric poem the sensations bred in the poet's mind by reading the Eastern tales. For this he had, one imagines, to *invent* a landscape, the unfolding description of which in the reader's imagination would do for the reader all that a long narrative did for him—and perhaps for no one else. Professor Paden, on the other hand, argues that Savary's *Letters*, also provided the 'scenery' of 'Recollections of the Arabian Nights'.

The poem, it will be recalled, describes how on reading the *Arabian Nights* in childhood the poet entered a delightful imaginary world far back in time, and remote in situation, the world presided over by 'good Haroun Alraschid', Caliph of Baghdad. We are immediately taken with him in memory on a night expedition down the Tigris, through Baghdad, and then

---

[1] For an excellent analysis, see H. M. McLuhan's article 'Tennyson and Picturesque Poetry' in *Essays in Criticism*, i (1951), p. 262.

up one of the clear canals leading from the main stream. This leads through flowery meadows, silvered with moonlight, and then beneath a dark and odorous bower of palms to a lake into which flow the waters of a fountain above. This lake lies among lemon-groves and palms in whose midst the nightingale sings. The banks of the lake are ornamented with huge, scented flowers in pots and urns. Seeing a blaze of light, he leaves his shallop and walks through the garden which is laid out with cedars, artificial mounds, tamarisks, bushes of wild roses, myrrh-thickets and obelisks 'graven with emblems of the time'. Unexpectedly he emerges before a pavilion brilliantly lit by a million tapers, which cast light far over the city. He steals up to a 'Persian girl alone',

> Serene with argent-lidded eyes
> Amorous, and lashes like to rays
> Of darkness, and a brow of pearl
> Tressed with redolent ebony,
> In many a dark delicious curl,
> Flowing beneath her rose-hued zone;
>   The sweetest lady of the time,
>   Well worthy of the golden prime
>   Of good Haroun Alraschid.

Seated on a raised throne is Haroun Alraschid himself. Both the girl and the prince are shown quite still, like sleeping figures. Nothing happens; the poem exists entirely in its suggestions, and consequently is quite different in effect from another poem in which sleeping figures are described—'The Sleeping Beauty', published in the same volume.

Although the Persian girl is really only part of the scene, it is to her that the night journey leads, and on this account alone, the original motive for the poem must in some way be connected with her. Something in the original tale must have made the situation of penetrating the forbidden garden of the Caliph and coming upon a beautiful woman specially significant. Tennyson helps us by having stated that the girl in the poem is the Fair Persian in the *Arabian Night* story of Noureddin and the Fair Persian. The 'Pavilion of the Caliphat' can be recognized as the Pavilion of Pictures described in the same story. The edition of the *Arabian Nights* Tennyson used was a translation of the old Galland version which excised the detailed descriptions retained by later translators. Professor Paden argues that to have composed his elaborate descriptions, Tennyson must have resorted to Savary's descriptions of the Nile, the gardens of Cairo, and the woods of Damietta. But the Galland version of the story supplied plentiful hints for the descriptions. Mention is made there of the gardens bordering the Tigris, a beautiful walled pleasaunce which could be entered from a canal leading from the river, that it contained a fountain and a pavilion with four score windows, so that its many lights shone over the city, that it appeared beautiful in moonlight and contained mounds and alleys and so on. But in any case a more important matter to decide is what there could have been in the story of Noureddin and the Fair Persian which could have caused Tennyson especially to remember it and to recreate it in a different form imbued with so much feeling. The effect of the descriptions is so luxurious as to seem dream-like, and it is in a sense a Near Eastern counterpart of the northern wood, likewise hushed and still, in 'A Dream of Fair Women'. We should not perhaps be far wrong if we were to regard this poem as a 'dream of a fair woman'.

In Galland's swiftly-moving tale we are not given many details of her physical charms; we are simply told that she is the most beautiful of women. She was originally bought from a Persian merchant at enormous cost, and for a rather interesting reason. The king of Basra had been convinced by his amiable Vizier Khacan 'that neither Beauty, nor a thousand other charming Perfections of the Body, were the only Things to be coveted in a Mistress, but they ought to be accompany'd with a great deal of Wit, Prudence, Modesty and Agreeableness; and if possible, abundance of Sense and Penetration'.[1] As a result the king commanded Khacan to seek out, at no matter what expense, a woman thus rarely endowed. The Persian merchant insisted upon a very high price because, he claimed, he had spent a fortune upon her education. She was in fact, in the words of her elated discoverer,

so surprisingly beautiful, that she excell'd all Women that his Eyes had ever beheld; And as for her Parts, and Learning, added

[1] *Arabian Nights Entertainments* (10th edn., Dublin, 1776), iii, p. 4.

he, the Merchant engages, that she shall cope with the finest Wits, and the most knowing Persons of the Age . . .

She plays upon all Sorts of Instruments to Perfection, she dances, sings, and writes better than the most celebrated Authors, understands Poetry, and in short, there is scarce any Book but what she has read, so that there never was a Slave of so vast a Capacity heard of before.[1]

In other words, she was fit for a king.

But her fate was surprisingly different, for before she could be formally presented to the king, she was seduced by Noureddin, the son of the Vizier. His enraged father insisted that he marry her. 'You are not,' he said, 'to look upon her any longer as a Slave, but as your Wife: and you will not sell her, nor ever be divorced from her: for she having an abundance of Wit and Prudence, besides much better Conduct than you, I am persuaded that she will be able to moderate those rash Sallies of Youth, which are enough to ruin you.'[2] Unfortunately this confidence was belied, but not through any deficiency in the Fair Persian. Noureddin was ruined through foolish generosity despite timely warnings from his wife, and obliged to fly from Basra.[3] Nevertheless the Fair Persian continued entirely faithful, prudent and self-sacrificing despite the most shabby treatment from Noureddin, one of those 'bursts of great heart' led him to give her away to a common fisherman; happily this fisherman turned out to be Haroun Alraschid in disguise and at his most amiable.

This, then, was the story which Tennyson felt moved to recall from his recollections of the *Arabian Nights*. As Hallam observed, his poem did not supply what many looked for in the tales, 'Viziers, Barmecides, Fire-worshippers, and Cadis; trees that sing, horses that fly, and Goules that eat ricepudding!'[4] Instead, its exotic Eastern landscape and glowing portrait of a desirable Persian girl were meant to stimulate in the reader a feeling as intense as his own; invention is used

[1] iii, p. 5. [2] iii, p. 15.
[3] Prof. Paden believes that Noureddin was probably the original of the poem 'Written by an Exile of Bassorah'—*Tennyson in Egypt*, p. 131, n. 103. If he is right, the attraction of this particular story would receive striking corroboration.
[4] *The Englishman's Magazine*, i (April–August 1831), p. 621.

on literary, not 'actual', materials for this purpose. (Taine was only the first to deduce—in his case from this very poem—that Tennyson was a dilettante, 'said to be rich, venerated by his family, admired by his friends, amiable without affectation, even unsophisticated', living amongst books and flowers.)[1]

The emotion which the poem conveys in terms of dream-landscape is of intense delight, and this, in my view, was prompted by admiration of the type of woman presented in the original story in the *Arabian Nights*, a woman possessed of beauty, intelligence and fidelity. This may seem, perhaps, improbable, but it must be remembered that 'A Dream of Fair Women' is explicitly concerned with the ill-usage suffered by women in their relations with men, and of this the tale of Noureddin and the Fair Persian is a notable example. Moreover, in another poem published in the 1830 volume called 'Isabel' he gives a portrait of a woman whom he describes as

> The stately flower of female fortitude,
> Of perfect wifehood and pure lowlihead.

> The intuitive decision of a bright
> And thorough-edged intellect to part
> Error from crime; a prudence to withhold;
> The laws of marriage character'd in gold
> Upon the blanched tablets of her heart.

This poem was written with the poet's own mother in mind, which is not the same thing as saying that she is exactly described. But we cannot fail to see a close resemblance between the qualities of Isabel and those of the Fair Persian. The Prince in Tennyson's later poem explained that he had been inspired to a lofty view of women's role in life by *his* mother, and the poet allowed that no one else than his own had been in his mind when he wrote

[1] H. A. Taine, *History of English Literature*, trans. H. van Laun (1906), iv, p. 433. See also *Memoir*, ii, p. 497. 'Mariana' is another poem conveying mood through scene-painting—also prompted, perhaps, by the poet's feeling for another deserted woman in a work of literature. 'The Lady of Shalott' is a more obvious example, and 'Oenone' likewise.

'Alone', I said, 'from earlier than I know,
Immersed in rich foreshadowings of the world,
I loved the woman . . .
Yet was there one thro' whom I loved her, one
Not learned, save in gracious household ways,
Not perfect, nay, but full of tender wants. . . .'

I suggest that among 'the rich foreshadowings of the world' in which as a boy the poet was immersed was the tale of the sufferings of the Fair Persian in the *Arabian Nights,* for in her is to be found the type of the Princess. As I hope to show, the exotic Near Eastern setting invented for the Persian girl is carried over into the later poem.

II. THE SUPPRESSION OF POETIC AMBITION

During the first painful days at the University, Tennyson wrote to his aunt, Mrs. Russell:

> I am sitting owl-like and solitary in my rooms (nothing between me and the stars but a stratum of tiles). The hoof of the steed, the roll of the wheel, the shouts of drunken Gown and drunken Town come up from below with a sea-like murmur. I wish to Heaven I had Prince Hussain's fairy carpet to transport me along the deeps of air to your coterie. Nay, I would even take up with his brother Aboul-something's glass for the mere pleasure of a peep. What a pity it is that the golden days of Faerie are over! What a misery not to be able to consolidate our gossamer dreams into reality![1]

This letter shows that at the back of Tennyson's mind there was a memory of a fantastic tale which was a serio-comic illustration of his present desire. It shows that he found real life much inferior to his gossamer dreams of his boyhood

> When the breeze of a joyful dawn blew free
> In the silken sail of infancy.

The poem 'Recollections of the Arabian Nights' is, however, not escapist; it is different in tone altogether from this letter. Though descriptive, its emotional overtones are more mature; its warmth and luxury of description combined with a lingering pleasure in the beauty of the Fair Persian have an erotic

[1] *Memoir,* i, p. 512.

184

quality. The *Arabian Nights* have their share of sexual interest; but Tennyson does not use their method. For narrative there is description.

When we look at other stories which he adapted, we find that those concerning sexual love are similarly transmuted. 'The Lady of Shalott' and 'Sir Launcelot and Queen Guinevere' are largely dependent for their effects upon descriptions; yet the tales on which they are based concern love, even forbidden love. In the poems this is not made clear; we are preoccupied with the descriptions of spring and summer landscapes. We might almost infer that at this time Tennyson was attracted to stories concerned with sexual love, but confined his poems based on them to highly-charged description; and this receives corroboration elsewhere. The power he has of charging a scene with the emotion of the character set in it is illustrated in many poems, and notably in 'Mariana' and *Maud*.

Despite his genius for dramatic and descriptive lyric, nowhere better illustrated than in the original blank-verse lyrics of *The Princess*, Tennyson desired from his youth to succeed with a long narrative poem. He suppressed this aspiration in 1838 on prudential grounds, as we have seen. But leaving out of account his boyhood efforts, we know that in his nineteenth year,[1] when he was already at Cambridge, and presumably while composing some of the poems appearing in the 1830 volume, he essayed a lengthy but incomplete work called *The Lover's Tale*, modelled upon a story in Boccaccio. This was only completed in later life and published in 1879 to avoid piracy. Furthermore in about 1833[2] he made a prose sketch for an epic on the Arthurian materials, together with an outline of the allegory intended: some time between 1833 and 1840 he planned a drama on the same subject. All this material was put aside. He went so far as to write down the quite short episode which he entitled 'Morte d'Arthur' shortly after the death of Hallam in September 1833;[3] but it had to

---

[1] The *Memoir* (ii, p. 239) says that it was composed in his seventeenth year, but this is certainly wrong since the Preface to the edition of 1879, which quotes the earlier intended preface, gives the poet's age as nineteen. It was to be published in 1833, but was withdrawn from the press.

[2] *Memoir*, ii, pp. 123–5.   [3] *Memoir*, i, pp. 109, 129, 131, 138, 142, 153.

wait during the 'ten years' silence' for publication in 1842, and even then was carefully introduced so as to allay prejudice against long narratives. Another poem, about Lancelot's quest of the Graal was not written down at all and was consequently lost.[1] 'Sir Galahad', which appeared in 1842, but was in fact written much earlier—at least by 19 September 1834[2]—illustrates his preference for brief rather than lengthy treatment of narratives lying under his hand. Even when he borrowed unromantic narratives from novels, as in 'Dora', suggested by Susan Ferrier's *The Inheritance*, his poems were short.[3]

Nevertheless, even in lyrics, the pleasure he took in exotic description continued in association with dramatic situations reminiscent of fairy tales of the *Arabian Nights* pattern. Some of these poems of 1842 show significant anticipations of *The Princess*. They centre upon the choice made by women between the difficult course of bravely accepting the demands of love and yielding to considerations of expediency. *The Princess* takes the issue further. Ida resists the demands of love not from any lack of moral heroism, but almost by force of it. Fundamentally, however, she is placed in the same dilemma, and the poet demands of the reader that he share his own belief that a woman's finest achievement is to respond to the highest claim made upon her—that of true love. Not everyone will agree with this belief, but that Tennyson made it a corollary of Hallam's theory that women were agents, by virtue of the love they could offer and accept, of a kind of divinely-sprung redemption, is I think sufficiently clear from the poems to which I propose to give brief consideration.

III. THE PATTERN OF 'THE PRINCESS'

A remarkable anticipation of *The Princess*, in several respects, is 'The Day Dream', a poem which appeared in 1842, though one of its sections had been previously published in 1830. The

---

[1] *Memoir*, ii, p. 125. [2] *Memoir*, i, p. 139.

[3] See *Memoir*, i, p. 196, where Tennyson explains that he felt the need to tell the tale of the nobly simple country girl in the simplest possible poetic language, which suggests that he was also resisting his tendency to supply exotic description, fully indulged in 'The Gardener's Daughter'. For Spedding's depreciation of the tendency, see *Memoir*, i, p. 96.

The Pattern of 'The Princess'

date of composition of this poem is fairly certainly fixed by a
note by Edward Fitzgerald in the copy of *Poems by Two
Brothers* in the library of Trinity College, Cambridge,[1] which
states that it was complete in 1835 save for the prologue and
the epilogue: the poet may even have completed it to this
point in the preceding year. Like *The Princess* it is a narrative
—though broken up into short lyrical sections to avoid over-
due length. It has a clear relation to a fairy tale,[2] and carries a
moral of like import.

From the prologue we learn that the tale is related by an
admirer to a Lady Flora, whom we meet reclining one summer's day at a lattice window. The speaker offers to relate 'the
reflex of a legend past' to entertain her as she sits at the em-
broidery frame to 'add a crimson to the quaint macaw'. The
legend which is told is a faithful version of the familiar fairy
story of 'The Sleeping Beauty', which was the title of the section published in 1830, describing the princess as she lay in a
profound sleep. The story provides several interesting parallels
with other poems by Tennyson. The description of the activities of the palace arrested in mid-career by the spell reveals
the poet's gift for describing the immobile, previously shown
in the 'Mariana' poems and 'The Lady of Shalott'. The passage
beginning

> Well—were it not a pleasant thing
>   To fall asleep with all one's friends . . .
> And every hundred years to rise
>   And learn the world and sleep again;
> To sleep thro' terms of mighty wars,
>   And wake on science grown to more,
> On secrets of the brain, the stars,
>   As wild as aught of fairy-lore,

shows an interest in the far future and the marvels of science
which occurs again in 'Locksley Hall'. The poem concludes

[1] Joyce Green, 'Tennyson's Development during the "Ten Years'
Silence" (1832–42)', *PMLA*, lxvi (1951), p. 677 n. 62. See also *Memoir*,
i, pp. 134, 151.

[2] Tennyson took some pains to learn more about fairy tales. After
leaving Cambridge he read Thomas Keightley's *The Fairy Mythology*,
which includes 'Sir Orfeo', a poem which seems to be echoed in 'The
splendour falls' from *The Princess*. See *Memoir*, i, pp. 129, 130.

that Lady Flora is herself asleep, asleep, that is, to the fullness of life. Her mind is

> all too dearly self-involved,
> Yet sleeps a dreamless sleep to me,—
> A sleep by kisses undissolved,
> That lets thee neither hear nor see:
> But break it. In the name of wife,
> And in the rights that name may give,
> Are clasp'd the moral of thy life,
> And that for which I care to live.

The speaker invites her to take the poem for its moral:

> take it—earnest wed with sport,
> And either sacred unto you.

It is important to notice that her awakening is seen to fulfil not only her own life but the speaker's too. On her decision depends the completeness of *two* lives. In general terms, the suggestion is that sexual happiness ultimately depends upon the resolve of the woman.

In this connection it is interesting to see how the fairy tale is fitted to the earnest theme. The story of the Sleeping Beauty turns upon the prince's bold penetration into a dangerous thicket surrounding the castle in which the princess lies asleep. In this thicket lie the bodies of those who have previously failed in their perilous bid to break the spell:

> The bodies and the bones of those
> That strove in other days to pass
> Are wither'd in the thorny close,
> Or scatter'd blanching on the grass.
> He gazes on the silent dead:
> 'They perish'd in their daring deeds.'
> This proverb flashes thro' his head,
> 'The many fail, the one succeeds.'

One can easily see a resemblance to the central situation in *The Princess*, where the Prince enters the College garden at some peril to his life; his Princess is likewise reluctant to fulfil her role. Such a situation is part of the stock-in-trade of fairy tales and does not surprise us. It is even present in 'Recollections of the Arabian Nights'—the penetration of the Caliph's

private garden in the original tale of Noureddin and the Fair
Persian was forbidden and customarily punishable by death.
But for Tennyson it seems to have held a particular charm. In
a poem not published until 1851, but written much earlier,
'Edwin Morris', it reappears in a modern setting.[1] The speaker
in this poem recalls to mind the happy days he spent as a young
man ostensibly sketching in North Wales, but really wooing
the daughter of a wealthy industrialist, Letty Hill. She lived
with her parents, 'newcomers in an ancient hold, Newcomers
from the Mersey, millionaires', in a Tudor-chimneyed house
built on an island in a lake. In the autumn she is betrothed

> to sixty thousand pounds,
> To lands in Kent and messuages in York,
> And slight Sir Robert with his watery smile
> And educated whisker . . .

Despite this, the young man, in response to a note from her
signed 'Your Letty, only yours', rows across the lake to the
island, and at the risk of detection, meets Letty:

> She moved,
> Like Proserpine in Enna, gathering flowers.
> Then low and sweet I whistled thrice; and she,
> She turn'd, we closed, we kiss'd, swore faith, I breath'd
> In some new planet. A silent cousin stole
> Upon us and departed. 'Leave', she cried,
> 'O, leave me!' 'Never, dearest, never: here
> I brave the worst;' and while we stood like fools
> Embracing, all at once a score of pugs
> And poodles yell'd within, and out they came,
> Trustees and aunts and uncles. 'What, with him!
> Go,' shrill'd the cotton-spinning chorus; 'him!'
> I choked. Again they shriek'd the burthen, 'Him!'
> Again with hands of wild rejection, 'Go!—
> Girl, get you in!'

The poem strikes a note of wistful comedy. In Letty Hill we see
another cousin Amy of Locksley Hall, a woman who failed to
respond to the demands of love when suddenly put before her.
The poem ends with

[1] In the *Memoir*, the date of composition is implied to be 1839. See
i, p. 174. Sir Charles Tennyson, op. cit., p. 211, gives 1845.

Anticipations

> I have pardon'd little Letty; not indeed,
> It may be, for her own dear sake, but this,—
> She seems a part of those fresh days to me.

The outcome of 'Locksley Hall' is quite different. Amy, having long concealed her love for her cousin, finally confessed it, whereupon

> Love took up the harp of Life, and smote on all the chords with
>   might;
> Smote the chord of Self, that, trembling, past in music out of
>   sight.

The two lovers often met in secluded places:

> Many an evening by the waters did we watch the stately ships,
> And our spirits rush'd together at the touching of the lips.

But Amy, like Letty, proved unworthy of the high claims of love; she was not of the heroic mould. The result was that the cynical bitterness of her lover became even more intense; he yearns for the hopes of his youth, aspires to the strength to bear his lot in the new age. The lover of Letty Hill overcame his disappointment, though he too as a young man had had a touch of the same *mal de siècle*.

> 'I have, I think,—Heaven knows,—as much within;
> Have, or should have, but for a thought or two,
> That like a purple beech among the greens
> Looks out of place. 'Tis from no want in her;
> It is my shyness, or my self-distrust,
> Or something of a wayward modern mind
> Dissecting passion. Time will set me right'.

In other words, he resembles the speaker in 'Locksley Hall' as much as Letty Hill resembles Amy. In one sense he resembles the speaker in *Maud* even more, for the latter too suffers from the same dislike of his times and a mistrust of love. He too penetrates a forbidden garden to keep tryst with Maud—another daughter of *nouveaux riches* who leaves a ball to meet him there. A similar meeting leads to a fatal duel. Like the lover in 'Edwin Morris', he is obliged to fly, but this time for his life.

The Pattern of 'The Princess'

In comparing these variations upon a fundamentally similar situation, we can see how certain elements are assembled.
Dissatisfaction with modern life, a neurotic or at least un-
balanced hero, women obliged to decide between love and
interest, an absorption in the discoveries of science; these disparate elements are fitted to a story of a young man's risks in
dangerous meetings with a woman. They all reappear in *The
Princess*, where the central situation is restored to its original
fairy-tale aspect. The 'weird seizures' of the Prince, the
scientific discussions, a 'dangerous' heroine, a risky trespass to
visit her—all these elements fill out a situation which had particular significance for the poet. It is, I suggest, a situation
which was always intended to relate to the role of women in
life. This, I think, is made quite certain by the discussions in
'Edwin Morris'. Before the account of the incident involving
Letty Hill this very topic is discussed. Edwin Morris, a poet,

> he that knew the names,
> Long learned names of agaric, moss and fern,
> Who forged a thousand theories of the rocks,

had described how his earliest love had been for Nature and
that this had mysteriously identified itself with the love he
felt for a woman:

> 'My love for Nature and my love for her,
> Of different ages, like twin-sisters grew,
> Twin-sisters differently beautiful.
> To some full music rose and sank the sun,
> And some full music seem'd to move and change
> With all the varied changes of the dark,
> And either twilight and the day between;
> For daily hope fulfill'd, to rise again
> Revolving toward fulfilment, made it sweet
> To walk, to sit, to sleep, to wake, to breathe.'[1]

[1] The lines
> My love for Nature and my love for her
> Of different ages like twin sisters throve,

were included in 'The Gardener's Daughter' at an early stage in its
composition, as can be seen from the Heath Commonplace Book in the
Fitzwilliam Museum. The entry is dated 1833. Arthur Hallam mentions
the poem in a letter dated 31 July 1833 (*Memoir*, i, p. 103).

Anticipations

This passage throws some light on the substitution of natural description for incidents involving forbidden love in earlier poems. Edwin Morris's idealistic report of his awakening to love for a woman is laughed at by another member of the party:

> Then said the fat-faced curate Edward Bull:
> 'I take it, God made the woman for the man,
> And for the good and increase of the world.
> A pretty face is well, and this is well,
> To have a dame indoors, that trims us up,
> And keeps us tight; but these unreal ways
> Seem but the theme of writers, and indeed
> Worn threadbare. Man is made of solid stuff.
> I say, God made the woman for the man,
> And for the good and increase of the world.'

In this poem occurs not only the same situation as was used in *The Princess*, with elements shared by *Maud* and 'Locksley Hall', but also a dialogue which would have been quite as appropriate to the Prince and his irascible father. The old King in *The Princess* is another Edward Bull: for him 'Man is the hunter; woman is his game'.

We can see, then, that in 'Edwin Morris', *Maud*, and to some extent 'Locksley Hall', a fairy-tale situation—which appears undisguised in 'The Day Dream' and *The Princess*— is used to illustrate a theme, the influence for good or evil of women. Consequently it would be rash to assume that the events described in them have any reality in Tennyson's own experience, even though it is possible that some of his own thoughts are transferred to the luckless lovers. Nevertheless, we may legitimately infer that the choice of the tale in the first place indicates that he felt that a worthwhile love could only be achieved in the modern age by a degree of courageous independence on the part of women.[1]

---

[1] Lionel Stevenson very convincingly argues in 'The "high-born maiden" Symbol in Tennyson', *PMLA*, lxiii (March-June 1948), pp. 234 ff., that in 'The Lady of Shalott' and 'The Palace of Art' among other poems, Tennyson was presenting, after Shelley, an allegory of his own soul by way of a woman-figure. He makes an interesting parallel with Jung's theory that the 'anima', a symbol for the unconscious, is frequently represented as a woman-figure, which with maturity is identi-fied with a real woman. To the list of poems in which he sees the poet

The Pattern of 'The Princess'

An earlier poem was published in the 1833 volume which was not reprinted in the poet's lifetime, nor included in any authorised editions until 1897. This poem, called 'Kate', portrays another Princess Ida:

> Whence shall she take a fitting mate?
> For Kate no common love will feel;
> My woman-soldier, gallant Kate,
> As pure and true as blades of steel.

The poem concludes:

> Kate saith 'the world is void of might.'
> Kate saith 'the men are gilded flies.'
> Kate snaps her fingers at my vows;
> Kate will not hear of lovers' sighs.
> I would I were an armed knight,
> Far-famed for well-won enterprise,
> And wearing on my swarthy brows
> The garland of new-wreathed emprise;
> For in a moment I would pierce
> The blackest files of clanging fight,
> And strongly strike to left and right,
> In dreaming of my lady's eyes,
> O, Kate loves well the bold and fierce;
> But none are bold enough for Kate,
> She cannot find a fitting mate.

making the transference—in some of which allegory is obviously intended—he adds 'Locksley Hall', *The Princess* and *Maud*. The parallels I have drawn between some of these poems is meant to lead to a more pedestrian conclusion, namely that Tennyson's attitude to sexual love was of a piece with his other heroic tastes, somewhat modified by experience of real life; and that he shared Arthur Hallam's belief in the high role of women in redeeming society from its errors. This view has the merit, I believe, of explaining the presence in these poems of passages of social criticism, of the portrayal of men out of harmony with the age, and of the hope that science could accelerate social improvement.

In 'The Flight', published in 1885, though said by Tennyson (*Memoir*, ii, p. 319) to be 'a very early poem', we are given a monologue by a young woman steeling herself to flee her tyrannical father's house on the eve of a forced match to a man she detests; she hopes one day to meet again her lover who has gone overseas. In stanza xv there is a clear allusion to Lucy Ashton in *The Bride of Lammermoor*, which may well have interested the poet in the pattern of events described in this chapter. The resemblance between the story of *Maud* and the plot of *The Bride of Lammermoor* is discussed by Andrew Lang in *Alfred Tennyson* (1901), pp. 88–9.

Anticipations

In some respects, the Princess of the later poem is foreshadowed in this very early poem. But to present her as heroine of the new feminism, and to make a criticism of it, demanded the telling of a tale which could not be reduced to detached lyrics, though they might still be incorporated. The unwillingness to undertake a long poem had to be put aside. The tale which had appeared in disguise before was admirably fitted to the theme and it only remained to adapt it to the need to introduce a woman's college of the kind foreseen by Kemble. What that tale very probably was will be discussed in the next chapter.

CHAPTER X

The Source

I. 'Maud', 'Rasselas' and the Oriental Tale

THE romantic stories Tennyson enjoyed in his youth
continued to give him pleasure in later life; before discussing their relevance to *The Princess* I should like to
say something about that part of the story of *Maud* which
indisputably derives from a tale in the *Arabian Nights*, for
this will help in deciding the sort of thing we can expect
to find in the story or stories to which *The Princess* was indebted.

Maud, it will be remembered, like other women in Tennyson's poems, had to decide between conforming with her
family's wishes and returning the love of a young man whose
almost neurotic condition expressed itself in savage criticism
of the state of contemporary English life. She decides for the
lover, but as the result of a duel which unhappily proves fatal
he is obliged to leave the country. After a period of insanity,
he is inspired by a dream in which Maud appears to him to
take up his life afresh and to join in a war which he feels to be
just and likely to remedy the social cancer at the heart of
English life. His old cynicism leaves him and at last he feels
committed to a cause, a cause which he knows to be good. He
feels a deep sense of relief that 'a peace that was full of wrongs
and shames' is at last ended, and that he can be one with his
kind again. The point we are to take is that his love was not
wholly thrown away and wasted. Though Maud is dead, the
knowledge of her integrity in love remains a source of healing
power to her lover. If she had failed him his resentment against
his kind would have been deepened not only by his obsession
that her father had cheated his father, but because he believed
that Maud had been betrothed to him from their infancy:

The Source

Did I hear it half in a doze
   Long since, I know not where?
Did I dream it an hour ago,
   When asleep in this arm-chair?

Men were drinking together,
   Drinking and talking of me:
'Well, if it prove a girl, the boy
   Will have plenty; so let it be.'

Is it an echo of something
   Read with a boy's delight,
Viziers nodding together
   In some Arabian Night?

Strange, that I hear two men,
   Somewhere, talking of me:
'Well, if it prove a girl, my boy
   Will have plenty; so let it be'.[1]

This enigmatic section of the poem hints at a pre-contract between the speaker's father and Maud's. Then they were still friends and business partners, thinking of providing for their sons, though Maud's father as yet had no children. When Maud was born she was not provided for; but this had been foreseen (in the conversation overheard by the speaker as a small boy) and circumvented by the suggestion that she should be married to the other partner's son. It is hardly surprising that this autocratic suggestion should have caused the son to wonder whether he had dreamed it, or unconsciously remembered a tale of

Viziers nodding together
   In some Arabian Night.

[1] Part I, vii. To clarify the point Tennyson later added another stanza in which occur the lines:

. . . Maud's dark father and mine
Had bound us one to the other,
Betrothed us over their wine,
On the day when Maud was born;
Seal'd her mine from her first sweet breath!
Mine, mine by a right, from birth till death!
Mine, mine—our fathers have sworn!

'Maud', 'Rasselas' and the Oriental Tale

In point of fact, the incident closely resembles one in a story from the *Arabian Nights*, the tale of Nourredin Ali and Bedreddin Hassan.[1] These two are brothers and joint-Viziers who resolve to marry sisters, and if their children prove to be of opposite sex, to pair them off when they come to age. They immediately fall out, however, over the matter of dowry and jointure; Nourredin thinks it prudent to take himself off. Each brother nevertheless has the expected son and daughter, and by magical intervention they meet and finally marry. The general parallel with *Maud* is obvious—yet in tone the stories are worlds apart. In the *Arabian Nights* story all is fantastic and supernatural. In *Maud* this incident is placed in a context which gives it psychological realism.

Now *The Princess* is much closer in spirit to the romantic tales of the *Arabian Nights*; but nevertheless the degree of transmutation we see in *Maud* should warn us not to expect more than a general resemblance between it and a source, with perhaps a good clue. Certain elements could not by any stretch of imagination be looked for. It was suggested in Chapter I that editors who have sought an original for *The Princess* have not always made a distinction between the story and the theme it illustrates; some have used much space in suggesting literary sources of the *theme* despite the evidence that contemporary feminist agitation supplied it ready-made. One of the most popular of suggestions of this kind was that the poem was developed from a single paragraph in *Rasselas*, Chapter XLIX:

> The princess thought that of all sublunary things, knowledge was the best: she desired first, to learn all sciences, and then purposed to found a college of learned women in which she would preside: that . . . she might raise up for the next age, models of prudence and patterns of piety.

This 'anticipation' was pointed out in print as long ago as 1861.[2] It hardly deserves much attention since it is really a

[1] The identification of this story was made by W. D. Paden in *Tennyson in Egypt*, p. 161, n. 238.

[2] *Notes and Queries*, 17 August 1861, p. 129. A fresh appearance of the suggestion occurs in John Robert Moore's 'Conan Doyle, Tennyson and *Rasselas*' in *Nineteenth Century Fiction*, vii (1952–3), p. 221.

source for the theme; there is not even a hint of the plot. All we have is a conjunction of the theme with a *princess*, and it must be admitted that this is rather arresting. We can easily see how the conjunction in *Rasselas* occurred. The idea of founding a women's college is one of many schemes of happiness formulated by the prince and his sister, and relates to Johnson's overall theme of the vanity of human wishes. This theme was fitted to an oriental tale because among the *Persian Tales* translated by Ambrose Philips there is a very similar account of a peregrination in search of happiness;[1] indeed oriental stories of this kind abound in incidents involving a prince or Caliph going among his people, often in disguise. It suited Johnson very well to follow the established plan, and treat his philosophic theme by way of a tale about a prince and princess journeying through the Near Eastern world in search of happiness. Since, as I hope to show, *The Princess* adapts a story from the *Persian Tales*, clearly its relation to *Rasselas* is one of common origin rather than of direct dependence.

II. THE PERSIAN TALES

The sort of story to be looked for as suggesting to Tennyson the plot of the poem need clearly have nothing to do with a woman's college, for this is an element which most likely came from Kemble. It will rather have some close relation with the attitude of the Princess towards marriage. It was argued earlier that the conclusion we are left with after reading the poem is that what Tennyson regarded as objectionable was the sex-antagonism and aversion to marriage of the Princess, not the College itself, the need for which he tacitly admitted. The tale which Tennyson probably had in mind would almost certainly have as its heroine one who had a similar aversion to marriage.

That he did not invent the story himself is a matter of no great importance, and in any case it should be understood that in attempting to identify the source of the plot I am anxious to avoid giving the impression that deliberate borrowing took

[1] See Geoffrey Tillotson, ' "Rasselas" and the "Persian Tales" ', *Essays in Criticism and Research* (1942), p. 111, and Gwin J. Kolb, 'The Structure of Rasselas', *PMLA*, lxvi (1951), p. 698.

place when most probably there was nothing of the sort. At the same time, I think that borrowing—of the unconscious kind we *can* imagine to have taken place—is not put out of the question by Tennyson's belief that the subject was original,[1] for 'subject' could refer more easily to theme than story. Nor need we too much shrink before his celebrated tirade on source-hunters:

> But there is, I fear, a prosaic set growing up among us, editors of booklets, book-worms, index-hunters, or men of great memories and no imagination, who *impute themselves* to the poet, and so believe that *he*, too, has no imagination, but is for ever poking his nose between the pages of some old volume in order to see what he can appropriate.[2]

The fact is that he was often glad to borrow stories and anecdotes, and Woolner, Jowett and Fitzgerald[3] all contributed. But he was at pains to insist that he owed no debt to any other *poet* after *Timbuctoo*,[4] and denied borrowing for *The Princess* from Shelley and Wordsworth; it is clear that what he objected to was the assertion that his poetry was not his own. To know the source of a work may help in its interpretation; this is particularly so with *The Princess*.

The fact that the intransigent heroine is a princess is, by analogy with *Rasselas*, a clue to the place where Tennyson read at one time or another some story or stories which were wonderfully capable of being adapted to the contemporary situation. A second clue is that between the Prince and the Princess there exists a betrothal contracted in childhood, a feature whose origin in the *Arabian Nights* has already been discussed in relation to *Maud*. Princes and princesses are often met in the stories of the *Arabian Nights*, for although the protagonist of a particular tale may be a humble fellow like

[1] The *Memoir*, i, p. 247, makes a distinction between 'subject' and 'story': 'The subject of "The Princess", my father believed, was original, and certainly the story is full of original incident, humour and fancy.' In *Materials*, the words 'as he invented it' came after 'story'. The later omission may be significant.

[2] *Memoir*, i, p. 258.

[3] Fitzgerald suggested in fun that he would never use a story *given* to him: it had to be left in his way. See *Memoir*, i, pp. 515–16.

[4] *Memoir*, i, p. 46 n.

The Source

Aladdin or Sinbad, the general romantic preoccupation with high life is satisfied by setting incidents in courts, where princes may play their parts as whimsical or unpredictable persons whose absolute powers often provide the fearful dilemmas which, together with magic, form the stuff of fairy tales.

Antoine Galland, the French orientalist, commenced issuing *Les Mille et Une Nuits* in 1704, the series being completed in 1717 in twelve volumes. So great was their success that the equally celebrated oriental scholar, Pétis de la Croix, who like Galland had been sent to the Near East under official auspices, published a set of *Persian Tales*, called *Les Mille et un Jours, contes persans*. These had been overseen in translation by LeSage, and how much of the French version of them is his work is unknown. They appeared between 1710 and 1712. Both sets of tales were quickly translated into English. The *Persian Tales* were translated by 'Dr. King and several other hands' in 1714, but this translation[1] was eclipsed by another made in the same year by Ambrose Philips. Others appeared in the course of the century, but that of Philips appears to have retained its popularity with the public.[2] Martha Conant distinguishes between the *Arabian Nights* and the *Persian Tales* thus:

> In general the *Persian Tales* resemble the *Arabian Nights* in the mingling of magic and reality, of strange enchantments and oriental customs almost as strange; in dramatic presentation of incident and background; in lack of characterisation, and, with few exceptions, of structural unity. But the *Persian Tales* is far more sentimental, more fantastic, more brilliant in colour. Here the reader is in a fairyland of charming or grotesque surprises, while in the *Arabian Nights*, despite the misty clouds of enchantment, there is substantial ground under foot. May this not be one reason why the *Arabian Nights* has always been a greater favourite in England than the *Persian Tales*; and why, in France, the popularity of the *Persian Tales* has equalled, if not surpassed, that of the *Arabian Nights*?[3]

[1] *The Persian and Turkish Tales, compleat*. The *Turkish Tales* were also the work of Pétis de la Croix.

[2] See Martha P. Conant, *The Oriental Tale in England in the Eighteenth Century* (Columbia, 1908), p. 273. She lists editions for Philips's translation for 1722 (3rd), 1738 (5th), 1750 (6th), 1765 (7th), 1781, 1783.

[3] op. cit., p. 25. French editions of the *Persian Tales* appeared in 1826, 1835 and 1844.

The Persian Tales

The number of English editions of Philips's translation shows that the tales were by no means out of favour during the eighteenth century, even though they were eclipsed by the *Arabian Nights* in the nineteenth.[1]

The *Persian Tales* are set within a frame-story similar in purpose to that of Scheherazade in the *Arabian Nights*, that is, to connect a large number of separate tales. It relates how a certain Princess Farruknaz is told a series of stories daily at her bath, in order that she may be persuaded that some men at least may be trusted. The teller of the stories is an old nurse, who is much distressed at her mistress's unwillingness to be wooed. The best account of the *Persian Tales* themselves is given by Ambrose Philips in the preface to the third edition of his translation (1722). There he writes:

Compositions of this Kind are never intended for the Entertainment of vulgar Spirits. They only are capable of being delighted with them whose souls are quickened with the Powers of Fancy, and warmed with generous Passions. There is no doubt, but to such the Pleasures of the Imagination are beyond all other Amusements in Life; which has been finely explained in a Set of Papers upon that Subject, in the *Spectator*.

The Design of these feigned Histories is to reduce a young Princess to Reason, who had conceived an unaccountable Aversion to Men, and would not be persuaded to marry. In order to this, each story furnishes a shining Instance of some faithful Lover, or affectionate Husband. And although every Tale pursues the same Drift, yet they are all diversified with so much Art, and interwoven with so great a Variety of Events, that the very Last appears as new as the First.

The Princess Farruknaz had succeeded in persuading her indulgent father never to oblige her to marry against her will. The reason for the princess's objection to marriage was fear occasioned by a curious dream of a doe who, having preserved a deer from a hunter's toils, was deserted by him when herself entrapped. This dream she interpreted as a true picture of the relations between the sexes. Nevertheless the king was anxious,

[1] The only nineteenth-century English edition listed in the British Museum *Catalogue of Printed Books* is one edited by J. M. McCarthy (1892). There were several lavish editions published in France. Prof. Tillotson (op. cit., p. 112) mentions an English edition for 1848.

The Source

for 'he was apprehensive, lest the Refusal of his Daughter should stir up the Princes to be his Enemies: and fearing the Oath he had made might draw upon him a troublesome War', he readily abetted her nurse's stratagem of trying to convert her to marriage by telling tales with an appropriate moral, that not all men are faithless.

Day after day, as the princess takes her bath, the subtle tales are told, until on the sixty-third day, that of Princess Tourandocte is narrated. This princess greatly resembles herself in situation, having, like Tennyson's Princess too, resolved not to marry. Indeed, the situation of such a story being told to a high-minded young lady and her court rather strikingly resembles that of the Prologue to Tennyson's poem, which might be thought of as a modern version of the ancient device immortalized in the *Arabian Nights* and *Persian Tales*. Lilia, the idealistic daughter of Sir Walter Vivian, whose son is entertaining his college friends, asks to be told a tale, a kind of Christmas entertainment out of season. The tale is told by each of the seven college friends in turn, instead of by one person, but it must be remembered that this was a necessary amendment of the old tale-telling device. Nineteenth-century gentlemen did not easily entertain a company by a narrative of such length. Consequently the story-telling had to be playful. Furthermore the introduction of the theme of a woman's college made it appropriate that it should be undergraduates who told the story in a way Tennyson knew to be authentic from his own experience at Trinity. Finally, of course, the poet tried to remove the inevitable defects of such a method by having one of the party, the poet, retell the whole tale as best he could. Fitzgerald was surely right to be apprehensive on hearing that the poet was proposing to insert 'characters' of the speakers before each section—unless they were all Tennysons—for as he maintained, they all speak with one voice.

If we see the nineteenth-century picnic as the equivalent of the Persian morning of leisure at the side of the scented bath, we shall be able to understand the modernizations of the tale itself. But first we may examine the tale of Tourandocte as Ambrose Philips relates it, always bearing in mind that *Maud* shows how far the poet could alter a story of this sort to suit modern situations, and the fact previously established, that all that concerns the college must not be expected in the tale.

Tourandocte, though heroine of a Persian tale, is in fact a princess of China, a circumstance that will not surprise readers of the *Arabian Nights*, where China also figures large, and is not notably out of character with the rest of the landscapes. The princess is of course beautiful, as befits the heroine of such a tale. But like the Fair Persian she is also notable for her learning. The distance of her father's kingdom from the other Asiatic principalities, however, does not permit this fact to be well known, and indeed the great agitation she creates in the minds of princes from near and far is largely caused by the circulation of certain miniatures, paintings which fall as far below her real beauty as most court-paintings deliberately flatter. Much emphasis is placed in the tale on this picture of the lady:

The Princess *Tourandocte* . . . is in the Nineteenth Year of her Age. She is so very beautiful, that the Painters, who have attempted her Picture, tho' the greatest Artists of the *East*, have all of them owned with Confusion, that they have been foiled, and that the Pencil of the most practised in beautiful Features, would never be able to express half the Charms of the Princess of *China*. Nevertheless, the different Paintings that have been made of her, though infinitely short of the Original, have caused great Havock in the World.

To her ravishing Beauty she joins a Mind so embellished, that she is Mistress not only of every Accomplishment, which is usually taught to Ladies of her Rank; but is likewise skilled in those Sciences which are proper only to Men. She can write the different Characters of several Languages; She is knowing in Arithmetick, in Geography, in Philosophy, in the Mathematicks, in the Law, and more especially in Theology . . . but all her bright Perfections are eclipsed by an unexampled Insensibility of Heart: She tarnishes her charming Merit by a detestable Cruelty.

It is now two Years since the King of *Thebet* sent to demand her in Marriage for the Prince his Son, who fell in Love with her upon the sight of a Picture of her, which came into his Hands.[1]

The lady has in fact enough talent to conduct a university single-handed, and rather dims the lustre of the Fair Persian

[1] *Persian Tales*, ii, p. 9.

The Source

(that other Eastern intellectual beauty), save in one important respect. She lacks what we would still call, I think, womanliness.

Tennyson's poem also has an eastern Princess,[1] and northern Prince, who, indeed, in the original opening line of the first part of the poem announced

> I was the prince and heir of Alibey,[2]

a realm which, though as obscure as could be desired, is patently an appropriate setting for such a potentate. The Prince in the poem also knew no more than the Prince of Thebet what his lady really looked like, and had to rely upon a miniature of her, clearly of recent date, and thus presumably brought to him by some painter of the foreign court. He confides:

> And still I wore her picture by my heart,
> And one dark tress; and all around them both
> Sweet thoughts would swarm as bees about their queen.
>
> .   .   .
>
> But when the council broke, I rose and past
> Thro' the wild woods that hung about the town;
> Found a still place, and pluck'd her likeness out;
> Laid it on flowers . . .

Towards the end of the poem, when the Princess is almost won over, this picture is again mentioned:

> > 'Never, Prince!
> You cannot love me.'
> >   'Nay, but thee', I said,
> 'From yearlong poring on thy pictured eyes . . .'

In the *Persian Tales*, the prince's name is Calaf: he has already travelled to the foreign court, and is told by the old hostess at

---

[1] Her kingdom is of the south, but she is clearly native to the 'eastern' world on the score of her leopards.

[2] I am indebted to Sir Charles Tennyson for the loan of a transcript of the poem giving much of the version which appeared in the MSS mentioned above p. 8, n. 1. For a reference to 'Alibey' as the prince's kingdom see his article 'Tennyson Papers: IV. The Making of "The Princess" ', *The Cornhill Magazine*, 153 (January–June 1936), p. 676.

The Persian Tales

the inn where he is staying the remarkable story of Touran-docte. (We may remember that Tennyson provides a host of an inn who tells the Prince about Ida, and helps him and his friends in their task.) Calaf learns from the hostess that the Princess Tourandocte has absolutely refused to marry the suitors from foreign courts who are constantly pressing their attentions upon her, and that her father has to send them back with a denial. In *The Princess*, it is a little different:

> My father sent ambassadors with furs
> And jewels, gifts, to fetch her. These brought back
> A present, a great labour of the loom;
> And therwithal an answer vague as wind.

Calaf by chance sees a picture of Tourandocte, and imme-diately decides to attempt to win her for himself, and is not dissuaded even by discovering that, in true fairy-tale manner, the princess, who prides herself upon her wit and learning, has imposed an ordeal upon her suitors. This is the solving of riddles, failure in which is to be rewarded by death. This very startling obstacle was agreed to by her father only because both his daughter and he felt that it was tantamount to a complete refusal on the princess's part to marry, but with the onus of declining transferred to the suitor.

Here, of course, it may be objected, *The Princess* is very different. Nothing like riddling is resorted to as a means of holding off suitors from the misanthropic beauty. But it must be remembered that Tennyson had to adapt his romantic story (whatever its source might be) to the contemporary theme of a woman's college.[1] I would suggest that, bearing this in mind, the situation in *The Princess* is in fact very close to that in the Persian tale, for the women's college of *The Princess* has one extraordinary and indeed fantastic rule—a death penalty for male intruders; and this clearly is nothing more than a capital veto on attempting to offer marriage to the Princess or her protégées:

[1] Tourandocte's intellectual pride naturally suggested to her setting riddles, since this not only got rid of her unwelcome suitors, but gratified her sense of superiority in intellect. In the poem, the College satisfies Ida's two desires of showing her intellectual power, and keeping herself unmarried.

The Source

'Wretched boy,
How saw you not the inscription on the gate,
LET NO MAN ENTER IN ON PAIN OF DEATH?'

The whole plot, in fact, hinges upon the Prince and his companions being exposed to a death penalty in the same manner as Calaf, when he aspired to Tourandocte's hand.

As I mentioned earlier, Calaf is not put off by the risks attending his suit:

> No, incomparable Princess, continu'd he, looking on the Picture with a languishing Air, no Obstacle shall hinder me: I will love you, spite of your Barbarity; and since I am permitted to aspire to the Possession of you, I will do all I can to obtain it. If I perish in so noble an Enterprize, all that will trouble me in Death will be the Thoughts of losing you![1]

After various delays, Calaf prevails in his determination to risk his life:

> Nay, I confess to you, there is a secret Charm even in the Princess's Cruelty, which pleases my Love, and flattering myself that I am perhaps the happy Mortal who is to triumph over her Pride . . . I cannot live unless I obtain Tourandocte.[2]

The princess enters the great chamber, filled with the glittering robes of mandarins, professors of the Royal College and doctors of known abilities. She makes no defence of her cruelty, but points out that any wooer has only himself to blame for the consequences. To confound him, she throws off her veil, and

> her Eyes shone brighter than the Stars, brighter than the Sun, when he shines in his full Glory at the opening of a black Cloud.[3]

Nevertheless, Calaf successfully guesses her riddles and she is thus under an obligation to marry him. But she still utterly refuses to do so, and for this is upbraided by her father. Very generously, Calaf promises to resign her if she guesses *his* riddle; otherwise she will be his. Tourandocte at this point is

[1] op. cit., ii, p. 28.
[2] Note the resemblance to the Prince's words in 'The Day Dream' when confronted with the perilous task of penetrating the thicket surrounding the Sleeping Beauty.
[3] op. cit., p. 51.

in a state of consternation at the prospect that her pride will have a fall. Her two slaves, whom she takes to be devoted to her, press their counsels upon her. Now in point of fact, Tourandocte has begun to soften from her iron mood, but her pride is still uppermost in her mind, and she cannot allow herself to be humiliated by defeat. But unknown to her, one of the two confidantes is disloyal to her because she has herself fallen in love with the prince. Her name is Adelmule; and she sees the prince secretly and admonishes him to fly the princess's cruelty—but really for her own advantage. This Adelmule was herself a woman of position in another land, and only found herself in the harem of Tourandocte because she had been saved from a rushing torrent by the soldiers of the princess's own father after she had been thrown in to preserve her from capture. Despite her blandishments, however, the prince will not give up hoping to win Tourandocte, whom he loves entirely; accordingly, he is overcome with grief when she correctly supplies the answer to his riddle. But strangely enough, despite her satisfaction at her triumph, Tourandocte feels remorseful at the effect this conclusive success has upon the whole court, which is plunged into the deepest gloom at the turn events have taken. She accordingly reveals her true womanliness of nature by confessing that she had really been unable to outwit the prince on his own terms, but had been aided by Adelmule who, disappointed at the failure of her intrigue, dies by her own hand.

The parallel with *The Princess* may now be shown. The Princess Ida is also betrayed by one of her closest and most trusted counsellors. This is Lady Psyche, who conceals her knowledge of the true identity of the Prince and his two companions, one of whom is her own brother, Florian, whom she is naturally anxious to protect. In other words, she plays the role of Adelmule in the Persian tale, save that her motive is an entirely respectable one. Like Adelmule she is a foreigner in the court—that she should be a compatriot of the Prince, and sister to one of his friends is the easiest of adaptations. Ida is quite deceived until, during a geological expedition, Cyril, the Prince's other companion, betrays their identity by singing a rather inappropriate ditty. In her anger, Ida falls into a raging torrent, and her life is only saved by the Prince's quick action. (This may, perhaps, be a reminiscence of the story of Adelmule.) Ida's sense of obligation to the Prince prevents her from carrying out her edict, but like Tourandocte, she has no intention, despite her having been betrothed to the Prince since childhood, of marrying him after all. Instead she agrees, again like Tourandocte, to stand by the outcome of a second means of arbitration. This is a joust, or rather mêlée, in mediaeval style, between her brothers and the Prince and his companions, each supported by knights of their respective entourages—for by this time the Princess's realm has been invaded by the old King, the Prince's father. Now it is as obvious, I suppose, as anything could be, that this curious episode, so out of harmony with the rest, is a graft upon the story: it occurs at the same point in the narrative as the second riddling in the Persian tale of Tourandocte, and, Tennyson makes quite plain, is equally inconclusive as far as the Prince is concerned:

> It needs must be for honour if at all;
> Since, what decision? if we fail we fail,
> And if we win we fail.

The Prince and his companions are defeated, but like Tourandocte, Ida quite unexpectedly forgoes her advantage, and eventually agrees to marry the Prince. This change is still surprising despite its more careful motivation in the poem, where a Lady Blanche (most ironically named) is made to bear full responsibility for all that is unhappy in the scheme for governing the women's college, though Ida and Psyche are genuinely enthusiastic for women's independence of the other sex.

Though it is not exactly relevant to the discussion of parallels, it may be helpful to mention here that the presence of Psyche's child has obvious thematic importance. The need to provide this child is the reason that Psyche is made a widow, a condition which does not disqualify her from being the object of Cyril's affections, a detail which is not very gracefully handled perhaps, since Cyril is made to appear as much interested in her property as in her person. But it is perhaps sufficient to remark here that the alteration in the character of Psyche to fit the theme does not disguise the fundamental similarity of her part in the poem to that of Adelmule in the story of Tourandocte.

This story was reprinted in 1812 by Henry Weber in a large collection of oriental stories called *Tales of the East*.[1] Weber spent much time in the Introduction to his three volumes listing analogues and tracing indebtedness in European literature. But despite his awareness of the wide dissemination of the stories he prints, he does not point out that some of the elements of the tale of *Calaf and the Princess of China* which we have been considering recur in the story of Ferokh-Faul, prince of Serendib, in Jonathan Scott's *Bahar-Danush, or Garden of Knowledge* (1799). This particular story tells of a prince, Ferokh-Faul, of whom it is prophesied that he will suffer much pain from loving a woman first seen in a portrait. He does in fact do so, and finds that it represents the queen of the Amazonian kingdom of Shunguldeep. This lady professed utter detestation of all men, yet exceeded in valour Rustum and Isfindiar. Despite this, the prince and a devoted companion resolve immediately to visit her kingdom; the companion provides female clothes as a disguise, and musical instruments. They set out, therefore, in the character of singing girls, and having arrived at the city where the queen is then residing, they find themselves at evening among a company of beautiful girls 'who appeared as so many hooris amusing themselves in the gardens of Paradise'. They tell them that they are foreigners attracted by the reputation of their sovereign, and that on that account have ventured to visit her. Their bashfulness overcome with wine, they entertain the girls with their singing.[2]

In this tale we already have a number of points in Tennyson's poem anticipated. The picture still plays its prominent part in unfolding the plot, but in addition we have the prince provided with a companion, the disguise in women's clothes,

---

[1] ii, p. 363.

[2] Jonathan Scott, *Bahar-Danush: or Garden of Knowledge* (Shrewsbury, 1799), iii, pp. 97 ff. (Scott had translated this collection of tales on reading that an earlier well-known translation of 1768 by Alexander Dow was inaccurate and incomplete.)

the musical performances to the assembled all-female court, though without the disastrous outcome perpetrated by Tennyson's Cyril trolling a tavern catch and betraying their sex. The danger of discovery by the Amazon queen remains as great, of course. The prince in the Persian story sees that he can do nothing more in disguise, so he takes a stern decision. He withdraws from the court with his friend, and they throw off their female attire. They then collect a band of chosen men, with whom they invade the queen's garden under cover of night. The next morning they slay her attendants, except one whom they send as a messenger to the queen. The queen is taken aback at this turn of events, and on sending a messenger to find the reason for the molestation of her territory, is told that the prince in his turn has a like destestation of females whom he has vowed to put to death. Whereupon the queen unexpectedly loses her animosity towards the prince and agrees to marry him.

The additional resemblance to the poem consists, of course, in the resort to arms on the part of the prince to settle the *impasse* reached after the failure of the disguised entry into the queen's territory. Taken in conjunction with the tale of *Calaf and the Princess of China*, it will be seen that the two tales of royal ladies who will not wed out of dislike for men provide nearly all the main incidents of Tennyson's poem, due allowance being made for the adaptation inevitable to the treatment of the theme.

We have, of course, only the internal evidence of the surely remarkable parallelism with the tales to suggest that Tennyson may have had them in mind when composing the story of *The Princess*. He would not have had to go very far to find them both together, however. In Weber's *Tales of the East*, where, as already stated, the story of Tourandocte is reprinted, that of the prince of Serendib and the queen of the Amazons is given in a very prominent place, namely in the form of a *résumé* in his Introduction, where, it will be remembered, emphasis is placed upon the wide diffusion of analogues.[1]

[1] p. xlvi. Weber placed it there with a number of other stories which Alexander Dow had omitted from his translation and Scott had subsequently supplied, though Weber thought so little of them that he would not give them a place in his main collection.

Tennyson and Persian Poetry

At a glance a reader could see together in one book two tales on the topic of a woman loth to wed, and dangerous to court, one of them passionately attached to her intellectual pre-eminence. I suggest that Tennyson had them in mind when composing his poem: not only were they remarkably apposite to the contemporary state of feminism; they provided an eastern setting in which to introduce the luxurious descriptions to which he was temperamentally disposed.

III. TENNYSON AND PERSIAN POETRY

In his early poetry, Tennyson adapted, and later transmuted, the descriptions and incidents he encountered in reading the travel books and fictions relating to the Near East. In the interval up to the writing of *The Princess* his interest in the literature of this region had not declined; and in *The Princess* itself he was given an opportunity of introducing detail derived from Persian literature to fill out the narrative drawn from Persian tales.

The earlier examination of Tennyson's pleasure in the Near East and its literature was not carried beyond the evidence of it in 'Recollections of the Arabian Nights'. That Tennyson owed an important debt to Sir William Jones's translation of the *Moâllakát* in his 'Locksley Hall' (1842) is, however, well known.[1] It is the first of the seven poems of the *Moâllakát*, that of Amriolkais, which provides a strong suggestion for the setting of the poem, that of a young man left by his comrades to commune with himself over the departure of his beloved.[2] The development the poet makes from this dramatic opening is quite different from that in the original, but if it be seen as a treatment of the theme of 'modern love', love inhibited in the materially-minded nineteenth century by worldly considerations, then it makes a strong contrast with the decidedly

[1] *Memoir*, i, p. 195. Jones gave not only a prose translation of this poem, but also the original Persian in roman script, and a full account of it in his *Poeseos Asiaticae Commentarii, Works* (1799), ii, pp. 393 ff., and iv, pp. 249 ff.

[2] A fragment of what Palgrave stated was the original MS containing some descriptive lines not published is inserted in the British Museum copy of the eighth edition (1853) of *Poems*. At the top it bears the note 'Roving Oriental'.

untrammelled affections remembered by the speaker in Amriolkais's poem. Indeed an awareness of an implied contrast of this nature is nearly as helpful towards understanding the poem as it is necessary to the comprehension of the twentieth-century treatment of the same theme in *The Waste Land*.

Evidence for the poet's continuing interest in Persian poetry after 1842 is not far to seek. The magnificent section xxII of Part I of *Maud* (1855) unquestionably draws upon the imagery of Persian love-poetry, which, as Jones elegantly observed, seems to rest its claim to beauty of effect upon the deft mingling of beautiful associations—of flowers, music, the tent of the heavens canopying the gardens where the poet praises the charms of his beloved. Jones's own translations provide numerous examples; and in 1854, a little before the composition of this section, Tennyson was reading Hafiz in the Persian, both alone, and afterwards with Fitzgerald's help.[1] Here it may be sufficient to quote Jones's own description of the kind of poetry upon which Tennyson is clearly modelling his own magnificent song:

> Les poëtes Asiatiques aiment extrêmement à personnifier des termes abstraits, et à douer les êtres inanimés de la voix de la raison. Ils se plaisent particulièrement à s'adresser aux objets insensibles, à les appeler pour sympathiser à leurs peines, ou pour partager leur joie en leur ordonnant de porter leurs messages à ceux qu'ils aiment, en leur comparant leurs beautés et leurs perfections aux charmes dont ils sont épris.[2]

For Tennyson's use of this pathetic fallacy I cannot do better than quote the familiar stanza vIII from this section of *Maud*:

> The slender acacia would not shake
> One long milk-bloom on the tree;
> The white lake-blossom fell into the lake
> As the pimpernel dozed on the lea;
> But the rose was awake all night for your sake,
> Knowing your promise to me;
> The lilies and roses were all awake,
> They sigh'd for the dawn and thee.

[1] *Memoir*, i, pp. 373, 374.
[2] *Traité sur la Poésie orientale* (*Works*, v, p. 445).

Tennyson and Persian Poetry

The last stanza of this section:

> She is coming, my own, my sweet;
> Were it ever so airy a tread,
> My heart would hear her and beat,
> Were it earth in an earthy bed . . .

echoes a common conceit of Persian poetry.

The beauty of the Persian imagery of lily and rose, the scents of the garden, wine and revel, and the tenderness expressed through the hyperbole of such lines as

> Shine out, little head, sunning over with curls,
> To the flowers, and be their sun,

which are quite in the Persian manner, are by no means lessened by transference to an English setting. These images are frequently of a mystical connotation in Hafiz and Jami. Occasionally they become wearisome through reiteration, but in Tennyson's poem they convey a sense of excitement and passion.

If these exquisite verses are nevertheless as completely natural to the landscape of Farringford in the Isle of Wight as the solitary musings of the speaker in 'Locksley Hall' are to the Lincolnshire coast, though both are transmuted from originally Persian settings, it is because Tennyson possessed a genius for fitting an apt *mise en scène* to his portrayals of deep feeling. We have already seen this at work in the earlier poems which convey passion through natural descriptions.

If we examine section XXII of *Maud* a little more closely, we can still see something of the originally Persian elements. The setting is dawn in a garden. Carefully placed allusions to the stars, the moon, darkness, the red rose, the white lily, the ever-increasing hush as the moment before dawn approaches and the carriage wheels of the revellers echo away, all suggest breathless quietude. Standing before the garden lake, listening to the faint tinkle of the brook, the speaker saw that, though the lilies and roses kept awake, the white lake-blossom had slipped below the surface; the slender acacia tree was utterly still, and the red blossom of the pimpernel was asleep. He waited, with trembling passion, the coming of his beloved in her ball dress,

213

The Source

> In gloss of satin and glimmer of pearls,
> Queen lily and rose in one.[1]

So skilfully selected are the images, so strong an impression of repressed excitement is suggested by the rhythm, that description and dramatic tension combine to create an almost sensible experience of the moment. One would imagine that it would be difficult to produce so strong an effect more than once, but I would suggest that it is in fact the situation met in the beautiful song from *The Princess* written a number of years earlier:

> 'Now sleeps the crimson petal, now the white;
> Nor waves the cypress in the palace walk;
> Nor winks the gold fin in the porphyry font.
> The fire-fly wakens; waken thou with me.
>
> 'Now droops the milk-white peacock like a ghost,
> And like a ghost she glimmers on to me.
>
> 'Now lies the Earth all Danaë to the stars,
> And all thy heart lies open unto me.
>
> 'Now slides the silent meteor on, and leaves
> A shining furrow, as thy thoughts in me.
>
> 'Now folds the lily all her sweetness up,
> And slips into the bosom of the lake.
> So fold thyself, my dearest, thou, and slip
> Into my bosom and be lost in me.'

The acacia is replaced by the cypress, the English garden by palace-walks. The lily slips once more into the lake, and although it is not the roses which remain sleepless this time, the firefly wakens in their stead. The lake is replaced by a porphyry font in which a golden fish gleams; the peacock droops like a ghost, giving a touch of 'milk-white' to the picture to

---

[1] The imagery used in *Maud* is interestingly discussed by E. D. H. Johnson, 'The Lily and the Rose; symbolic meaning in Tennyson's *Maud*', *PMLA*, lxiv (1949), p. 1222: and by Roy P. Basler, 'Tennyson the Psychologist', *South Atlantic Quarterly*, xliii (1944), p. 143, reprinted in his *Sex, Symbolism and Psychology in Literature* (New Brunswick, 1948).

replace the 'milk-bloom' in the other. The garden lies beneath a great vault of star-strewn sky, across which a meteor silently slides. Just as Maud had come out to her lover in glimmering satin, the beloved of the eastern poet 'glimmers' through the blue night towards him. We have, in fact, two distinct poems suggested by a single emotional stimulus—an imagined picture of a woman coming toward her lover at night in a garden. In *Maud*, it is an English garden; in *The Princess*, it is a Persian one.

I am now able to approach more squarely the other connections *The Princess* has with Persian literature. Allowing that there is a similarity, and thus a looking forward, to the Persian-inspired section of *Maud*, we have to consider the possible reason for the inclusion of so unmodified a kind of Persian love-lyric in *The Princess* at all. The oriental *Stimmung* of 'Now sleeps the crimson petal' has not been replaced with an English equivalent. While its erotic overtones are of a different order from those of Hafiz, the imagery of the cypress, peacock, lily and rose is obviously Persian. Moreover, there can be no real doubt that the form of the poem, seven distichs arranged to provide an opening and closing quatrain and three central distichs, all repeating a final identical word, is a variation upon the form of the Persian ode or *ghazal*, a love poem of the kind much practised by Hafiz and Jami. When it is remembered that the poem is read by the Princess Ida from a volume of the poets of *her own land*, we are led to ask whether the poet could have intended that another 'Persian' connection was to be observed by his readers.

There are various strong indications that Ida is to be regarded as a southern, indeed oriental, princess.[1] Although consistency is not to be expected in a poem whose geography, for instance, is so ideal, there is an unaccountable luxuriousness

---

[1] Perhaps it would be more accurate to say that we are from time to time meant to see her in that light. At other times she is the ideal medieval heroine of both sorts, the Bradamante-Britomartis kind and that appropriate to the ideals of 'courtly love'. At one moment she is a poet; at another, she is a philosopher; and of course towards the end she comes nearer to the conventional ideal of the age. Though not everyone may feel that this changing aspect of her character is artistically satisfactory, no one can doubt that Tennyson had a reason for allowing it.

in the descriptions. Ida's 'mother-city' is reached by crossing
tilth and grange, passing vines and blowing bosks of wilder-
ness, and does not seem much more exotic than, say, Carcas-
sonne. The College, on the other hand, is suggestive of a
gracious climate, possessing

> a court
> Compact of lucid marbles, boss'd with lengths
> Of classic frieze, with ample awnings gay
> Betwixt the pillars, and with great urns of flowers.
> The Muses and the Graces, group'd in threes,
> Enring'd a billowing fountain in the midst.[1]

In the College garden,

> One walk'd reciting by herself, and one
> In this hand held a volume as to read,
> And smoothed a petted peacock down with that.
> Some to a low song oar'd a shallop by,
> Or under arches of the marble bridge
> Hung, shadow'd from the heat; some hid and sought
> In the orange thickets; others tost a ball
> Above the fountain-jets, and back again
> With laughter.

This surely suggests not the Backs, at Cambridge, though they
were clearly enough the model, but eastern

> High-walled gardens green and old,[2]

where the poet's 'shallop' had previously ventured, not on the
Cam but the Tigris. There are no orange trees or peacocks in
the gardens of the good Haroun Alraschid as there are in the
Princess's, though they might seem rather more appropriate
there; but in both there are central fountains and tamarisks
and great urns of flowers. Indeed one of the first things encountered by the Prince on arrival at the College was the

> splash and stir
> Of fountains spouted up and showering down
> In meshes of the jasmine and the rose.

---

[1] It was, on Tennyson's own authority, an idealisation of Nevile's
Court, Trinity College, Cambridge. See *Memoir*, ii, p. 152.
[2] 'Recollections of the Arabian Nights.'

Tennyson and Persian Poetry

Later, as he stood above the 'empurpled champaign' on the terrace 'ranged along the northern front', he drank the gale,

> That blown about the foliage underneath,
> And sated with the innumerable rose,
> Beat balm upon our eyelids.

These descriptions of jasmine and roses are reminiscent of Persian poetry, where delicious perfumes are frequently mentioned. But perhaps the most oriental scene in the poem is that immediately after the geological expedition to the cliff-face above a waterfall. Above the fall itself, the landscape was northern, with mention of a dark crag, a cliff, copses, lean and wrinkled precipices, a coppice-feathered chasm; but on descending to where the 'pavilion' had been pitched, the Prince tells how they

> dipt
> Beneath the satin dome and enter'd in,
> There leaning deep in broider'd down we sank
> Our elbows; on a tripod in the midst
> A fragrant flame rose, and before us glow'd
> Fruit, blossom, viand, amber wine, and gold.

The scene is strongly reminiscent of a Persian *divan*; it is more of a setting perhaps for a damsel with a dulcimer than for one looking

> on the happy autumn-fields,
> And thinking of the days that are no more.

The Princess herself is very decidedly suited to the exotic situations just described. Indeed she retains an eastern appearance in our minds although our impression of the landscape is sometimes that it is far from oriental.[1] For example, she has

---

[1] The description of the fall is alpine, e.g.

> And, o'er a bridge of pinewood crossing, came
> On flowery levels underneath the crag,
> Full of all beauty.

Tennyson visited Switzerland in 1846 with Moxon and composed 'Come down, O maid' with Lauterbrunnen and Grindelwald in mind; see *Memoir*, i, p. 252. The passage describing the maidens crossing the park, illumined by patches of sunlight (a favourite picture of Tennyson's) is as English as 'The Gardener's Daughter'.

tamed two leopards, which play about her sandal. She has handmaidens to comb out her long black hair. She has a magnificent dark beauty in complete contrast with that of the Prince, with full lips and luminous eyes. On her forehead, she wears a single jewel. She has not the languorous appearance and nature of the beauties of the desert, however, but the proud *hauteur* and regal magnificence of the ladies of the *Arabian Nights*.[1] As already mentioned, she reads a *ghazal*; she is also acquainted with the Persian legend of the love borne for the rose by the bulbul. When the Prince imitated the singing of a woman,

> 'Not for thee', she said,
> 'O Bulbul, any rose of Gulistan
> Shall burst her veil.'

Though it may be conceded on the foregoing evidence that Tennyson did intend to provide a Persian air to give his eastern heroine a correct setting,[2] it may legitimately be asked whether there is evidence that the poet was especially interested in Persian literature at the time of the composition of *The Princess*. Ever since the poem 'Now sleeps the crimson petal' was recognized as a *ghazal*, this question has posed itself, though not so far as I am aware, in any larger connection. Many readers of the poem familiar with any of the *ghazals* adapted by Goethe, Rückert and Count Platen in German or by Sir William Jones and Richard Chenevix Trench in English might have immediately recognized Tennyson's model. Those unfamiliar with these examples might, a few years after the poem's appearance, have learned the fact from another source, for in 1856, Fitzgerald's friend E. B. Cowell, the Persian scholar, in giving specimens of the *ghazals* of Jami, made specific reference to the model for Tennyson's poem in a footnote: '. . . we can distinctly recognize the Persian measure,

---

[1] W. D. Paden, *Tennyson in Egypt*, p. 132, n. 103, characterises the women of the *Arabian Nights* in a very brief space.

[2] The *Persian Tales* are notably lacking in local colour. See, for instance, Martha P. Conant, op. cit., p. 92. Tennyson's own inclination to supply picturesque detail where it is absent from his source is exemplified in 'Recollections', as has already been shown.

even though stripped of its rhyme, in Tennyson's beautiful ode in *The Princess*[1] which he then quoted.

Although the means whereby the poet became familiar with the *ghazal* has been disputed, no one has seriously questioned Cowell's claim that the poem *is* an imitation of that form. Indeed the claim as given above is modestly expressed. The poem possesses the requisite number of couplets, the repetition of a single final word at short intervals to produce what is tantamount to rhyme, and uses the standard images and ornaments of the Persian love poem, roses, lilies, peacocks, the stars, the cypress.

Tennyson's earlier study of Persian poetry in connection with his contributions to *Poems by Two Brothers* and in his 'Locksley Hall' may have provided him with a knowledge of the Persian *ghazal*, for Sir William Jones's *Works* contain several references to the characteristics of the form.[2] There is the further possibility that he had seen Goethe's *West-oestliche Divan*,[3] or Richard Chenevix Trench's *Poems from Eastern Sources* (1842).[4] For the present purpose, its mere presence in

[1] E.B.C., 'Jámi, the Persian Poet', *Fraser's Magazine*, liv (July–December 1856), p. 603.

[2] See, for example, *A Grammar of the Persian Language* (*Works*, ii, p. 235 and p. 240), *The History of the Persian Language* (*Works*, ii, p. 237), *Poeseos Asiaticae Commentarii* (*Works*, ii, p. 404), *Traité sur la Poésie orientale* (*Works*, v, p. 463). Tennyson's poem has seven distichs divided into five sections, so that while retaining the features of a *ghazal*, it approximates to a sonnet.

[3] Goethe's celebrated work does not provide any particular resemblance to Tennyson's poem, but does give examples of the *ghazal*. Tennyson did read the collection (*Memoir*, ii, p. 233), but when is uncertain.

[4] Trench's volume, which has one or two pleasant pieces, was published by Moxon in 1842. He writes in his note to 'Chidher's Well', p. 116: 'On this poem I may observe that it is the first of several in the volume written with an arrangement of rhyme hardly familiar to the English reader, which yet is that of a great part, as I believe, of the lyric poetry of the East, and which may not, perhaps, be unworthy of a place among us. According to the laws of the Ghazel,—for poems in this metre are so entitled,—the two first lines must rhyme, and then this rhyme repeats itself in the second line of each succeeding couplet, which is in fact a new stanza, till the end of the poem,—the termination in each of these following couplets being left free. This simple rule of the one repeated rhyme being observed, the Ghazel admits otherwise of the greatest possible variety. . . . In Germany, the Ghazel has been perfectly domesticated. Rückert and Count Platen are, I believe, considered to have cultivated it with the greatest success.'

the poem of *The Princess* is significant, for without at all
suggesting that the Princess is meant to be consistently Persian, it seems almost certain that the indications of her eastern
character already examined, taken in conjunction with the
luxurious descriptions and her singing the *ghazal*, are meant to
provide a strand in the medley which is explained by the
nature of the source. Having selected a fairy tale from the
Persian Tales for the central incident of a Princess reluctant to
marry and adapted it to the theme of women preferring higher
culture to marriage, it seems quite logical that the poet should
have provided appropriate decoration to the romantic part of
his poem in the shape of Persian descriptions and imagery,
already dear to his heart on their own account.

This will become more evident when we consider a question
which has provoked interest recently, namely whether Tennyson can be said to have occupied himself with learning Persian
at a date nearer to the composition of *The Princess* than about
the time of the writing of *Maud*. The *Memoir* makes no mention of any attempt to learn the language earlier than 1854,
more than six years after *The Princess* appeared, when in a
letter to Forster dated 29 March the poet reported that his
eyes had suffered a sudden disorder after three hours' reading,
or trying to read, small Persian text[1] in a small printed
grammar, Hafiz and other Persian books. A little later, probably in April, Fitzgerald came to stay at Farringford for a
fortnight, and in the evenings, he interspersed his playing of
Mozart with translating Persian odes for Tennyson.[2] As the
poet settled down for work on *Maud* after a tour in Somerset
and Dorset in August[3] of the same year, it seems not unreasonable at first sight to infer that the Persian-inspired section of
the poem discussed earlier was suggested by his later efforts
in the language. But since the poem 'Now sleeps the crimson
petal' in the first edition of *The Princess* seems to anticipate
it, then we are to suppose that the poet had an earlier suggestion for his Persian manner than this.

In 1898, Cowell asserted that he began to teach Tennyson a
little Persian as early as 1846. He wrote that he had spent a
few days in London and had gone with Edward Fitzgerald to

[1] *Memoir*, i, p. 373.   [2] ibid., p. 374.   [3] ibid., p. 377.

see Tennyson in his bachelor lodgings: 'He wanted to read some Hafiz, so I translated an ode with an interlinear translation; but the character daunted him. He took to Hafiz.'[1] This date is early enough to explain the inspiration for 'Now sleeps the crimson petal'. W. D. Paden has, however, questioned the accuracy of Cowell's memory in this matter, pointing out that in a letter that can be dated by its contents October or November 1848, Fitzgerald wrote to Cowell in terms which show that in that year Cowell was still unacquainted with the poet.

> A. Tennyson is now residing in London at 25 Mornington Place, Hampstead Road, a short walk from me. I particularise all this, because should you come to London, you can call upon him without further introduction. I have often spoken about you to him, and he will be very glad to make your acquaintance.[2]

Indeed, he might have added another piece of evidence that shows that Cowell was wrong over the date of meeting Tennyson for the first time. Writing to his poet friend Bernard Barton in December 1848, Fitzgerald remarked:

> I shall be at Brighton till Wednesday: then return here, when I *hope* I shall find my law matters forward towards completion— Edward Cowell proposes to be in London about the same time, when I am to show him two literary lions in the persons of A. Tennyson & Carlyle—the latter of whom is more rabid than ever.[3]

Both pieces of evidence make it clear that even up to 1848 Tennyson had had no help from Cowell.

This, however, is not the only evidence on the matter. Aubrey de Vere wrote in the journal from which I quoted earlier (Chapter I) as follows. The entry is dated 1 July 1845:

> Driving in from Hampstead I met Alfred Tennyson, who was little pleased to see me, and seemed living in a mysterious sort of way on the Hampstead Road, bathing and learning Persian.[4]

[1] G. Cowell, *Life and Letters of Edward Byles Cowell* (1904), pp. 373–4.

[2] W. D. Paden, 'Tennyson and Persian poetry once more', *MLN*, lx (1945), p. 284. The case for some influence upon a number of Tennyson's poems from a first-hand knowledge of Persian is made by J. D. Yohannan, 'Tennyson and Persian Poetry', *MLN*, lvii (1942), p. 83, and very effectively answered by W. D. Paden, 'Tennyson and Persian Poetry Again', *MLN*, lviii (May–December 1943), p, 652, and the first-named article.

[3] *Some New Letters of Edward Fitzgerald*, ed. F. R. Barton (1923), p. 167.   [4] Wilfrid Ward, *Aubrey de Vere, a Memoir*, p. 87.

This establishes that at a time when *The Princess* was being composed Tennyson was sufficiently interested in Persian literature to be taking the trouble to learn the language. Not only may his renewed studies have been the reason for his attempting an English version of the *ghazal*, but they may also have provided him with the materials for the oriental background he desired to give his fairy tale drawn from Persian tales. Indeed, he may originally have had the source of his story through looking at the Persian grammar which had longest been within his reach, that is, the one bound up in those *Works* of Sir William Jones which we see he read to such good purpose. Sir William Jones's Grammar was an extremely elegant production, drawing its illustrations from the best literature in the Persian language. It is almost certain that one as interested in the language and its literature as Tennyson shows himself to have been would have looked to see what texts were available to him in translation. In the Appendix to *A Grammar of the Persian Language* called 'A Catalogue of the Most Valuable Books in the Persian Language', we see recommended: 'The Persian Tales of a thousand and one days, translated into French by Petit de la Choix.'[1] That Jones had cast over the gay stories the lustre of his eminent learning may perhaps have caused Tennyson to read the tale of the learned princess whose antagonism to marriage so curiously matched that of some of the women of the Victorian age.

IV. TURANDOT

It was shown in Chapter VI (p. 138) that the position of women in the East was often considered relevant to the discussion of women's rights in the early nineteenth century, together with that of the working class and negro slaves. The oriental tale was still looked upon as a means of learning about the social habits of the eastern nations. Weber, for instance, makes the

[1] The works of Pétis de la Croix were not altogether unknown in the Tennyson household. Yale possesses a copy of *The History of Genghizan the Great . . . by the late M. Pétis de la Croix . . . now faithfully rendered into English* (1722) that bears on the inside of its front cover, 'Geo. Clayton Tennyson/Febr 1807/ A. Tennyson'. Noted by W. D. Paden in his *Tennyson in Egypt*, p. 128, n. 85.

point that the customs portrayed in his huge collection had
been proved by the reports of travellers to the regions in question to be faithful representations. Earlier, Scott had written
to like effect. He deplored the occasional freedom of behaviour
encountered in the stories he had translated, but pleaded in
mitigation:

> They show, however, (for they are certainly just pictures of
> eastern manners) the cruel tyranny of the haram, and shameful
> ignorance in which women are kept in Asia, to be destructive to
> purity of mind and conduct, and prove the superiority which
> liberty, education and well-merited confidence give the fair sex of
> this happy island and other unrevolutionized parts of Europe.[1]

This complacency was not shared by all his female com-
patriots, as we have seen; but his remarks do illustrate the
way in which oriental tales prompted reflection upon the position of women at the beginning of the century and afterwards.[2] His remarks lend some support to my contention that
the Fair Persian of the *Arabian Nights* may have been to
Tennyson a symbol of oppressed womanhood like any of the
heroic women of 'A Dream of Fair Women'. In fact he was not
the first to perceive that the fairy-tale heroines of these
stories, and notably Tourandocte herself, had a significance
for his age, in that their attitude to men and marriage came
close to that entertained by a number of the braver spirits
among young women of the day.

In fact it is of some interest in this connection to trace some
of the changes undergone by the Persian tale of Turandot—as
I shall henceforth call the princess. In France, Italy and Germany, during the century succeeding its first publication, the
story was adapted for stage representation; and oddly enough
some critics have seen signs of dramatic quality in Tennyson's
The Princess too. For instance, Sir Charles Tennyson writes:
'What distinguishes it from all Tennyson's earlier work is its
persistent use of a dramatic method which gives it a liveliness

---

[1] Scott, op. cit., Translator's Preface, i, p. v.
[2] We may recall, incidentally, the eastern settings of a number of very
different works having feminist tendencies, e.g., Lawrence's *Empire of
the Nairs*, Lady Morgan's *Ida of Athens*, Shelley's *The Revolt of Islam*
and Monckton Milnes's *Palm Leaves*.

and power not present in anything he had previously written. Scene after scene, particularly in the later sections, are so written that they could with hardly any change be translated into dramatic form.'[1] Hugh I'Anson Fausset makes the same point less sympathetically; speaking of the burlesque part of the poem, he writes:

> Such incidents in comic opera could be relied on to bring down the house. In a poem of luxuriant lyrical sentiment, which professes also to propound and solve one of the deepest problems of human life—the essential reality of man and of woman in the high adventure of love—they are almost insultingly irrelevant.[2]

Whatever we may think of this point of view, at least it suggests that the poem had dramatic possibilities, even if only of the standard of comic opera, an observation the truth of which is admittedly exemplified by the existence of Gilbert's 'respectful parody', *Princess Ida*, and a number of forgotten adaptations for stage performance. If, however, the dramatic quality is considered a new feature in Tennyson's work, we may inquire whether there was a similar quality in the original Persian tale which could possibly have contributed to its presence in the poem as well. We have seen that most of the episodes can be found in two tales, *Calaf and the Princess of China*, and the tale of Serendib and the Queen of the Amazons. It will suffice for the present purpose to examine the first as being the more celebrated.

It will be recalled that Pétis de la Croix was assisted in his work of first presenting the *Persian Tales* to a French public by the celebrated LeSage, author of *Gil Blas*. LeSage seems to have seen the dramatic possibilities of the tales almost immediately, and with D'Orneval, a prolific author of minor plays successfully performed at the Foires de Saint Germain and Saint Laurent, edited a collection of the pieces performed at

---

[1] *Alfred Tennyson*, p. 222. The same point was well made by W. E. Gladstone in a review of Tennyson's poems in *The Quarterly Review* for October 1859, reprinted in *Famous Reviews*, ed. R. Brimley Johnson, p. 241: 'The author has termed it a "medley": why, we know not. It approaches more nearly to the character of a regular drama, with the stage directions written into verse, than any other of his works . . .' (p. 242).

[2] Hugh I'Anson Fausset, *Tennyson, a Modern Portrait* (1923), p. 130.

the Foires. In this collection we find an operetta called *La Princesse de la Chine, Pièce en Trois Actes*, composed by the editors and said to have been performed in 1729 at the Foire S. Laurent.[1] This little operetta is in fact a version of the story of Turandot, though it does not use her name. Calaf and Altoun Khan, the Princess's father, keep theirs, but all but a vestige of their original character disappears, since they are cast amongst the traditional figures of Italian farce.

This little work at least shows how early the dramatic qualities of the story were appreciated, and also how soon the opportunity was taken to introduce a good deal of low comedy into what was in the original a consistently sober narrative.

This tradition was continued in Italy by the dramatist Carlo Gozzi,[2] who triumphed over his rivals, Goldoni among them, by infusing new life into the nearly extinct *commedia dell' arte* by adapting it to *fiabe*, which were simply dramatized fairy tales. These, while no longer wholly extempore and wholly farcical, were nevertheless still given partly in the dialect spoken by the traditional characters of the *commedia dell' arte* like Pantalone, Brighella, Tartaglia and Truffaldino. One of the 'fairy tales' Gozzi adapted was that of *Calaf and the Princess of China*, from the *Persian Tales*, and he called it *Turandot*.[3] Richard Garnett, in *A History of Italian Literature* (1898), quotes J. A. Symonds's opinion that Gozzi's *fiabe* would make excellent operatic libretti. Puccini's opera *Turandot*, based upon Gozzi's play, was by no means the first to justify this claim.[4]

Gozzi was for some time eclipsed in his own country, but his play *Turandot*, printed in a poor version at Berne in 1777, was avidly read in Germany, a circumstance which has been seen as evidence of a beginning of romantic interests in that country. As a result, no doubt, of this popularity, no less a dramatist than Schiller translated the play afresh in 1802 with

---

[1] *Théâtre de la Foire* (Paris, 1731), vii, p. 122.
[2] Born 1720, died 1808.   [3] 1762.
[4] Not all the operas called *Turandot* are based upon Gozzi. There were at least five versions performed in Germany and Austria between 1810 and 1888—see *Dictionnaire des Opéras* by Clément and Larousse (Paris, 1897), s.v. Another of Gozzi's *fiabe* was adapted as an opera in 1921, viz., *L'Amour des Trois Oranges*, music by Prokoviev.

The Source

full acknowledgment to Gozzi.[1] His version was close to Gozzi's, and retains the characters of the *commedia dell' arte* grafted on the original Persian tale by the Italian playwright. A comparison of the versions of the tale by Gozzi and Schiller reveals that surprisingly little adaptation was necessary to turn it into a most satisfactory drama. It contained enough fairy-tale material to produce very strong situations (notably the central one of the guessing of riddles under a risk of death), yet no magical events that would be completely incredible on the stage. The characters had to be reduced in number both to simplify the plot and intensify its pathos. Adelma, as Adelmule is called in these plays, is aided in her betrayal of the Princess by the counterparts of Lady Blanche and the Host in Tennyson's poem, and the Prince's father is made to fall into the hands of the Princess. These adjustments may be thought by some to be weakenings of the original. An improvement, perhaps, is to have Adelma forgiven, as Lady Psyche is in the poem; her suicide casts an unexpected air of tragedy over what could easily have been a happy ending.

This account of the dramatic history of the story of Turandot has been given not only to illustrate its potentialities for stage performance, but also because it is not impossible that the poet may have read Schiller's play. He seems to have devoted himself to learning German at Somersby after having gone down from Cambridge, and certainly knew it well enough in 1842 to be able to read it. By 1847 he could do so fluently, despite a modest disclaimer to a perfect acquaintance with the language to his German translator, the poet F. Freiligrath. When in Switzerland in 1846 he had quoted Goethe to a young lady in Lucerne, who had reciprocated by 'spouting Schiller's *William Tell*'.[2] In 1848, he spoke to a Miss Rundle about Schiller, saying that he was 'one-sided, schwärmerisch, yet

---

[1] Schiller's play appeared as *Turandot, Prinzessin von China*, Ein tragicomisches Märchen nach Gozzi von Schiller (Tübingen, 1802). It appears in the *Sämtliche Schriften von Schiller*, general editor Karl Goedeke (Stuttgart, 1870), xiii and xiv (in one), p. 373. For Gozzi's interest for German writers, see H. H. Rusack, *Gozzi in Germany* (Columbia, 1930).

[2] *Memoir*, i, pp. 124, 213, 271, 232.

Turandot

Schwärmerei better than mere kalter Verstand, not dramatic, but could not agree with some who thought him nothing'.[1]

If Tennyson did read Schiller's play as well as the Persian tale, he must certainly have been interested in one great development that the character of the Princess herself had undergone. In the *Persian Tales* as originally translated by Pétis de la Croix, the motive for Turandot's reluctance to marry was simply pride in her own ability to confound the ablest doctors. She had no sympathy for the wooers who succumbed to her charms because they brought their fate upon themselves.[2] In Gozzi's play, a more rational justification of her cruelty is supplied. She is made to say, on first greeting the Prince:

Heaven knows that those tongues which call me cruel are lying. An absolute detestation for your sex makes me do all I can to live far away from its hateful members. Why may not I enjoy that liberty which everyone should enjoy? Who obliges you to make me cruel against my will? If prayers avail, I humble myself to pray to you. Give up, prince, the trial. Do not try my test, for it is only of that I am proud. Heaven has graciously given me wit and ability. I should be dead if in the divan I should be shamefully vanquished in a public test of my powers. Go, give up considering the riddles. There is still time. You will lament your approaching death in vain.[3]

Here the quality of exaggerated intellectual pride is retained, but there is an admixture of protest at the loss of liberty which marriage with the other sex implies. She loves two things instead of one, not solely her acuity, but also her personal liberty.

Schiller, however, goes much further, as will be seen from his version of the same speech:

Heaven knows that those tongues are false which call me cruel and pitiless. I am not cruel—I only insist upon a free life, and will not be subject to another. That natural right, learned in our mother's womb and conceded to the vilest of men, I, the daughter of a king, shall keep. Throughout all Asia I see woman debased and

---

[1] *Materials*, i, p. 358. [2] *Persian Tales*, ii, p. 50.
[3] *Turandot*, by Carlo Gozzi, Act II, scene 5. In the *Teatro Classico Italiano* (Lipsia, 1829), p. 637.

condemned to servitude; and I have resolved to avenge my insulted sex upon this insolent race of men who cannot boast any superiority over the tenderer woman than that of mere brute strength. But nature has given me imagination and subtlety as weapons with which to defend my liberty. I shall have nothing to do with men. I hate them and despise their arrogance and pride. They lustfully seek to possess everything precious, especially if it pleases their senses. Nature was generous to me in graces and intellect. Why is it the fate of the noble things in the world to be the prey of the rude hunter, when the vulgar are concealed by their very baseness? Must beauty be the prey of one man? It is really as free as the sun in its glory, the source of light, the joy of all eyes, the property of none.[1]

Here Turandot is no longer a mere fairy-tale heroine; hers is the voice of all women aspiring to be free. Her grounds of dislike for men are rational, and her vindictiveness is the more justified when we consider that Schiller causes her specifically to mention the condition of women in *Asia*, which Jonathan Scott the English translator of the *Bahar-Danush*, found a subject for sympathy three years before. Without regarding Schiller's play as a mere feminist tract disguised as a play—Turandot's subsequent fate in his play is the same as in Gozzi's, and has no moral whatever—we cannot fail to notice that the original heroine of the fairy tale has been changed into an ardent supporter of women's rights. (One wonders how much the playwright was influenced by Lawrence's *Empire of the Nairs*, which we know he read in 1800, only two years previously.) Later in the play, when she has been frustrated by the Prince's correct guessing of the riddles, she again condemns men. In Gozzi,[2] she reviles the sex for inconstancy and promiscuity. In Schiller, she says:

He is a man. I detest him, and I must detest him. They are all deceivers, all faithless; they are only swayed by self-love. A wicked sex on which the heart of woman wastes fidelity, constancy, affection and sympathy, like gems thrown into the sea. A grovelling slave when he seeks to conquer us; but very different, a violent oppressor, when we are in his clutches. He gives the name of love, attention and respect, to obstinacy, pride, and bitter, wicked

[1] Schiller, *Sämtliche Schriften*, xiii/xiv, p. 384.
[2] Act III, Scene 2; *Teatro Classico Italiano*, p. 640.

thoughts; and these disordered impulses of a wild animal lead him
to deeds which the ferocity of an animal does not come to. The
true faith and love in the single, gentle heart of woman are well
known. Be silent, then. If this unknown prince proves successful in
this second test, death will be less distasteful than the discomfiture.
Shall I let the world see me subjected to the disdainful yoke of
common women? Let it see me give my free hand to a man, to a
tyrant? No, that shall never be! Turandot shall never fall into that
quagmire. Be his bride! I would sooner throw myself into the tomb
than into the arms of a man . . .[1]

These are words which equal in violence any of those uttered
by the agitators for female rights, yet they only express what
could easily come into the minds of some of the most rebellious
of the women who espoused the extreme form of the cause.
There is no evidence that Tennyson had read this play, and it
is much easier to believe that he had read the original tale in
the oriental collections we have discussed. But the fresh motivation Schiller provides for his Princess is a very significant
sign of the times. What in the eighteenth century was originally
an entertaining story with a familiar fairy-tale *motif* at its
centre has become a drama wherein one of the most arbitrary
elements, the hatred of men and marriage combined with intellectual pride on the part of what we may call a leader of
society, has ceased to be part of the good joke, and taken on
the air of deadly earnest. If I am right in suggesting that
Tennyson's poem and Schiller's play derive ultimately from
the same source (and, in Tennyson's case, a possible variant)
we can, I think, see the force of Tennyson's remark concerning
The Princess: 'You have seen amongst other things that if
women ever were to play such freaks, the burlesque and the
tragic might go hand in hand.'[2]

---

[1] *Sämtliche Schriften*, xiii/xiv, p. 407. The critic Franz Horn criticized
Schiller for the extended motivation thus: 'Schiller produced a hybrid
type—a combination of novel and fairy-tale,—when he motivates
Turandot's hatred for men. This ought not to have been done. A fairy-
tale does not psychologize.' Quoted by Rusack, op. cit., p. 73.

[2] *Memoir*, i, p. 256.

CHAPTER XI

'The Princess' and Evolution

B ECAUSE the Princess is recognizably a 'Persian' heroine, in a frequently exotic setting, an unexpected note is struck by, among other things, the presence in the poem of a good deal of scientific allusion. This takes various forms. The curriculum of the women's college, for instance, includes not only the traditional male diet of classics and mathematics but something also of

> the mind,
> The morals, something of the frame, the rock,
> The star, the bird, the fish, the shell, the flower,
> Electric, chemic laws, and all the rest . . .

Ida had long made mathematics and astronomy her special interest; we are told that she passed whole nights with Psyche in a tower, talking of 'sine and arc, spheroid, azimuth and right ascension'. As we have seen, one of the major incidents of the poem is occasioned by a geological expedition to a nearby river gorge where the party chattered

> stony names
> Of shale and hornblende, rag and trap and tuff,
> Amygdaloid and trachyte . . .

These allusions are prepared for by the scientific revels of the Mechanics' Institution in the Prologue. The touch of extreme modernity which they bring undoubtedly affects the tone of the poem; consequently it may be assumed that they were inserted for a good reason. It was not essential for the poet to have gone into detail over the scientific bias of the college curriculum or to have given so prominent a place to a scientific expedition. It might perhaps be that he considered scientific discoveries potentially picturesque—'Locksley Hall' establishes that he was not afraid of using 'modern' imagery. Possibly he thought they were sufficiently like marvels from fairy tales to be easily fitted into the one he was adapting for the plot of the poem; I shall show later that there is good reason for taking this to be a correct assumption, because in 1839 the notion was more generally current than it is today. In 'Locksley Hall' the speaker says:

> Here about the beach I wander'd, nourishing a youth sublime
> With the fairy tales of science, and the long result of time.

In 'The Day Dream' the story-teller dilates upon the pleasure of sleeping a hundred years in the manner related of the Sleeping Beauty:

> To sleep thro' terms of mighty wars,
> And wake on science grown to more,
> On secrets of the brain, the stars,
> As wild as aught of fairy lore.

Alternatively he may have introduced the scientific details because he had in mind the preoccupations of the Socialists not only with industrialism and feminism, but also with the positive use of scientific methods in ascertaining the 'laws' of society as well as of the physical world. We might in fact believe he was illustrating the kind of education women might demand in the universities they would one day establish, an education which would enable them to come closer to understanding the way society was developing. Earlier, mention was made of the resemblance between the Saint-Simonian concept of distinct 'epochs' developing from earlier ones, and, on the other hand, the later scientific theory of distinct species developing from simpler ones. Ida seems to believe, as we shall see, that society had undergone a fundamental change, and it is accordingly of interest to see what the Saint-Simonians had to say on this subject. I shall therefore again quote from Robert Southey's article on the Saint-Simonians in the *Quarterly Review* for 1831. He is speaking of Comte's theory of organic and critical periods of history and is observing that it regarded revolutions not as evils but as necessary parts of social development:

These alternations are necessary parts of the great system, appointed from the beginning, for the development of collective humanity, a being which grows from generation to generation, as an individual from year to year, but with this difference, that it is subject to no decay. For the human race never has retrograded; it has continually advanced in obedience to its own physiological law, the law of progressive development, the law of human perfectibility. This law is 'so essential a condition to the existence of our species, that whenever a people who were at the head of the human race have become stationary, the germs of progressiveness, which were stifled in their bosom, have immediately been transplanted elsewhere, to a soil where they could expand: and it has been constantly seen that such a people, having rebelled against the law of mankind, have sunk and been annihilated, as if crushed under the weight of a curse.[1]

I think it will be agreed that this is very like the language of what was to become the theory of the evolution of *animal* species. Southey recognized that the Saint-Simonians were putting before the world the idea that races and nations progressively developed from one distinct stage to another, and that this was in accordance with a physiological law. Any attempt to frustrate this natural process would eventually cause a total collapse of the social organism; and, in practical terms, they saw the denial of legitimate influence to the working class and to women as likely to have this dangerous effect. I believe that Tennyson was arguing along similar lines in *The Princess*, and that the scientific discussion is directed to the conclusion that the future of the race turns upon allowing women to realize their intellectual aspirations without jeopardizing the marriage relationship, which is viewed as an essential instrument in forwarding human development.

Now the scientific allusions in the main part of the poem all concern astronomy and geology. An evolutionary theory had been advanced long before to explain certain observed phenomena in both fields; but the time had not yet come when geological evidence for animal evolution was sufficient for a similar theory to be generally accepted for it, too, though one had in fact been advanced. Before Darwin, the hypotheses of Herschel and Laplace that stars and planets originated in the condensation of inter-stellar gases, seen as nebular patches

[1] xlv (April–July 1831), p. 431.

through the telescope, led both to surmise that the universe 'evolved' into its observable condition. Psyche's lecture on the subordination of women, leading up to the vision of equality whereby men and women might together 'sound the abyss of science, and the secrets of the mind' begins its survey of man's social development with a reference to the fact that this world

> was once a fluid haze of light,
> Till toward the centre set the starry tides,
> And eddied into suns, that wheeling cast
> The planets.

She meant to suggest that since the inanimate world developed, so must man expect to develop; and, more to the point, women must also expect to take a part in the process. Today this reads oddly; conscious participation in evolution is no part of the theory.

To understand exactly what Tennyson may have had in mind in *The Princess*, his scientific interests up to the date of its composition must be examined. Jowett recorded that

In the first years of his [Tennyson's] childhood his great-grand-father had taught him some of the wonders of the starry heavens, in a manner which remained with him throughout life. Some paragraph in a newspaper or magazine about a comet or fixed star, would often catch his eye: these he would invest with a light and life which he himself gave to them . . .[1]

Hallam Tennyson noted that two of his father's earliest lines were

> The rays of many a rolling central star,
> Aye flashing earthwards, have not reach'd us yet,[2]

and that in a Somersby notebook he found a fragment of a poem describing the surface of the moon mixed up with astronomical diagrams. Tennyson's assimilation of Herschel's teaching as a boy is shown in his remark to his elder brother Frederick who was nervous at the thought of attending a dinner party: 'Fred, think of Herschel's great star-patches, and you will soon get over all that.'[3] He once alluded to the nebular hypothesis in the first version of 'The Palace of Art' in the

[1] *Memoir*, ii, p. 462.   [2] ibid., i, p. 20.   [3] ibid.

following lines describing the erring soul's joyous vision of the heavens from her watch-tower:

> Regions of lucid matter taking forms,
>   Brushes of fire, hazy gleams,
> Clusters and beds of worlds, and bee-like swarms
>   Of suns, and starry streams.
>
> She saw the snowy poles of moonless Mars,
>   That marvellous round of milky light
> Below Orion, and those double stars
>   Whereof the one more bright
>
> Is circled by the other.[1]

As already mentioned, the early evolutionists made the nebular hypothesis part of their argument, though it was by no means generally accepted. Ida was up to date: her early astronomical studies and revulsion against 'romantic' attitudes like that displayed in the song 'Tears, idle tears, I know not what they mean', both show themselves in her greeting of a sunset:

> 'There sinks the nebulous star we call the sun,
>   If that hypothesis of theirs be sound . . .'[2]

While Tennyson was at Cambridge, he encountered another scientific discovery which turned his thoughts to the possibility of evolution, and this time in connection with animal species. He quickly introduced it into 'The Palace of Art':

> 'From change to change four times within the womb
>   The brain is moulded', she began,
> 'So through all phases of all thought I come
>   Into the perfect man.
>
> 'All nature widens upward. Evermore
>   The simpler essence lower lies,
> More complex is more perfect, owning more
>   Discourse, more widely wise.

[1] Cf. *Memoir*, i, p. 120. Satellites ('moons') of Mars were discovered in 1877. The lines were originally given in a footnote in the 1833 volume.

[2] See E. A. Mooney's article, 'A note on astronomy in Tennyson's "The Princess" ', in *MLN*, lxiv (1949), p. 98.

'The Princess' and Evolution

'I take possession of men's minds and deeds.
I live in all things great and small.
I sit apart holding no forms of creeds,
But contemplating all'.

So ran the lines in the 1833 edition. In 1842 the first of these stanzas was altered to

'From shape to shape at first within the womb
The brain is modell'd' she began,
'And thro' all phases . . .'

—the difference being that the idea of *four* changed shapes is dropped and that of an unspecified number substituted. The two following stanzas remained practically unchanged in all editions down to 1853, when the first of them was dropped, and the second considerably modified. As the lines were originally published the poet was alluding to the discovery of resemblances between the foetal brains of humans at various stages in their growth and the brains of other vertebrates, like fishes, reptiles, birds and the lower mammalia. Now to have evidence that the brain in its growth before birth progressively resembles those of different creatures lower in the animal scale is enough to provoke some doubts about the conventional theological explanation of man's origin, and that this was so with Tennyson might well be inferred from a letter written by Arthur Hallam which seems to have been in reply to one of Tennyson's discussing this subject. Tennyson had asked how one could distinguish the operations of God in oneself from motions of one's own heart. Hallam, seemingly taking up specific points, replied as follows:

Is God less God because He acts by general laws when He deals with the common elements of nature? . . . That fatal mistake which has embarrassed the philosophy of mind with infinite confusion, the mistake of setting value on a thing's *origin* rather than on its character, of assuming that *composite* must be less excellent than simple, has not been slow to extend its deleterious influence over the field of practical religion.[1]

The allusions to 'general laws' governing the combination of 'the common elements of nature', the reference to setting

[1] *Memoir*, i, p. 44.

importance on a thing's *origin*, and to compositeness, seem very probably to relate to earlier discussion of science and religion, with particular reference to the awkward implications of the discovery of analogies between the human embryo brain and the brains of creatures lower in the animal scale. Immediately after this letter, as if commenting upon it, Hallam Tennyson wrote in the *Memoir* as follows:

My father seems to have propounded in some college discussion the theory that the 'development of the human body might possibly be traced from the radiated, vermicular, molluscous and vertebrate organisms.' The question of surprise put to him on this proposition was 'Do you think that the human brain is at first like a madrepore's, then like a worm's, etc.? but this cannot be for they have no brain.'[1]

Hallam Tennyson was misled by the anatomical terminology of this passage into reconstructing Tennyson's words inaccurately.[2] Clearly what Tennyson propounded referred to the human *brain*, not body, and was an extension of what was alluded to in 'The Palace of Art'. We can see from the passage thus altered—it was reconstructed from a surviving letter of Arthur Hallam's and I suspect the same one—that although he had written the lines

'From shape to shape *four times* within the womb
The brain is moulded', she began . . . ,

in reference to the fourfold analogy between the brains of the vertebrates (the highest anatomical class), he was also prepared to believe that there was a possibility that the human brain had possibly developed from the rudimentary nervous systems of organisms falling into Cuvier's lower divisions. The objection that in such forms of life there is no such thing as a 'brain' misses the point, and throws into emphasis the fact that he had somehow come to relate the discovery that the human brain seemed to develop through stages analogous to the permanent forms in fishes, reptiles and birds before reaching the recognizably human form, to the very much more

[1] ibid.
[2] This is made certain by reason of his attributing different words to his father in *Materials*, i, p. 55.

startling idea that the human brain had developed—in the quite different sense of 'evolved'—from the very simple nervous systems of Cuvier's *radiata*.

The discovery of the fourfold resemblances of the foetal human brain to the brains of other vertebrates was made by Friedrich Tiedemann,[1] (Professor in the University of Heidelberg, who published his findings in 1816) and further investigated by E. R. A. Serres. The details of the discovery were naturally of a highly technical character, and Tiedemann's work did not find a translator into English until 1826, when W. Bennett, M.D. published *The Anatomy of the Foetal Brain* at Edinburgh. Although Tennyson undoubtedly did read scientific works from time to time, I do not think he could have read this one. The evidence that his poetry supplies is that he did not go in search of such specialized treatises or of fixed opinions on any of the issues presented to him, but took isolated theories, even if mutually contradictory, to throw light upon the human condition. For this, quite general accounts of scientific progress were sufficient, and it seems obvious that on this subject of the development of the human brain he had read some account which led him beyond Tiedemann's discovery to a much broader consideration of the structures of the nervous systems of organisms from the lowest to the highest points in the scale accessible to investigation. Moreover, this more popular source of information must have suggested to him two conclusions—if it is to relate, that is, to the views advanced in the poem and the college discussion. One is that there is a continuity of some sort throughout the scale—no radical changes in structure; the other that ascendancy in the scale is accompanied by complexity in nervous organization:

> More complex is more perfect, owning more
> Discourse, more widely wise.

I think that there can be little doubt that Tennyson read about these 'secrets of the brain' in two articles in successive

[1] *Anatomie und Bildungsgeschichte des Gehirns im Foetus des Menschen* (Nurnberg, 1816). The identification was made by W. R. Rutland, 'Tennyson and the theory of evolution', *Essays and Studies*, xxvi (1940), p. 7.

'The Princess' and Evolution

numbers of the *Westminster Review*, issued while he was at Cambridge—those for January and April 1828. They were devoted to a number of fairly recent works on the nervous system, and provided a general and relatively untechnical account of their contents and implications. Among the works reviewed in the second article was Tiedemann's. The articles were written by no less an authority than T. Southwood Smith; they were published under the general title of the 'Nervous System'.[1] In the first of the articles he discusses the ascertained kinds of nervous tissue and nerves, and remarks:

It was formerly supposed that there was the same complexity of structure in the lowest, as in the highest, animal. It was even imagined, that the minutest and the simplest being possessed every faculty that belongs to any animal, only in a less perfect degree. A more careful examination of nature has shown the incorrectness of this opinion. On looking deeper into her plan, it is found, that the progress of the animal frame from its state of greatest simplicity to that of its highest complexity is remarkably gradual. There is nothing, indeed, more wonderful than the strictness with which that progression is graduated. We have seen, that the structure of the vegetable is much more simple than that of the animal, and we have shown the reason why the organisation of the latter must necessarily be more complicated than that of the former. We have seen that the animal is distinguished from the vegetable by the possession of two additional faculties; namely, those of sensation and voluntary motion, and that the gradual complication of the animal frame arises from the more perfect provision which is successively made for the more perfect exercise of these functions: it being a general law of the animal economy, that the more extensively and perfectly any function is exercised, the more complex the apparatus becomes by which it is performed.[2]

The last few lines of this passage provide a strict parallel to the verses from 'The Palace of Art' already quoted:

'All nature widens upward. Evermore
The simpler essence lower lies,
More complex is more perfect, owning more
Discourse, more widely wise.'

[1] *The Westminster Review*, ix (January–June 1828), pp. 172 and 451. The author was identified by George L. Nesbitt, *Benthamite Reviewing*, p. 181.   [2] p. 176.

The article then continues with an examination of the nervous system in the rest of the animal kingdom taken successively by classes according to Cuvier's classification. First mention is made of the zoophytes, which fall into the class *radiata*, then of the *articulata*, by way of the leech and earthworm, then of the *mollusca*, and finally of the *vertebrata*, as exemplified by fish, reptiles, birds and finally mammals. The purpose of this survey is to demonstrate that throughout all the forms of animal life, from zoophytes right up to mammals, there is traceable a consistent development in the nervous system, a greater and greater complexity without any departure from the fundamental plan of organization.

The correctness of this view of the nervous system, exhibiting throughout the animal kingdom, wonderfully diversified as it is, one and the same connected whole, is most clearly and strikingly verified by the results of the recent researches which have been instituted relative to the foetal development of the nervous system in the different orders of vertebrated animals . . . If the account we are about to give of these unexpected and singular phenomena be extremely brief and general, still we hope it will be intelligible to the unprofessional reader, and will enable him better to understand, and induce him to take a greater interest in, the exposition that is to follow, of the functions of the nervous system.

Then follows a detailed account of the appearance at different stages of embryonic brains of various vertebrates, from which certain conclusions are drawn, among which are the following:

In the progress of its development in the superior classes, the nervous system passes successively through the different forms which constitute its permanent state in the inferior classes.

The elementary parts of the nervous system in all the classes are identical . . . ; the differences increase as the animal rises in the scale; and if, in the progress of its evolution, any cause occur to arrest the development of any part of its nervous system, the animal may be born with the nervous system proper to a different class.

Southwood Smith is in no way concerned to explain this remarkable fact that the nervous system possessed by the highest animals seems to possess direct relationship with that of the inferior classes. Nothing in the way of an evolutionary theory is even hinted at: the article ends by even pointing out the difficulty of holding that the brain is the seat of the intellectual faculties despite the fact that an increase in the complexity of neural organization always accompanies higher powers. Yet there can, I think, be little doubt that Tennyson had the facts in these articles in mind when writing his poem. It seems quite certain, even from Hallam Tennyson's garbled reconstruction of the sense of his father's remarks at a college discussion, that the poet had ventured to assert that the human brain (not 'body' as Hallam wrote) may have developed, i.e., evolved, through the stages represented by Cuvier's fourfold classification of the animal kingdom on the basis of anatomical structure. This belief could well have been reached by reading Southwood Smith's articles, since they pointed unerringly to it, incredible though it seemed.

Hallam's letter arguing that God is no less God because, in dealing with the common elements of nature, he works by general laws, and that, consequently, the *origin* of anything complex has nothing to do with its *character*, seems to me to be directly related to the problem which immediately presents itself on considering an evolutionary theory, namely, What are we to think of our spiritual life, our religious promptings and our concept of the soul? The letter, it will be remembered, was here answering Tennyson's inquiry about distinguishing the operations of God from motions of our own hearts; 'The Palace of Art' is an allegory of an erring Soul believing itself to be at the ultimate stage of development, and seeking to dwell apart

> holding no form of creeds,
> But contemplating all.

That the Soul is shown to be plagued with despair as a consequence of attempting to sever itself from God demonstrates that the poet finally accepted Hallam's viewpoint;[1] or at any rate saw that revealed religion could not be allowed to suffer as a result of doubts bred by an infant science. Indeed, he

---

[1] It was Hallam's case in his *Theodicœa Novissima*.

240

sought to exorcise those raised by Tiedemann's theory by making the erring Soul foolishly base its own hubristic confidence upon it.

Bearing in mind that Tennyson seems to have pondered these articles sufficiently to have discussed one of their most significant implications with the Apostles, and to have incorporated it into a poem of the deepest value in establishing his view of the correct balance between art, science and religion, one cannot fail to see the importance of the similarity between the words of Southwood Smith on the development of animal species and those of Southey on the Saint-Simonian concept of the development of social 'organisms'. The former observed that if in the progress of the evolution [i.e. foetal development] of a superior class of animal any cause occurred to arrest the growth of any part of its nervous system, the animal might be born with the nervous system appropriate to a different, i.e. lower class. The Saint-Simonians, according to Southey—and we have seen how familiar the Apostles were with their doctrines—believed that the human race had continually advanced in obedience to its own physiological law, the law of progressive development, the law of perfectibility, and, moreover, that when a highly-developed community refused to progress, it sank back, 'as if crushed under the weight of a curse'. The point I wish to make is that the idea of continuous development of species and of nations, with a corollary that development might be interrupted, was one with which Tennyson was familiar at a very early stage in his career. The significance of this will appear later.

Tennyson's interest in science sprang from his interest in the poet's true subject—man. He concerned himself with books and articles on scientific topics in no dispassionate manner as becomes the scientist. As scientific evidence of one sort and another came to his notice he dwelt not on its implications for the further development of science, but on the hints it afforded concerning man's nature and his place in a mysterious universe. He seems to have weighed the hypotheses advanced to explain the host of new facts daily discovered without attempting to decide between them. As a consequence there are in the scientific allusions in his poems notable contradictions and inconsistencies. For example, the evidence which could lead to a belief that evolution was a possibility might also suggest no more than that each species had been *created* one after another on the basis of the experience gained from the working of the lower ones, thus explaining the seeming duplication and adaptation of members. Some such idea occurs in *The Princess*. When the geological party come upon the fossilized bones of a prehistoric mammoth exposed by the cutting back of a waterfall,[1] the Princess

> gazed awhile and said,
> 'As these rude bones to us, are we to her
> That will be.'

But the Prince interposes an objection:

> 'Dare we dream of that,' I ask'd,
> 'Which wrought us, as the workman and his work,
> That practice betters?'

The Princess has her answer ready:

> 'To your question now,
> Which touches on the workman and his work.
> Let there be light and there was light; 'tis so,
> For was, and is, and will be, are but is,
> And all creation is one act at once,
> The birth of light; but we that are not all,
> As parts, can see but parts, now this, now that,
> And live, perforce, from thought to thought, and make
> One act a phantom of succession. Thus
> Our weakness somehow shapes the shadow, Time;
> But in the shadow will we work, and mould
> The woman to the fuller day.'

This effectively disposes of the Prince's objection—the creation was to God a single act out of time. We who live in time, the shadow cast by God's light, can have no adequate concept of his processes. But the implication is obviously that the creation is still incomplete and is proceeding; and, moreover, that we can participate in it by *working* in the shadow. The

[1] Lyell discussed the significance of the cutting-back of Niagara and the entombment of a mastodon in his *Travels in North America* (1845), pp. 27–53.

word 'mould' is significant in this connection; it occurred in 'The Palace of Art':

> 'From change to change four times within the womb
> The brain is moulded', she began . . .

In both poems it occurs in a context giving it a special sense connected with evolution, but in *The Princess* the means whereby evolution will occur is left undefined, save that in this instance something is thought to be left to men and society to contribute towards it. The same idea is present in *In Memoriam*, though there many other notions are explored, some of them contradictory.

At this point it becomes necessary to consider the order of composition of *The Princess* and *In Memoriam*. In the first chapter it was mentioned that when Edmund Lushington first heard of *The Princess* in the summer of 1845 at Eastbourne, he was told by Tennyson that his marriage to Cecilia Tennyson had been brought in at the end of *In Memoriam*, many of the cantos of which were completed.[1] Lushington wrote these details at the end of his life,[2] and it seems almost certain that he consulted a diary to be so sure of the year in question (which is corroborated by Edward Fitzgerald) and the precise place. In 1845, however, the title *In Memoriam* had not yet been adopted, and the poems were usually referred to as the 'Elegies', even up to 1850, the year of publication.[3] The question arises whether Lushington altered what was actually said only to the extent of supplying the name by which the poem came to be known, or whether he was constructing the rough sense of the remark from distant memory. The positiveness over the time of year and small circumstantial details which suggest the use of a diary lead one to think that he may have recorded the remark also. If so, and Tennyson really said that it was at the *end* of the poem that the marriage was introduced, then we may believe that save for additions and alterations,

---

[1] *Memoir*, i, p. 203. See above, p. 10.

[2] On his deathbed, according to *Materials*, i, p. 245. The *Memoir* omits several passages from Lushington's reminiscences which were printed in *Materials*. These make it almost certain that he was consulting a diary and private letters.

[3] See e.g. *Memoir*, i, p. 297. The title *The Princess* seems not to have been in use either in 1845. See above, p. 9.

'The Princess' and Evolution

the order of completion of *In Memoriam* and *The Princess* is the reverse of the order of publication.[1] If we take it that the difficulties raised in *In Memoriam* by, among other things, the geological evidence for an (eventual) evolutionary theory were 'resolved' by considerations affecting a marriage celebrated in a poem composed at the very time that *The Princess* was resumed, then it might be believed that the poet had come upon an idea which gave him special interest in the married state, which is the true preoccupation of the latter poem. To some people the conclusion of *In Memoriam* appears abrupt; the seriousness of the last Part of *The Princess* is certainly in remarkable contrast to the air of badinage present at the beginning. This suggests that in the summer of 1845, when *In Memoriam* was seemingly not long concluded and the composition of *The Princess* resumed, the poet had come to see that in marriage there was something so significant that it could assuage the despair recorded in the poems of *In Memoriam* and justify the intrusion of deep feeling in *The Princess*. To see how this may have come about, the scientific allusions in *In Memoriam* must be briefly reviewed.

The use of the unpalatable evidence for possible 'development' of the human brain as the ground of a wicked pride in the erring Soul in 'The Palace of Art' shows that Tennyson came to hold an equivocal view of the value of scientific knowledge for settling moral and metaphysical questions. Many other passages confirm this. In 'Love thou thy land' he says:

[1] Of course the poem does end *In Memoriam* as we have it, but the possibility has to be considered that it was only adapted for this position afterwards; Lushington might have said what he did about Tennyson's remark because he knew from the published version that it stood there. But I believe that it is so clearly a fit resolution of the poem's discordant heart-searchings that it was always intended to end it, and that Lushington was reporting Tennyson's actual words, save for the title. But apart from this, Lushington mentions several poems intended for *In Memoriam* (and on one occasion the poet's own estimate of one of them); he shows a lively awareness of the difference in order of composition and that of publication. Moreover, it is clear, prior to writing the passage under examination, that *In Memoriam* had no title; he speaks of 'memorial poems' (*Memoir*, i, p. 202), and the volume 'which now constitutes the book called *In Memoriam*'. (*Materials*, i, p. 246.) It was probably only to avoid the inconvenience of this periphrasis that he inserted '*In Memoriam*' (and '*The Princess*') in the passage.

Make knowledge circle with the winds;
But let her herald, Reverence, fly
Before her to whatever sky
Bear seed of men and growth of minds.

In *In Memoriam* he writes:

Who loves not Knowledge? Who shall rail
Against her beauty? May she mix
With men and prosper! Who shall fix
Her pillars? Let her work prevail . . .

Half-grown as yet, a child, and vain—
She cannot fight the fear of death.
What is she, cut from love and faith,
But some wild Pallas from the brain

Of demons? fiery-hot to burst
All barriers in her onward race
For power. Let her know her place;
She is the second, not the first.

Again, in the introductory stanzas to the poem, dated 1849,
he has:

Let knowledge grow from more to more,
But more of reverence in us dwell;
That mind and soul, according well,
May make one music as before.

Ida's ingenious answer to the Prince's 'metaphysical' point,
that geology seems to teach that the creator improved in his
work like any common artisan, is really no more than an extension of these same views. Worldly knowledge only seems to
supply the truth: and reverence is still due to the creator,
whose vision is of a single act. Arthur Hallam had really supplied this solution when he asked what difference it made that
in dealing with common elements God proceeded by general
laws. But Ida's words were written after a period of what
appears, by the record of *In Memoriam*, to have been one of
doubt as to the answer.

This doubt was partly prompted by uneasiness over these

same geological evidences, seemingly supporting earlier hypotheses in the fields of astronomy and embryology.

> They say,
> The solid earth whereon we tread
>
> In tracts of fluent heat began,
> And grew to seeming-random forms,
> The seeming prey of cyclic storms,
> Till at the last arose the man;
>
> Who throve and branch'd from clime to clime,
> The herald of a higher race,
> And of himself in higher place,
> If so he type this work of time
>
> Within himself, from more to more . . .

These lines, resembling those of Psyche's lecture, refer once again to the nebular hypothesis, but also to what is usually called the 'cataclysmic theory'. By this, it was suggested that the resemblances between the anatomical structures of present-day animals and fossils of extinct species were to be explained by the occurrence of fresh creations after each of a series of cataclysms, of which the Flood was perhaps one. The theory was, at the date these lines were written, by no means new, having been propounded by Cuvier himself. What is of especial interest is Tennyson's addition of the idea that man was 'herald of a higher race', provided only that he followed the example time had brought to light concerning the rest of the animal kingdom. How this could be without his being totally destroyed and re-created is difficult to see. But as I said earlier, Tennyson did not restrict himself to a single hypothesis to explain the evidences of 'development'. He did not for instance consider only the cataclysmic theory. In 1837 he occupied himself with Lyell's *Principles of Geology*,[1] and there can be little doubt that he was considerably influenced by it, for it dealt in large measure with the topics I have been discussing. Lyell devoted a whole chapter[2] to refuting the

---

[1] *Memoir*, i, p. 162. References are to the fourth edition, 1835.
[2] Book 1, chapter 9.

cataclysmic theory in the light of the discovery that vertebrates had been found in the most ancient European sedimentary formations, when according to the theory they should not appear until much later in geological time. He himself followed James Hutton (*Theory of the Earth*, 1788) and John Playfair (*Illustrations of the Huttonian Theory*, 1802) in believing that the world was formed at one date and altered in its conformation by unending igneous activity and erosion. Hutton and Lyell, though not subscribers to the theory of the German 'Neptunists' that *all* rocks were of a sedimentary type, held that marine erosion and deposition were important agents in creating major land-forms. Indeed Sir John Thomson saw a reference in *In Memoriam* to Lyell's theory:[1]

> There rolls the deep where grew the tree.
> O earth, what changes hast thou seen!
> There where the long street roars hath been
> The stillness of the central sea.
>
> The hills are shadows, and they flow
> From form to form, and nothing stands;
> They melt like mist, the solid lands,
> Like clouds they shape themselves and go.

Obviously this theory, taken as an explanation of the origin of sedimentary formations in which fossil remains are found, is at complete variance with the cataclysmic theory referred to in the same poem. Yet Tennyson may be assumed to have realized the enormous potentiality of marine erosion—its capability of forming major land-masses—from other lines in the poems:

> The moanings of the homeless sea,
> The sound of streams that swift or slow
> Draw down Æonian hills, and sow
> The dust of continents to be.

Of course the poet was exploring the terrible significance of either of the alternatives, which made the age one in which one could ask whether this was not

[1] J. A. Thomson, *The Science of Life* (1899), p. 243.

'The Princess' and Evolution

'A time to sicken and to swoon,
   When Science reaches forth her arms
   To feel from world to world, and charms
Her secret from the latest moon?'

Gone are the days when science told delightful fairy tales!

... all the phantom Nature stands
A hollow form with empty hands.

Lyell's book also provided information on the workings of
natural law in the survival of species. He rejected Lamarck's
theory of Functional Reaction, which was to the effect that
'The production of a new organ in an animal body results from
a new need which continues to be felt, and from a new movement which this need originates and sustains',[1] and did so
because in his view it rested upon the assumption that species
were not fixed, but only convenient, man-made classifications
which could be rendered obsolete by developments in accordance with his famous law. Lyell, on the contrary, believed
that species were fixed within narrow limits:

The entire variation from the original type, which any given kind
of change can produce, may usually be effected in a brief period of
time, after which no further deviation can be obtained by continuing to alter the circumstances . . . the least possible excess
beyond the defined limits being fatal to the existence of the individual.[2]

Tennyson touches upon this in his lines

Are God and Nature then at strife,
   That Nature lends such evil dreams?
   So careful of the type she seems,
So careless of the single life.

Lyell had written a little earlier in the same section:

If we consider the vegetable kingdom generally, it must be
recollected that even of the seeds which are well ripened, a great
part are either eaten by insects, birds and other animals, or decay
for want of room and opportunity to germinate . . . In the universal struggle for existence, the right of the strongest eventually prevails.[3]

[1] ibid., p. 221.   [2] Book 3, p. 21.   [3] Book 3, p. 9.

248

'The Princess' and Evolution

In the same section of *In Memoriam*, Tennyson has:

> . . . I, considering everywhere
> Her secret meaning in her deeds,
> And finding that of fifty seeds
> She often brings but one to bear,

> I falter where I firmly trod . . .[1]

Lyell's explanation of the apparent 'development' of species was that they were simultaneously created, and in the course of time were gradually eliminated by the struggle for existence he had remarked upon. He devoted several chapters[2] to the tale of mutual destructiveness of organisms, and the resultant equilibrium, which had been disturbed from time to time by changes of climate and like phenomena, and more recently by man's increased power of altering or modifying his environment by using his intellect. This new factor, which he calls 'moral', introduced no situation inexplicable by the established physical laws of nature, and might be accounted for without resort to any theory of external intervention in the established order of things. Man is only conforming with the laws of the survival of the strongest: the survival of species has always depended on the balance of power between natural enemies:

> Every species which has spread itself from a small point over a wide area, must . . . have marked its progress by the diminution or entire extirpation of some other, and must maintain its ground by a successful struggle against the encroachments of other plants and animals.[3]

Tennyson's poem continues in the next section:

> 'So careful of the type?' but no.
> From scarped cliff and quarried stone
> She cries, 'A thousand types are gone;
> I care for nothing, all shall go.'

Man, the poem argues, is deluded in believing that God is love, and love is the law of creation, for he himself is as destructive

---

[1] *In Memoriam*, LV. Douglas Bush points out a remarkable parallel in Butler's *Analogy*. See his *Science and English Poetry* (1950), p. 122 n.
[2] Book 3, chapters VIII, IX, X.   [3] Book 3, p. 139.

as other creatures, and if he had only looked at what was going on about him he would have seen that

> . . . Nature, red in tooth and claw
> With ravine, shriek'd against his creed.

Man, in fulfilling Lyell's principle of an equilibrium of destructiveness, is

> . . . A monster then, a dream,
> A discord. Dragons of the prime,
> That tare each other in their slime,
> Were mellow music match'd with him.

Lyell's calm contemplation of the scene of fell purposes was not shared by Tennyson. The poet's notion of humanity's development from lower species, itself disagreeable but at least capable of being integrated into a total metaphysical scheme, as Hallam had shown in the Cambridge days, was entirely rejected by Lyell who, though aware of the facts uncovered by Tiedemann, would not accept an evolutionary hypothesis to explain them. Lyell had thus destroyed a dream only to substitute a nightmare. But Tennyson, be it observed, did not immediately refrain from republishing the lines in 'The Palace of Art' mentioning the discovery. In 1842, five years after reading Lyell, they were altered a little, as I have mentioned, but transferred to a more prominent position; and there they remained until 1853. We can only infer that he was not unwilling to keep in his mind three mutually exclusive theories—the cataclysmic, the uniformitarian (Lyell's) and the quasi-evolutionary.

Lyell was not so Olympian that he was unaware of the metaphysical problem his argument produced. He wrote:

> Why the working of this machinery [he is speaking of earthquakes] should be attended with so much evil, is a mystery far beyond the reach of our philosophy, and must probably remain so until we are permitted to investigate . . . other parts of the moral and material universe with which they may be connected.[1]

Tennyson felt that the position science had reached was tantalizing; it had moved a great way, but had done little but

[1] Book 2, p. 291.

uncover difficulties which undermined confidence in traditional spiritual values. He felt that there was a solution and that it was science which would eventually suggest it. One can understand why he imagined the delights of sleeping a hundred years to wake to science grown to more,[1] and why he lamented that the race between science and social ills appeared to be a losing one, even if in his heart he believed with the Saint-Simonians that a time of upheaval was inevitable and not devoid of hope:

> Science moves, but slowly, slowly, creeping on from point to point.

> Yet I doubt not thro' the ages one increasing purpose runs,
> And the thoughts of men are widen'd with the process of the suns.[2]

The inner belief that there was still ground for hope is repeated in *In Memoriam*, where the poet states his belief that time does not merely produce a series of fortuitous events:

> I see in part
> That all, as in some piece of art,
> Is toil coöperant to an end.[3]

This belief is indeed one of those most characteristic of Tennyson's whole attitude, and though assailed, is always ready to reappear.

The exact dating of many of the poems forming *In Memoriam* is not possible, but Hallam Tennyson makes a point of

---

[1] In 'The Day Dream'.   [2] 'Locksley Hall'.

[3] *In Memoriam*, cxxviii. This belief was questioned in 'The Two Voices', where it appears as

> He seems to hear a Heavenly Friend,
> And thro' thick veils to apprehend.
> A labour working to an end.

(The last line was also used in a poem called 'Youth' which was not published—see *Memoir*, i, p. 112.) The idea reappears in 'Love thou thy land' (*c.* 1834):

> Even now we hear with inward strife
> A motion toiling in the gloom—
> The Spirit of the years to come
> Yearning to mix himself with Life.

'The Princess' and Evolution

observing in a note[1] on a reference to Robert Chambers's
Vestiges of the Natural History of Creation (1844), that the sections of the poem which deal with evolution had been read by
his father's friends some years before the publication of this
work. Bearing in mind that Chambers's book is a thorough-
going advocacy of an evolutionary theory of the origin of
species, the inference we are to draw from this is that Tennyson had genuinely anticipated something of it before Chambers's well-known book appeared. It is difficult to decide how
many of the stanzas are to be included under the heading.
Those already discussed certainly have parallels rather in
Lyell than in Chambers; but some others may derive from
Chambers all the same. Hallam's view could well have been
that they are not exactly evolutionary in the Darwinian sense
of the word. For example, the stanza

> I trust I have not wasted breath:
> I think we are not wholly brain,
> Magnetic mockeries; not in vain,
> Like Paul with beasts, I fought with Death,

which seems from its first line to have been late in the series
may have derived from Chambers's account of the seemingly
electrical nature of nervous and cerebral action:

> There are many facts which tend to prove that the action of this
> apparatus is of an electrical nature, a modification of that sur-
> prising agent, which takes magnetism, heat, and light, as other
> subordinate forms, and of whose general scope in this great system
> of things we are only beginning to have a right conception.[2]

Nevertheless, in general, when the facts underlying those
stanzas which are most justly called evolutionary can be found
in Lyell's work (even though this was anti-evolutionary in
intention), we can have no grounds for questioning Hallam's
statement.

The problem of ascertaining how much there was in Chambers's book for which Tennyson himself felt sympathy is
greatly simplified by the circumstance that included in the

---

[1] *Memoir*, i, p. 223.
[2] *Vestiges of the Natural History of Creation* (1844) [by Robert Cham-
bers], p. 333.

'The Princess' and Evolution

Memoir is a letter, written in November 1844 to Edward Moxon, in which the book is asked for. 'I want you to get me a book which I see advertised in the *Examiner*: it seems to contain many speculations with which I have been familiar for years, and on which I have written more than one poem. The book is called *Vestiges of the Natural History of Creation.*'[1] I think it can be accepted that Tennyson really did hold some theory of an evolutionary character from his interest in, and personal interpretation of Southwood Smith's articles, but that he should have had in advance so clear a notion of what Chambers's book contained that he was able to determine that it discussed a topic on which he had written 'more than one poem', makes it clear that the advertisement must have been extremely detailed. Yet the files of the *Examiner* show that the advertisements for both the first and second editions (in November 1844) give only the barest details; consequently it could not have been an advertisement at all that the poet saw. He must instead have been referring to a long notice of the book inserted in the book-review section of the paper in the issue for 9 November 1844.[2] This notice is highly laudatory where many to come were not, and is remarkable for its having selected for quotation many passages of especial interest for the student of Tennyson; indeed it might be said that to read the notice is to read all that is necessary for understanding the significance of Chambers's book for the poet. Bearing in mind that it was Tennyson's habit to reflect upon scientific matter in newspapers and magazines—we have seen to what effect in the passage from 'The Palace of Art'—it might not be too much to say, perhaps, that the impression made upon him by the notice could have been greater than that of the book itself. Nor would this be surprising, since the effect of compressing the argument yet giving copious extracts from it, is to make the whole incisive and easily comprehended. Moreover, the writer of the notice insists throughout that the idea of a developing creation is not irreligious, but the very reverse. He enthusiastically develops Chambers's own point that to pursue the manifold evidences that decay and supersession are

[1] *Memoir*, i, p. 222.
[2] Because it is not readily accessible, it is given in an Appendix, p. 279 below.

compensated for by the rise of new and more perfect forms of life, is to uncover the majestic workings of an intelligence which extends to the greatest and the least of natural phenomena. Chambers was far from blind to the implications of evolution and he saw them in much lighter colours than did Lyell; the notice quotes his words:

> I would say . . . there may yet be a faith derived from this view of nature sufficient to sustain us under all sense of the imperfect happiness, the calamities, the woes, and pains of this sphere of being. For let us but fully and truly consider what a system is here laid open to view, and we cannot well doubt that we are in the hands of One who is both able and willing to do us the most entire justice. And in this faith we may well rest at ease, even though life should have been to us but a protracted disease, or though every hope we had built on the secular materials within our reach were felt to be melting from our grasp.

The reviewer applauds this view of things, seeing it to reflect 'the noblest thoughts and the loftiest aspirations that have consoled and elevated the hopes of humanity in this world':

> What is the comfortable faith and trust to which the mere unassisted truths of natural science have led this ardent and sincere investigator, if it is not that which the Religion of Christ has assured to its humble and undoubting followers—that this Present Existence is the preparation for a Better, and that the road leading thither is the love of God and Man, the practising every virtue, the living reasonably and justly while we are here, the proportioning of our esteem to the value of things, and the so using the world as not to abuse it.

The evolutionary theory that Chambers postulated took much less account of the mutual destructiveness of species than did Lyell's hypothesis, which had described the struggle for survival without attaching it to any theory of development of species. It utterly rejected cataclysms, of course, and also Lamarck's concept of development in response to needs, which Chambers called one of 'the follies of the wise'. His view was that God is bringing creation into existence slowly, but according to a pre-arranged plan. Species, moreover, develop from one another in accordance with this central purpose, and mutual destructiveness is not invoked as an explanation of the disappearance of species. The hand of the grand author of the design is apparent, not in any day-to-day intervention in its workings, but in the operations of ascertainable *laws*. Indeed, if we but try, we may see law underlying the apparently most unpredictable events, like the incidence of crime in cities.[1] We may not expect to be exempted from these laws whatever our pleas: consequently it behoves us to learn them, and apply them to our advantage. The parallel this concept holds with Ida's speech in *The Princess*, where she explains creation as both a single act and a process, will be obvious; it is prompted, it will be remembered, by the sight of the fossil bones of an extinct mammoth exposed by the waterfall. There are other significant parallels between Chambers's book and Tennyson's poem. First, however, we must establish what appeared in the review in *The Examiner* which led Tennyson to see that *Vestiges* contained speculations with which he had been familiar for years, and on which he had written more than one poem.

First, we may take it that the stanzas in the first version of 'The Palace of Art' dealing with the Herschel-Laplace nebular hypothesis were not written in ignorance of the implication that the galaxies were in process of being created: this receives explicit treatment in the Review at *A* (in the Appendix): furthermore, the reference to binary stars in the same passage of the poem may well imply knowledge of the simple theory of their production occurring at *B* of the Review. Tiedemann's theory of the development of the foetal brain is given a prominent place in the Review at *C*. Tennyson's concern for the possibility of individual immortality despite the carelessness for the single life implied by the evolutionary theory finds an echo in Chambers, and is repeated in the Review at *H*. In these important respects, Tennyson was familiar with the evidences, and probably the 'speculations' contained in the book, the review of which he read in November

---

[1] Here he is indebted to that same essay 'Sur l'homme et le développement de ses facultés' by L. A. J. Quetelet, from which Lady Morgan drew for her *Woman and her Master* (1840). See above, p. 123, n.1.

1844. Within a few months he seems to have written the conclusion of *In Memoriam* and resumed *The Princess*.[1]

If we examine the concluding stanzas of *In Memoriam*, I think we can see that Tennyson had assimilated a good deal of Chambers's doctrine. The last four lines of the whole work describe

> That God, which ever lives and loves,
> One God, one law, one element,
> And one far-off divine event,
> To which the whole creation moves.

God seen as fundamentally benign in purpose, despite the casualties created in the process of continuous creation, God who shows himself in the workings of laws initiated an infinite time ago and intended to continue indefinitely the slow, purposive amelioration of species—including man—this was also Chambers's vision. Somehow, by mysterious laws, man himself might be improved in the course of generations, and the dreams of a nobler race of men, at peace, enjoying world-government, engaged in peaceful commerce over the whole surface of the earth, realized.[2] Chambers wrote as follows on this idea, and the passage was quoted in full in the Review in *The Examiner* (at *F*):

Is our race but the initial of the grand crowning type? Are there yet to be species superior to us in organization, purer in feeling, more powerful in device and act, and who shall take a rule over us? There is in this nothing improbable on other grounds. The present race, rude and impulsive as it is, is perhaps the best adapted to the present state of things in the world: but the external world goes through slow and gradual changes, which may leave it in time a much serener field of existence. There may then be occasion for a nobler type of humanity, which shall complete the zoological circle on this planet, and realize some of the dreams of the purest spirits of the present race.

---

[1] Lushington came down to Eastbourne to see Tennyson in July 1845 during the vacation from Glasgow University. The conclusion, which mentions his marriage, may have been written earlier, but resemblances in phraseology to Chambers's book suggests that it was not much earlier.

[2] See 'Locksley Hall' for this vision of the future, which was earlier shown to resemble that of the Saint-Simonians.

Tennyson's conclusion to *In Memoriam* describes the marriage of his sister to Lushington, and after their departure visualizes, in verse which gives sublimity to the occasion, the moon which hangs over the North Downs also lighting the shores

> By which they rest, and ocean sounds,
>   And, star and system rolling past,
>   A soul shall draw from out the vast
> And strike his being into bounds,
>
> And, moved thro' life of lower phase,
>   Result in man, be born and think,
>   And act and love, a closer link
> Betwixt us and the crowning race
>
> Of those that, eye to eye, shall look
>   On knowledge; under whose command
>   Is Earth and Earth's, and in their hand
> Is Nature like an open book;
>
> No longer half-akin to brute,
>   For all we thought and loved and did,
>   And hoped, and suffer'd, is but seed
> Of what in them is flower and fruit;
>
> Whereof the man that with me trod
>   This planet was a noble type
>   Appearing ere the times were ripe . . .

Here we see another allusion to Tiedemann's theory, no longer attributed to an erring Soul, but uttered by the poet himself in lines which set it in close association with an evolutionary hypothesis, which, by virtue of the similarity of phrasing, was almost certainly supplied by Chambers's book, even if it had been present earlier in Tennyson's own mind. It is not difficult to see why Chambers's mention of the possibility that mankind as it now is might possibly be the initial of the 'grand crowning type' should have appealed to the poet as a suitable theme for the culmination of his Elegy upon his friend. He had already written for it, on suggestions provided by Lyell's book, poems which raised the awful metaphysical problem of man's inborn aspirations to virtue during life and spiritual immortality despite corporeal death. Chambers's theory of evolution adumbrated the possibility that the evidences of physical development of man from lower species were not reason for despair, but simply proof of God's majestic scheme of continuous creation. The mystery of pain and death was not removed, but at least God could not be said to have deserted the giant mechanism, for in a sense it was an aspect of God's presence; and, who knows, God's benevolence, as manifested in the physical evidence not of mere supersession of species but also of their *improvement* might extend to a form of compensation after death. Milton's lines exactly express this view:

> All is best, though we oft doubt
> What the unsearchable dispose
> Of highest wisdom brings about,
> And ever best found in the close.[1]

More than this, Tennyson's belief in the near-divinity of Hallam, so often expressed in the poems of *In Memoriam*, could easily be fitted into the reasoned argument for the probable appearance of a higher type of man, the Christ that is *to be*.

The strength of the belief he came to hold in the possible development of a higher type of man, a man who would realize the moral ideal of philosophers of all ages, as well as 'of the purest spirits of the present race', may be measured from his lines in *Maud*:

> A monstrous eft[2] was of old the lord and master of earth,
> For him did his high sun flame, and his river billowing ran,
> And he felt himself in his force to be Nature's crowning race.
> As nine months go to the shaping an infant ripe for his birth,
> So many a million of ages have gone to the making of man:
> He now is first, but is he the last? is he not too base?[3]

The turn which he here gives to the evolutionary theory in *Maud* is characteristic: the improvement of man he looks for is not merely physical and intellectual (which after all is all

[1] *Samson Agonistes*, ll. 1745–8.
[2] 'The great old lizards of Geology' (Tennyson): see *Works*, p. 957.
[3] *Maud*, Part I, iv (vi). Compare Chambers (*F* in the Review): 'The gestation of a single organism is the work of but a few days, weeks or months; but the gestation, so to speak, of a whole creation is a matter probably involving enormous spaces of time.'

that is implicit in it), but moral: man must grow morally better. Bearing this in mind, we can understand the relevance to the poem of the fulminations against immoral commercial practices—in which it is hinted that Maud's own father shared. Remembering, too, Tennyson's series of poems on the near-obligation of women to redeem their despondent lovers—who are in revolt against the commercial spirit of the age—we can see more clearly why the speaker in this poem finds reconciliation with his world in having had his love for Maud returned, even in such tragic circumstances. This, I suggested in an earlier chapter, is the pattern of ideas associated with *The Princess*.

In *In Memoriam* Tennyson bids us

> Contemplate all this work of Time,
> The giant labouring in his youth;
> Nor dream of human love and truth,
> As dying Nature's earth and lime . . .

and goes on to say, in lines I have quoted earlier, that man appeared on an earth which itself had evolved from nebulae, and then

> . . . throve and branch'd from clime to clime,
> The herald of a higher race,
> And of himself in higher place,
> If so he type this work of time
>
> Within himself, from more to more . . .

Lady Psyche's lecture repeated the same tale of terrestrial evolution: but it was left to the Prince to connect it specifically with feminism. Speaking to Ida of the grand expectations he had of the effect of woman's true emancipation, he first says that men and women must grow together.

> Yet in the long years liker must they grow;
> The man be more of woman, she of man;[1]
> He gain in sweetness and in moral height,
> Nor lose the wrestling thews that throw the world;
> She mental breadth, nor fail in childward care.

[1] In one of the beautiful poems describing Hallam in *In Memoriam* occur the lines:

'The Princess' and Evolution

The vision of the married pair is then elevated in his imagination: they approximate the archetypal figures of the Christian myth; but they exist in the future, not the past:

> And so these twain, upon the skirts of Time,
> Sit side by side, full-summ'd in all their powers,
> Dispensing harvest, sowing the to-be,
> Self-reverent each and reverencing each,
> Distinct in individualities,
> But like each other even as those who love.[1]

The sublime concept of the equal union of the sexes then finds its culmination in the belief I have already examined in *In Memoriam* and *Maud*:

> And manhood fused with female grace
> In such a sort, the child would twine
> A trustful hand, unask'd, in thine,
> And find his comfort in thy face.

See CIX. Tennyson attributed to Christ a union of male and female qualities, what he called 'the man-woman' in him (*Memoir*, i, p. 326 n). In 1869 he said 'They will not easily beat the character of our Lord, that union of man and woman, sweetness and strength' (*Memoir*, ii, p. 69). The idea that the sexual characters were shared—an idea advanced by John Goodwyn Barmby in *The New Moral World*, described in Chapter III, also finds expression in Tennyson's poem 'On one who affected an effeminate nature' (1889):

> I prize that soul where man and woman meet,
> Which types all Nature's male and female plan . . .

[1] The verse 'Distinct in individualities' appeared originally in 'The Ante-Chamber', a poem intended to serve as a prologue to 'The Gardener's Daughter'. The version printed in the *Memoir* (i, p. 199) omits it, but it remains in the copy of the poem included in the Heath Commonplace Book now at the Fitzwilliam Museum, Cambridge. 'The Ante-Chamber' gives an imaginary portrait of a painter who took delight in the infinite variety of individual human character, action and expression. It is interesting to note that one of the splendid sections of *In Memoriam* recalling incidents which revealed the charm of Arthur Hallam's personality (LXXXIX) dwells particularly upon his keen eye for what went on around him, and his dislike of the 'social mill' (of life in London) for its tendency to merge

> in form and gloss
> The picturesque of man and man.

Tennyson transfers the idea to the passage in *The Princess* without difficulty because it stood in 'The Ante-Chamber' in a context which strongly implied man's conformity with complex genetic laws.

Then comes the statelier Eden back to men;
Then reign the world's great bridals, chaste and calm;
Then springs the crowning race of humankind.
May these things be!

The Princess demurs: she had been capable of meeting the
metaphysical difficulty of reconciling faith in a Creator and
acceptance of evolution; indeed this dream had once also been
hers, but the setback of her attempt to surmount the first
practical step by herself had disillusioned her.

Sighing she spoke, 'I fear
They will not'. 'Dear, but let us type them now
In our own lives . . .
either sex alone
Is half itself, and in true marriage lies
Nor equal, nor unequal. Each fulfils
Defect in each, and always thought in thought,
Purpose in purpose, will in will, they grow,
The single pure and perfect animal,
The two-cell'd heart beating, with one full stroke,
Life'.[1]

In these lines the idea that man is a developing animal is
fully brought out; in order to emphasize the evolutionary aspect of marriage, Tennyson has risked injuring the tone of the
climax of his poem. In addition, there is a strong suggestion
that it is the duty of men and women to try to approach in
their lives the moral standard they desire to be fully realized
in the 'grand crowning race'. It is difficult to resist the conclusion that Tennyson is here admitting the notion for which
Chambers had derided Lamarck—that species are improved
in response to a felt need. This would hardly be surprising in
view of his eclecticism in regard to scientific hypotheses[2] and

[1] The word 'type', like 'mould' clearly has a meaning connected with
evolution. This passage and the previous one suggest that Tennyson
thought of the evolutionary theory in terms of a reversal of the story in
Genesis. Man and woman could in time move further and further from
their fallen condition until they entered an Eden.

[2] In *In Memoriam* his half-formed theory of evolution is not only
opposed by quite different scientific explanations of the evidence like
the cataclysmic and uniformitarian theories, but occasionally fuses with
alien notions altogether. When in 1837 Tennyson left Somersby, his
home for more than a quarter of a century, he dreamt of sailing down a

his frequently avowed impatience with the progress of nature's workings. For example, he makes Princess Ida herself say:

> Would, indeed, we had been,
> In lieu of many mortal flies, a race
> Of giants living each a thousand years,
> That we might see our own work out, and watch
> The sandy footprint harden into stone.

Indeed, if we see *The Princess* carrying into practical affairs some of the teachings of Chambers, then we must admit that the poet was misapplying the evidence of evolution to the extent of immensely shortening the period within which any real change of the kind discussed by the evolutionists could occur. His yearning for the moral improvement of individual men as a necessary preliminary to the reform of society at large (displayed in the noble speech attributed to Pallas in *Oenone* and later developed in *Idylls of the King*) overbore his realization of the slowness of the workings of natural processes.

Some of Chambers's own social applications of his evolutionary theory were seized upon by the reviewer in *The Examiner*. Remembering that Tennyson had the theme of both *In Memoriam* and *The Princess* running in his head at this time (November 1844), and that within a few months of reading the Review may possibly have concluded the former and have entered upon steady work on the latter, we can see that the following passage takes on special significance. Chambers is speaking of man's need to observe the laws of social existence as well as those of the physical world. One of these laws, he

river accompanied by maidens in a 'shallop' to meet Hallam in a great ship. The imagery makes it clear that the river is the river of life (compare 'The Dying Swan', 'The Lady of Shalott', 'Crossing the Bar'. The maidens remind us of 'Morte d'Arthur'). During the progress, the poet and maidens both grow in stature,

> As one would sing the death of war,
> And one would chant the history
> Of that great race which is to be,
> And one the shaping of a star.
> (*In Memoriam*, cɪɪɪ)

In other sections it appears as though transmigration ('From state to state the spirit walks') and a Dantean cosmogony are considered (Sections ʟxxxɪɪ and xcɪɪɪ).

believes, is to the effect that each individual, society or nation must interfere as little as possible in the activities of others:

> The same rule applies between one great body and class of men and another, and also between nations. Thus if one set of men keep others in the condition of slaves—this being a gross injustice to the subjected party, the mental manifestations of that party to the masters will be such as to mar the comfort of their lives: the minds of the masters themselves will be degraded by the association with beings so degraded: and thus, with some immediate or apparent benefit from keeping slaves, there will be in a far greater degree an experience of evil.[1]

Neither Chambers nor the reviewer probably thought of women when writing these words: but to Tennyson, preoccupied with the claim to women's rights, the thought of slaves, masters and resultant degradation by concealed influence would, I suggest, have had immediate association with feminism. It must be remembered that the emphasis falling on this paragraph in the Review is much greater than in the book: in the position it occupied in the former the passage jostles so closely the descriptions of cosmic processes and the solemn pronouncement upon man's obligation to conform with the social law under pain of dire consequences, that it could hardly fail to strike very forcibly one prepared for it by surprise at the substantiation of so many of his own speculations. We have seen that Tennyson would invest with a life and a light of his own a scientific discovery in 'some paragraph in a newspaper or a magazine'. The theory that evolution might fulfil the dream of 'a grand crowning race' gave particular importance to marriage and the family, for the Review specially emphasized that the operation of the law of development depended entirely upon the 'generative system'. It is in consequence of this, I suggest, that a marriage concludes *In Memoriam*; in marriage we come closest to participating in the cosmic purpose, though we must continuously seek to 'type' the qualities we desire to make permanent in man. Similarly,

---

[1] See *G* of the Review given in the Appendix. I quote from the Review in preference to the book which is its subject so that the context may be examined more easily. For example the passage quoted here continues with a condemnation of commercial malpractices.

though the intention of *The Princess* from the first was to oppose sex-antagonism and recommend marriage, the influence of the article may well have been to impose upon it a weight of feeling and scientific allusion it was not originally intended to bear. If we can recreate in imagination something of Tennyson's concern at Lyell's picture of man as merely the most successful contestant in a bitter struggle for a seemingly purposeless existence, it is not difficult to realize how profoundly he must have been affected by the equally 'scientific' vision of Chambers. It is then possible to view the conclusion of *In Memoriam* as a proper resolution of the poem's re-enactment of a mind's twistings and turnings in the net of evidences hostile to its ardent desire to believe that death is not the last word in a meaningless farce. Though much is still to be borne, the evidences formerly taken to be inimical to the poet's spiritual aspirations no longer prevent him from finishing the poem with a song of joy, an epithalamium celebrating not only an ordinary marriage but also a miraculous participation in the development of man.

The same point is made again in *The Princess*, where the love of the Prince and Princess is shown to be no inferior cast from a heavenly mould, but humanity's means of entering a Paradise that never was. This remarkable view, fit culmination to the painful reflections of *In Memoriam*, has a didactic purpose in *The Princess*, wherein Tennyson thought to influence directly the course of public thinking on a major social issue. That he should have adapted his art to the social problem of his day—despite his dislike of the present—was a natural consequence of the doctrine he was recommending, that we should live our lives so as to 'type' in them the qualities we desire to see generally prevail in the far future. The artist's duty was clear; when he perceived that society had to make a choice affecting its own destiny, he should seek to give it vivid actuality and suggest consequences.

It may be thought that although Chambers's book discussed the general connection between development and generation, this is hardly enough to cause Tennyson to write as feelingly as he did on feminism in *The Princess*. Earlier I mentioned that Southey and Southwood Smith alike believed that both societies and organisms were liable to revert to more primitive types if their natural development were inhibited. Chambers shared this view, and the reviewer in *The Examiner* quoted his very words (at *E* in the Appendix):

It is fully established that a human family, tribe, or nation, is liable, in the course of generations, to be either advanced from a mean form to a higher one, or degraded from a higher to a lower, *by the influence of the physical conditions in which it lives* . . . Prominence of the jaws, a recession and diminution of the cranium, and an elongation and attenuation of the limbs, are peculiarities always produced by these miserable conditions, for they indicate an unequivocal retrogression towards the type of the lower animals. *Thus we see nature alike willing to go back or to go forward.* Both effects are simply the result of the operation of the law of development in the generative system. Give good conditions, it advances: bad ones, it recedes . . . Monstrosities are nothing more than *a failure of the power of development in the system of the mother, occasioned by weak health or misery.*

Taking this passage with the one previously quoted, I think it clear that Tennyson must have been given pause by this passage. In a review which discussed many of the problems he was touching upon in one unfinished poem (*In Memoriam*), some highly relevant facts related to the theme of another (*The Princess*). The Review quotes, and consequently gives great prominence to, two passages from Chambers's book which have a direct bearing upon feminism. The first discusses in general terms the evils present in keeping classes of societies in an unjust subordination; the other takes this much further by stating as an indisputable fact that if women suffer weak health or misery, they may fail to transmit acquired characteristics to their children, and the whole society will in time revert to a lower condition; and it is this last-mentioned consideration which could explain Tennyson's willingness to deepen the tone of *The Princess*, despite the awkwardness of having specially to justify his doing so. That Chambers's suggestions were not lost on him is shown by the language used towards the end of the poem:

The woman's cause is man's: they rise or sink
Together, dwarf'd or godlike, bond or free.

'The Princess' and Evolution

> For she that out of Lethe scales with man
> The shining steps of Nature, shares with man
> His nights, his days, moves with him to one goal,
> Stays all the fair young planet in her hands—
> If she be small, slight-natured, miserable,
> How shall men grow?

The very close resemblance of the thought and expression of this to the passages quoted by the reviewer in *The Examiner* shows, I think, that it was not intended to form a merely grandiose climax, an inflated piece of false-sublime to lull the Princess and others like her into one more renunciation of their rights as complete human beings. Yet such, sometimes, has been the view of critics hostile to Tennyson. Although we may not be able to accept his evolutionary argument because we are possessed of deeper knowledge, we must recognize that his early grasp of the sociological relevance of then staggering hypotheses and his earnest endeavour to give it expression in a poem which would be widely read, deserves better recognition.[1] *The Princess* may not be among Tennyson's masterpieces, but at least it merits being thought of as an honest and far-sighted plea for the emancipation of women along lines which have in fact been followed.

[1] Prof. Arthur O. Lovejoy argues that Robert Chambers also deserves more credit for his *Vestiges* than has generally been allowed. See *The Popular Science Monthly*, lxxv (July–December 1909), pp. 499 and 537.

CHAPTER XII

Reflections of an Age

In the first chapter I suggested that *The Princess* afforded a glimpse of the aspirations of its age in the colours in which they presented themselves to the mind of the poet. I think that it will be agreed that Tennyson adapted the suggestions he received from Kemble and Chambers with great swiftness. Within a year or so of the first controversy over a women's college, the plan of the poem was fixed upon. In even less time after the reading of the notice of *Vestiges* he was actively continuing composition and incorporating the evolutionary implications of his theme. The beginning and the end of the poem, the parts where the fairy tale and the scientific interest are respectively most prominent, are clearly remarkably topical, even if at first sight they seem disparate. Although the incidents from Persian tales and the scientific matter both apply to the theme most aptly, they otherwise strike us as having little in common. And this applies, too, to the incident occupying an important place in the middle of the poem—the mediaeval tournament. Tournaments to win a lady's hand certainly illustrate a past attitude to the relations of the sexes—but what reason could Tennyson have had for including one in a poem which already disregarded the conventional requirements for poetic unity? I shall try to show in this chapter that what may strike us as only tenuously connected, at the time when the poem appeared would have seemed to many besides the poet to be surprisingly but clearly interrelated.

The interest Tennyson felt in fairy tales in one sense explains the selection of the plot of the poem; indeed, over and over again one sees how ingeniously the poet turned his own interests to account in handling this theme. But there are other considerations to be taken into account. He wished to reach a wide audience, and particularly women readers. Now at the time when he began composition, the *Arabian Nights* type of story was achieving an unprecedented popularity in England. In 1839, when the plan of the poem was worked out, no less than six new editions of the *Arabian Nights Entertainments* came up for review in the *London and Westminster Review*. Leigh Hunt on that occasion wrote an article[1] which is of great interest, for it helps to show how aware were Tennyson's contemporaries of the strange changes which were coming over society. These changes were producing the oddest paradoxes, one of which was this very popularity of the *Arabian Nights*—in an age of unprecedented progress in science and engineering.

Well may the lovers of fiction triumph over the prophecy, that was to see an end put to all poetry and romance by the progress of science;—to care for nothing but what the chemist could analyse, and the manufacturer realize; and take no further delight in nymphs and gnomes, because Sir Humphrey Davy had made a lamp; nor in the story of Iris because, as Peter Parley has it, the public was learning to know 'all about' rainbows.

It was over the last twenty years that the stories of the *Arabian Nights* had become so enormously popular. Hunt wrote that although it

has been the most practically and stupendously scientific in the history of the world, the love of fictitious writing has absolutely grown with its growth, and strengthened with its strength . . . as though Nature herself, through the medium of art, had resolved to see fair play to all the faculties of man, and to let no merely mechanical utility arise that should not be accompanied with a like amount of feeling and fancy.

He goes on:

And now, behold the Brighton coach running, or about to run, its thirty miles an hour; behold all England 'starting' every day for its triumphs over time and space, and the little children knowing all about *strata*, and prisms, and maps of the 'universe',—and behold, at the same time, fiction never so triumphant! Behold poetry

[1] xxxiii (October 1839–March 1840), p. 101. The author was identified by George L. Nesbitt, *Benthamite Reviewing*, p. 172.

never so rich since the time of Milton, novels and circulating libraries never so invincible, fairy tales never so honoured with republication and embellishment, and behold edition upon edition pouring forth all over Europe (for such is the fact) of the book which, forty years ago, Mr. Hole apologized for admiring,—now the glory of old readers as well as young, and the rapture of the critics!

After mentioning that after all we are indebted to the very same nations for our knowledge of both these delightful tales and the chemistry which was to undo the rainbow, he observes that in point of fact modern science has produced wonders that vie with the wildest fancies of the *Arabian Nights*.

In short, what is more romantic than the steam-engine itself,— the steam-carriage (the 'locomotive', as they ridiculously call it, with a romantic Latin pedantry) 'swallowing the ground' at the rate of thirty, forty, or sixty miles an hour, faster than Job's war-horse with all his 'fierceness and rage', bringing distant places into neighbourhood, and promising to bring an end to *war* by mixing up civilized nations in useful and beautiful intercourse! Was ever brazen steed in poet or romancer more wonderful, at first sight, to look at? Did Leviathan or Behemoth, when a hook was put in its nostrils, ever snort more formidably at his first impatient setting-out, with those short, sharp, and perilous-sounding vaporous pantings, as though the mysterious power within him disdained to be thus mastered? Did Hippogriff ever fly swifter through the air, or more startle the natives of this very valley of Thames, when Ariosto's knight rode him hither across the Channel, and saw the British chieftains mustering to a review?

What is significant for my present purpose is Hunt's comment on the new enthusiasm for such stories. He recalls that when they were first introduced to the English public they were looked upon 'as fit only to entertain children or their "mothers", the "superior intellects" of the other sex not having yet discovered how in this, as in greater instances, there lay a still superior instinct of wisdom in the childish nature'. He agrees with Sismondi that it is from these fictions

that we have derived that intoxication of love, that tenderness and delicacy of sentiment, and that reverential awe of women, by turns slaves and divinities, which have operated so powerfully on our chivalrous feelings. We trace their effects in all the literature of the South, which owes to this cause its mental character.

This connecting of the interest of the tales with chivalric feeling for women suggests one good reason why Tennyson chose such a story in illustration of his theme; another reason is to be found in Leigh Hunt's remarks on the parallel offered by modern science to the marvels of the *Arabian Nights*. But of course there is nothing in his remarks to suggest any direct connection between science and feminism; all he says is that developments in both have *accompanied* the growth of a taste for tales of the *Arabian Nights* variety. Nevertheless, Tennyson was not alone in relating scientific theory to judgments on the true position of women, and it may be convenient at this point to give an example or two of other opinions on the subject. An interesting one is provided by 'Shepherd' Smith, one-time editor of Owen's *Crisis*. He not only asserts that with the progress of science the emancipation of women is certain to proceed, but connects this development with European as opposed to eastern conditions:

> Nature is veiled in the East, and so is woman, her image and representative. She is crippled in China, concealed and imprisoned in Persia and Turkey, and regarded as a chattel, or private property, in every country in the world. But her veil is partly removed in Europe, for there the secrets of Nature are being discovered— there the Mother God is beginning to reveal herself, as alone she can be revealed, in the demonstrations of physical science.[1]

This passage illustrates very well part of the connection between feminism, science and Socialism which, I have suggested, underlies *The Princess*. The Socialists, like Tennyson, were always on the look-out for new scientific discoveries or theories which they could use to reinforce their social criticism. I showed earlier that Tennyson's interest in the discovery of Tiedemann concerning the analogies presented by the human embryo brain led him to reflect upon the possibility of human development, and indirectly to the feminism of *The Princess*. In the issue of Owen's newspaper *The New Moral World* for

---

[1] W. Anderson Smith, op. cit., p. 160, quoting *The Shepherd* for 1 February 1837.

10 February 1838,[1] Tiedemann's findings are invoked in a discussion of the justice of enslaving negroes, whose position at this time was often compared with that of women, if only because of the Oberlin agitation. But perhaps the most striking example of Socialist thought on the bearing of science on *feminism* is provided by an article written by William Thompson, who was discussed in Chapter IV as the author of *The Appeal of Women*, a disputant with J. S. Mill, and a supporter of Robert Owen. In 1826, William Thompson wrote an article in *The Co-operative Magazine and Monthly Herald* which he entitled 'Physical argument for the *equal* cultivation of all the useful faculties or capabilities, mental or physical, of men and women'.[2] The conclusions of this article remarkably anticipate those put forward by Tennyson in *The Princess*, but whereas Tennyson was indebted to Chambers's book, Thompson reached his opinion as a consequence of reading the writings of Lamarck, whom he quotes as follows:

Everything that Nature has caused to be acquired, or to be lost by individuals, by the influence of the circumstances to which their race has been for a long time exposed; and consequently by the influence of the preponderating employment of a particular organ, or by the constant want of the use of a particular part, it preserves, by generation, to the new individuals proceeding from those who have experienced such changes, *provided that the changes acquired are common to the two sexes, or to those who have produced these two individuals*.

Thompson went on to moralize upon the implications of this:

What stupendous intellectual and moral effects may we not expect to be produced in the human species, when the physical and mental powers of both the parents shall be equally cultivated, amongst whom even now, education operating on improved susceptibilities can effect such wonders as we every day see it to produce? particularly when we take into account the facts lately ascertained and placed beyond doubt by the philosophical enquirers into the mode of operating and developments of the brain, that changes produced by education inducing new social and intellectual qualities, produce analogous changes in the structure of the brain as

---

[1] iv, p. 122.
[2] i, no. 8, p. 250 (August 1826).

indicated by changes of form in its external bony covering, the cranium?[1]

From these specimens of contemporary social thought I hope to have shown that not only do the incidents and ideas in Tennyson's medley have a strong connection with advanced contemporary speculation but that although the result may seem disconnected, yet to those who were familiar with this speculation some considerable inter-connection (I would not say unity) would have been apparent. Reference to the East, a heroine drawn from a story of the *Arabian Nights* sort, the evidences for human development, allusions to Socialist activities, sympathy for higher education for women—all these matters were being widely discussed at the time of the poem's composition; but Tennyson seems to have desired to present them in a way which would most effectively reach his special audience. Even the tournament would have seemed to a contemporary both topical and relevant; indeed it might have given the best clue to the way in which the whole poem was to be read.

In 1839, the newspapers carried reports of preparations for a real tournament, held in September by the earl of Eglinton and Winton at his castle at Eglinton, a fine example of Scottish Baronial, *plus féodale que le moyen âge*. It was realistic in so far as the participants were not mere actors in a *tableau vivant*: they were young men of high birth who wore antique armour and followed as exactly as possible the rules of the joust. The combats concluded with a mêlée like that described in the poem. The beautiful Lady Seymour, a Sheridan and sister of Caroline Norton, graced the tournament as Queen of Beauty, a title she bore long afterwards,[2] and Louis Napoleon distinguished himself among the aristocratic visitors. The historian of the event wrote:

Those who were in London in the spring of 1839 must well remember the 'sensation' which the rumour of such a thing excited. Inquiries were being made everywhere, where intelligence could be

[1] pp. 251, 256. In 1880, S. Tolver Preston contributed 'Evolution and female education' to *Nature* (xxii, 23 September), in which the same deduction is made from the evolutionary theory of Darwin.

[2] *Record*, iii, p. 36.

gained, into the particulars of the reported fact, and as soon as it was ascertained to be true, the most intense curiosity arose on all sides to be acquainted with the details.[1]

At first the project was viewed by some as a piece of aristocratic folly. *The Examiner*, for instance, at first followed *The Times* in thinking it 'somewhat dull and altogether silly':[2] but popular enthusiasm carried the day, and the reporting moved through a phase of non-committal description to the point where the *Glasgow Argus* was rebuked in a leading article for suggesting that the large expenditure was an insult to the poor.[3] Much of the initial tardiness in approving the undertaking undoubtedly sprang from the fact that the competitors *rehearsed* for their parts on a tilting ground to which the public had access. This was at the Eyre Arms tavern at the top of St. John's Wood; practices were for a time carried on every Tuesday and Saturday,[4] and consequently it is quite possible that Tennyson, then residing at High Beech, Epping, could have seen incidents actually resembling those he eventually included in the poem he was at about this time planning. A contributor to *Tait's Edinburgh Magazine* for November 1839 remarked:

> The expectation of the whole world was on tiptoe—the curiosity, as well as the hopes of people of all ranks, conditions and ages, were raised to the highest pitch; and the interchange of questions and speculations became louder and more incessant the nearer the time approached. We scarcely ever remember any coming event, which—casting not its shadow, but its sunshine before it—so much occupied the minds of men; and still more, perhaps, the minds of women also.[5]

The interest of the event for women is the point to which I wish to draw attention, since it stamps it with the character borne also by the type of story into which a similar tournament

---

[1] [The Rev.] John Richardson, LL.B., *The Eglinton Tournament* (1843), p. 1. An illustration of the mêlée is included, showing pavilions and lists.

[2] *The Examiner*, 14 July 1839, p. 441.

[3] See the issues for 1 September, p. 555, and 8 September, p. 562.

[4] *The Examiner*, 14 July 1839, p. 441.

[5] vi, p. 697.

was introduced by the poet.[1] In confirmation of this interest I again quote from the historian of the event, who is himself quoting a morning newspaper:

As an exercise of mere animal dexterity and prowess, it is a most interesting spectacle; but when there is added to all that, the indispensable accompaniment of the presiding charm of beauty, and the virtuous influence of woman, all civilized men must admit that the interest of the spectacle is greatly enhanced. Even the mighty genius of Milton did homage at the throne of the 'Queen of Beauty', when he sang of the scenes:

'Where ladies' eyes
Rain'd influence, and judged the prize
Of wits or arms, where all contend
To win her smile whom all commend.'

The scene of the Tournament was graced by the fairest women of Scotland, and among them was the noble mother of the chivalrous host. It is not one of the least recommendations of such a scene that it cannot be considered complete without the presiding attractions of the fair sex. And, surely, in all times and countries there has been no such incentive to deeds of high emprise and honourable estimation as the virtuous influence of women.[2]

I think that it will be evident that to one considering the position of women in a changing world the interest provoked in 1839 by the Eglinton tournament, especially among women, would have seemed bizarre in the extreme. At a period in

[1] It is a fact perhaps not without significance that Shakespeare's *Pericles* has as one of its episodes a tourney for the hand of a princess occurring not long after a scene in which Pericles attempts to solve a riddle, under pain of death, in the hope of winning the hand of another princess, the daughter of the King of Antioch. It may be that Tennyson, obliged to find a substitute for the two sets of riddling in the Persian tale, decided to take a hint from Shakespeare and replaced the second by a joust which, while seeming to be equally romantic and unexpected as that in *Pericles*, in fact had the same relevance to the contemporary world as all the rest of his fantastic story. The mention in the Prologue of the Shakespearian precedent for a winter's tale would thus gain rather more point.

[2] Quoted in the Concluding Remarks by John Richardson. The article incidentally inveighs against 'the sordid, heartless, sensual doctrines of utilitarianism' and praises the Middle Ages for having at least 'led power captive in the silken chains of woman's finest influence'. This view is opposed to that of J. S. Mill and other of the supporters of women's rights; but it may be that Tennyson meant the mediaeval episode to suggest some such idea.

Reflections of an Age

history when Englishmen were deeply conscious of a need to consider their established institutions afresh, almost as if society could no longer look to the past for a precedent, here was an extraordinary demonstration of the vitality and meaningfulness of that past. To the author of 'Oriana' and 'Morte d'Arthur' this must have seemed especially significant. It would have suggested that the age was itself a medley, the present being not wholly new, the past oddly pre-figuring what was to come. It is this recognition which makes two contemporary reviews of *The Princess* especially interesting. Aubrey de Vere, writing in the *Edinburgh Review* in 1849, said:

> If a man were to scrutinise the external features of our time, for the purpose of characterising it compendiously, he would be tempted, we suspect, to give up the task before long, and to pronounce the age a Medley. It would be hard to specify the character of our Philosophy, including as it does fragments of all systems, sometimes at open war, and sometimes eclectically combined. Not less various is the texture of Society among us, in which time-honoured traditions are blended with innovations which a few months make antiquated. The Political condition of our day is a war of great principles. As heterogeneous in character is Art amongst us. Here we have an imitation of the antique, there a revival of the middle ages; while sculpture itself is sometimes compelled to relax its severity, and copy the rude attire of our northern yeomen. By what term could we describe the architecture of the day? In our rising cities we find a Gothic church close to a Byzantine fane or an Italian basilica; and in their immediate neighbourhood a town-hall like a Greek temple, a mansion like a Roman palace, and a club-house after the fashion of Louis XIV. The age in which we live may have a character of its own; but that character is not written in its face.
>
> In this respect Mr. Tennyson's poem 'The Princess', not without design if we may judge by the title, resembles the age.[1]

Very much the same view is taken by Charles Kingsley in a review published the following year.

> In this work, too, Mr. Tennyson shows himself more than ever the poet of the day. In it more than ever the old is interpenetrated

[1] *The Edinburgh Review*, xc (July–October 1849), p. 388.

275

Reflections of an Age

with the new—the domestic and scientific with the ideal and sentimental. He dares, in every page, to make use of modern words and
notions, from which the mingled clumsiness and archaism of his
compeers shrinks, as unpoetical. Though, as we just said, his stage
is an ideal fairy-land, yet he has reached the ideal by the only true
method,—by bringing the Middle age forward to the Present one,
and not by ignoring the Present to fall back on a cold and gal-
vanized Mediaevalism; and thus he makes his 'Medley' a mirror of
the nineteenth century, possessed of its own new art and science,
its own new temptations and aspirations, and yet grounded on,
and continually striving to reproduce, the forms and experiences of
all past time.[1]

It has been suggested[2] that this interpretation may have been
inspired by Tennyson himself in conversation. Certainly the
bizarre medley of incidents drawn from fairy tale, science and
mediaeval chivalry is in fact nothing other than a light-hearted
representation of the extraordinary complexity of contemporary thought and taste. We should be justified, I think, in
saying that Tennyson deliberately sought to disarm those who
looked upon all feminist proposals with passion and prejudice by casting his own view of the woman-question in the
form of a serio-comic poem. Its eclecticism in choice of materials represented the state of current taste and thinking. But
to give the hint that more was seriously meant than met the
eye, he composed a Prologue and Conclusion which, while
forming two of his most attractive Idylls, are notwithstanding expressions of his feelings on social relations as they
then existed. They seem to do little more than show how easily
nineteenth-century feminist aspirations could be made to
appear the idle inventions of a summer afternoon. But they
are meant to show his readers how things could and ought to
be. In the park in Kent which looked upon the English
Channel, there met that lazy afternoon, the 'two nations' at
their pleasures. These are very different, but do not clash.
The Mechanics' Institution at their festival are investors in the
future; Sir Walter Vivian's other guests, undergraduate friends
of his son's, are heirs to the past. The story they tell of the

---

[1] *Fraser's Magazine*, xlii (July–December 1850), p. 250.
[2] Shannon, p. 112 and p. 209, n. 42.

defiant Princess appears a wild, inconsequent fantasy; yet it was all suggested by contemporary events and what they saw and heard in the park. The Mechanics' festival was based upon a real festival; the story-telling was based upon Tennyson's own experience as an undergraduate. The real and the ideal are difficult to separate. Sir Walter himself is a recognizable contemporary figure—a gentleman farmer interested in an improved, scientific agriculture. His generosity in opening his park to the townsfolk shows a sympathetic understanding for the needs of another section of the community, an understanding which was needed by all possessed of wealth and influence.[1]

In the Conclusion, as darkness gathers over the countryside of wheat-field and grove, hamlet and tower, the friends meditate upon their fantasy. The poet among them has learned that we should not dismiss what first strikes us as fantastic without considering that

maybe wildest dreams
Are but the needful preludes of the truth.

This gentle rebuke was in answer to the insular scorn of his friend towards the events of 1848 in France, events prepared by the Saint-Simonians, among others. But we can see that the attitude was also to apply to the whole of life. Tennyson is suggesting that if a college for women seems fantastic, that is no reason why it should not be considered with an open mind. Scientific hypotheses may oblige us to re-think our hitherto unquestioned positions on many questions. If we understand that in *The Princess* Tennyson was attempting through an experiment to make his readers think about social

---

[1] Chapter VI, 'The Loss of Playgrounds', in J. L. and Barbara Hammond's book, *The Bleak Age* (revised edn., Pelican Books, 1947) forms an admirable comment upon the significance of Tennyson's portrayal of Sir Walter. In 1845, the year in which composition of *The Princess* was resumed, the General Enclosure Act was passed, 'making it easier to convert land that was still available for public enjoyment into private property'. At this time the introduction of improved drainage and imported fertilizers promised an enormous increase in the acreage under wheat, a matter of vital concern in view of the Corn Law controversy at this date. The fact that enclosure of common land would deprive townspeople of any place for country amusements received scant regard. The pleasure factory workers took in the countryside is well illustrated by the opening chapter of *Mary Barton*.

questions in an unprejudiced and intelligent way, we shall not be led to regard him as stupid or hypocritical, but very much the opposite. *The Princess* was, in fact, Tennyson's attempt to give artistic expression to some of the beliefs and ideals of his age.

Every artist submits in some measure to the exigencies of contemporary taste, while the function of some works is to make an age visible to itself. Such works may lead to the creation of others of lasting value. Of such a kind was *The Princess*, a poem attempting by way of an experiment in form to portray a critical age. By understanding what went into its making, we are, I think, better able to enjoy those of Tennyson's poems which, though in some measure coloured by the hopes and feelings of the same age, yet live on into another as part of the canon of great art.

APPENDIX

Review of Robert Chambers's *Vestiges of the Natural History of Creation*, published in *The Examiner* for 9 November 1844, p. 707.

In this small and unpretending volume we have found so many great results of knowledge and reflection, that we cannot too earnestly recommend it to the attention of thoughtful men. It is the first attempt that has been made to connect the natural sciences into a history of creation. An attempt which presupposes learning, extensive and various; but not the large and liberal wisdom, the profound philosophical suggestion, the lofty spirit of beneficence, and the exquisite grace of manner, which make up the charm of this extraordinary book.

To say that the writer of such a book is as modest as he is bold, is in other words to say that he has earnestly investigated Nature. Bacon's remark of Aristotle, *Audax simul et Pavidus*, applies to all such men. They are bold, in an assured certainty of the Laws which govern everything to which knowledge can penetrate; they are humble, in an awful contemplation of the Divine Author of those Laws.

'We advance from law to the cause of law, and ask, What is that? Whence have come all these beautiful regulations? Here science leaves us, but only to conclude, from other grounds, that there is a First Cause to which all others are secondary and ministrative, a primitive almighty will, of which these laws are merely the mandates. That great Being, who shall say where is his dwelling-place, or what is his history? Man pauses breathless at the contemplation of a subject so much above the finite faculties, and only can wonder and adore!'

In this spirit the book before us is written. It contains much that at a first reading may startle a devout and religious mind; it contains nothing that such a mind will do well to reject on more calm and full reflection. We believe nothing to be so certain as the assumption on which the writer proceeds: that while we give a respectful reception to what is revealed through the medium of Nature, we can at the same time fully reserve our reverence for all we have been accustomed to hold sacred, 'not one tittle of which it may ultimately be found necessary to alter'. Let all be welcome who bring new truths, if so they can be proved. Let the confident hope animate us, that these new truths will in time be found harmonious with the old. Error is the only thing we need to be afraid of: it is useless to fear or to persecute in any other direction. We may for ever force the Galileos on their knees to renounce the motion of the earth, but on their lips as they arise, the *e pur si muove* will still be found.

This is not the place for any detailed examination of the opinions set forth in the volume; and in abstaining, we would not be understood to assent to all that it contains. But we will endeavour to show its general drift and purpose.

A

It opens with a chapter on the arrangement and formation of the Bodies of Space, and on the wonderful relationships that exist between the constituents of our system. The result of the reasoning in this chapter would seem to be, that the formation of bodies in space is *still and at present in progress*, and that, among the thousands of worlds suspended there in all stages of formation, there is evidence, altogether apart from human traditions, for the probability of the comparative youth of our system, as one whose various phenomena, physical and moral, *as yet lie undeveloped, while myriads of others are fully fashioned and in complete arrangement.* The constituent materials of the earth and other bodies of space are next considered, and from this there is natural transition to the earth's first formation and settlement.

We take one or two familiar illustrations from these early chapters to show the simplicity of the writer's manner, and the beauty of his style.

EXTENT OF THE SOLAR SYSTEM

'The mind fails to form an exact notion of a portion of space so immense; but some faint idea of it may be obtained from the fact, that, if the swiftest race-horse ever known had begun to traverse it, at full speed, at the time of the birth of Moses, he would only as yet have accomplished half his journey.'

Yet the distance of other known stars which do not belong to our system, Syrius for example, is seven times as great as this! And the elder Herschel computed distances beyond Syrius, thirty-five thousand times more remote than even that star!! Observe, in connection with these immensities, the

Appendix

SUBLIME SIMPLICITY OF NATURE

'The law which causes rotation in the single solar masses, is exactly the same which produces the familiar phenomenon of a small whirlpool or dimple in the surface of a stream. Such whirlpools are not always single. Upon the face of a river where there are various contending currents, it may often be observed that two or more dimples are formed near each other with more or less regularity. These fantastic eddies, which the musing poet will sometimes watch abstractedly for an hour, little thinking of the law which produces and connects them, are an illustration of the wonders of binary and ternary solar systems . . . The tear that falls from childhood's cheek is globular, through the efficacy of that same law of mutual attraction of particles which made the sun and planets round. The rapidity of Mercury is quicker than that of Saturn, for the same reason that, when we wheel a ball round by a string, and make the string wind up round our fingers, the ball always flies quicker and quicker as the string is shortened. Two eddies in a stream, as has been stated, fall into a mutual revolution at a distance of a couple of inches, through the same cause which makes a pair of suns link in mutual revolution at the distance of millions of miles. There is, we might say, a sublime simplicity in this indifference of the grand regulations to the vastness or minuteness of the field of their operations.'

The formation of the earth is described in its various eras. We have the Era of the Primary Rocks, and the commencement of organic life. The Era of the Old Red Sandstone, and of the Secondary Rocks. We have the formation of land and the commencement of land plants; the New Red Sandstone Era, and the commencement of land animals; the Oolite Era and the commencement of mammalia; and we have the various incidents which belong to the Cretacious, Tertiary, and Superficial Formations. The geological revelations of the earth's wondrous history are thus laid succinctly before us: their narrative closing suddenly as man is about to enter on the scene.

THE EARLIEST LIVING CREATURES ON EARTH

'And what were those creatures? It well might be with a kind of awe that the uninstructed inquirer would wait for an answer to this question. *But nature is simpler than man's wit would make her*, and behold, the interrogation only brings before us the unpretending forms of various zoophytes and polypes, together with a few

Appendix

single and double-valved shell-fish (mollusks), all of them creatures of the sea. It is rather surprising to find these before any vegetable forms, considering that vegetables appear to us as forming the necessary first link in the chain of nutrition: but it is probable that there were sea-plants, and also some simpler forms of animal life, before this period, although of too slight a substance to leave any fossil trace of their existence.'

The Origin of Life it is indeed difficult to approach without a 'kind of awe'. But it is well perhaps to divest ourselves of it, as much as may be. The world on which we live is no such mighty matter, when we think of it, as this book teaches us to think of it, in its relations to its mighty Creator. We are inhabitants of but a little planet; third of a series which is but one of hundreds of thousands of series; the whole of which again form but one portion of an apparently infinite globe-peopled space, where all seems analogous!

Remembering this, let us listen with humility to such suggestions as a wise and earnest inquirer has to offer, on *the mode* in which the Divine Author has proceeded in the Organic Creation.

'The fact of the cosmical arrangements being an effect of natural law, is a powerful argument for the organic arrangements being so likewise, for how can we suppose that the august Being who brought all these countless worlds into form by the simple establishment of a natural principle flowing from his mind, was to interfere personally and specially on every occasion when a new shellfish or reptile was to be ushered into existence on *one* of these worlds?'

But it is not a matter of general likelihood, simply; science supplies facts which bring the assumption more nearly home to nature; and in the philosophical application of these facts, we observe the most striking feature of originality in the work under consideration. It will be well that the student should bring to this part of it, not only the modesty which is always useful in inquiries of this kind, but some recollection of past historical experiences.

'There is a measure of incredulity from our ignorance as well as from our knowledge, and if the most distinguished philosopher three hundred years ago had ventured to develop any striking new fact which only could harmonise with the as yet unknown Copernican solar system, we cannot doubt that it would have been universally scoffed at in the scientific world, such as it then was, or at the best interpreted in a thousand wrong ways in conformity with deas already familiar.'

The hypothesis of the origin of life admitted (as the Result, not of any immediate or personal exertion on the part of the Deity, but of Natural Laws which are expressions of His will), we proceed to that of the development of the vegetable and animal kingdoms. The general fact of an obvious gradation among the families of both vegetable and animal kingdoms, from the simplest up to the highest orders, is not disputed we believe, by any inquirer. The author of this book reasons, therefore, from the examples that have led to this inference, for the fundamental unity, in one system (the whole creation of which must have depended upon one law or decree of the Almighty, though it did not come forth at one time), of all the various organic forms of our world. He believes the whole train of animated beings to be *a series of advances of the principle of development*; he believes those advances to have been arranged from the first in the counsels of the Divine Wisdom, as under necessary modifications gradually to take place (a system foreshadowed by Plato); and he lays down the first step as of advance, under favour of these peculiar conditions, from the simplest forms of Being to the next more complicated, 'through the medium of the ordinary process of generation'.

We cannot within our limits exhibit, with any justice to the writer, his courage of reasoning to this remarkable hypothesis. But we will give one or two examples of the more striking order of his facts.

C   THE STAGES OF ORGANIC LIFE

'An insect, standing at the head of the articulated animals, is, in the larva state, a true annelid, or worm, the annelida being the lowest in the same class. The embryo of a crab resembles the perfect animal of the inferior order myriapoda, and passes through all the forms of transition which characterise the intermediate tribes of crustacea. The frog, for some time after its birth, is a fish with external gills, and other organs fitting it for an aquatic life, all of which are changed as it advances to maturity, and becomes a land animal. The mammifer only passes through still more stages, according to its higher place in the scale. Nor is man himself exempt from this law. His first form is that which is permanent in the animalcule. His organisation gradually passes through conditions generally resembling a fish, a reptile, a bird, and the lower mammalia, before it attains its specific maturity. At one of the last stages of his foetal career, he exhibits an intermaxillary bone, which is characteristic of the perfect ape: this is suppressed and he may then be said to take leave of the simial type, and become a true human creature. Even, as we shall see, the varieties of his race are represented in the progressive development of an individual of the highest, before we see the adult Caucasian, the highest point yet attained in the animal scale.'

Of these truths of physiology, strange as they may seem, there is no doubt. Each animal has been found to pass, in the course of his germinal history, through a series of changes resembling the *permanent forms* of the various orders of animals inferior to it in the scale. The changes indicated in the human being are in his brain and heart, which in their progress to complete formation are found to assume the various conditions of the insect, the fish, the reptile, the bird, and the lower mammalia. A difficulty remains, however, in what we see around us of the apparently invariable production of like by like. But the writer argues with great force that this can be held for no other than the ordinary procedure of nature *in the time immediately passing before our eyes.* He gives a remarkable suggestion, from some data of Mr. Babbage's calculating machine, that this ordinary procedure may be subordinate to a higher law which only *permits* it for a time, and in proper season interrupts and changes it.

D

'The gestation of a single organism is the work of but a few days, weeks, or months; but the gestation (so to speak) of a whole creation is a matter probably involving enormous spaces of time. Suppose that an ephemeron, hovering over a pool for its one April day of life, were capable of observing the fry of the frog in the water below. In its aged afternoon, having seen no change upon them for such a long time, it would be little qualified to conceive that the external branchiae of these creatures were to decay, and be replaced by internal lungs, that feet were to be developed, the tail erased, and the animal then to become a denizen of the land. Precisely such may be our difficulty in conceiving that any of the species which people our earth is capable of advancing by generation to a higher type of being. During the whole time which we call the historical era, the limits of species have been, to ordinary observation, rigidly adhered to. But the historical era is, we know, only a small portion of the entire age of our globe. We do not know what may have happened during the ages which preceded its commencement, as we do not know what may happen in ages yet in the distant future.'

In the phenomena of the generation of bees there is a curious illustration of the principle of development, so far as varieties of sex are concerned, which gives something like a distinct support to

Appendix

these parts of the author's reasoning. And how pregnant with matter for reflection, in the present condition of the world, are his remarks on the changes of the human family!

E

'It is fully established that a human family, tribe or nation, is liable, in the course of generations, to be either advanced from a mean form to a higher one, or degraded from a higher to a lower, *by the influence of the physical conditions in which it lives* . . . Prominence of the jaws, a recession and diminution of the cranium, and an elongation and attenuation of the limbs, are peculiarities always produced by these miserable conditions, for they indicate an unequivocal retrogression towards the type of the lower animals. *Thus we see nature alike willing to go back or to go forward.* Both effects are simply the result of the operation of the law of development in the generative system. Give good conditions, it advances: bad ones, it recedes . . . Monstrosities are the result of nothing more than *a failure of the power of development in the system of the mother, occasioned by weak health or misery.*'

The general result to which we are brought by the close of the investigation is, that the simplest and most primitive type of organic life, under a law to which that of like-production is subordinate, gave birth to the type next above it, that this again produced the next higher, and so on to the very highest. Applying this to the wonderful system of circular analogies and affinities in nature, (of which Macleay is the principal author) it is found that *the only appearance of imperfection,* as though in this direction the laws of life were not yet accomplished, *is in the circle to which man belongs.* Doubtless the ideas which rise in consequence are not a little startling.

F

'Is our race but the initial of the grand crowning type? Are there yet to be species superior to us in organization, purer in feeling, more powerful in device and act, and who shall take a rule over us? There is in this nothing improbable on other grounds. The present race, rude and impulsive as it is, is perhaps the best adapted to the present state of things in the world: but the external world goes through slow and gradual changes, which may leave it in time a much serener field of existence. There may then be occasion for a nobler type of humanity, which shall complete the zoological circle on this planet, and realize some of the dreams of the purest spirits of the present race.'

Appendix

The writer seems but little cognizant of the notions of the Greek philosophers, and it is the more strange to what an unconscious and large extent he corroborates many of their most striking views. The idea of a higher race was held by Pythagoras, who connected it with that view of more consummate worlds in space, inhabited in their turn by beings more perfect and beautiful than those of earth, which we have, in an earlier part of this notice, seen to be in some sort sanctioned by the results of astronomical inquiry. Another idea of the philosopher of Samos may be said to form the basis on which the writer of this volume, unconsciously, has raised its whole philosophical structure. Pythagoras held the world to be an harmonical development of the First One, advancing from the less beautiful and good to the better and more beautiful.

Two remarkable chapters which follow those we have named are on the Early History of Mankind and the Mental Constitution of Animals.

MENTAL ACTION

'Simple electricity, artificially produced, and sent along the nerves of a dead body, excites muscular action. The brain of a newly-killed animal being taken out, and replaced by a substance which produces electric action, the operation of digestion, which had been interrupted by the death of the animal, was resumed, showing the absolute identity of the brain with a galvanic battery. Nor is this a very startling idea, when we reflect that electricity is almost as metaphysical as ever mind was supposed to be. It is a thing perfectly intangible, weightless. Metal may be magnetized, or heated to seven hundred of Fahrenheit, without becoming the hundredth part of a grain heavier. And yet electricity is a real thing, an actual existence in nature, as witness the effects of heat and light in vegetation—the power of the galvanic current to reassemble the particles of copper from a solution, and make them again into a solid plate—the rending force of the thunderbolt as it strikes the oak; see also how both heat and light observe the angle of incidence in reflection, as exactly as does the grossest stone thrown obliquely against a wall. So mental action may be imponderable, intangible, and yet a real existence, and ruled by the Eternal through his laws.'

THE MIND OF MAN

'We have faculties in full force and activity which the animals either possess not at all, or in so low and obscure a form as to be equivalent to non-existence. Now these parts of mind are those which connect us with the things that are not of this world. We have veneration, prompting us to the worship of the Deity, which the animals lack. We have hope, to carry us on in thought beyond the bounds of time. We have reason, to enable us to inquire into the character of the Great Father, and the relation of us, his humble creatures, towards him. We have conscientiousness and benevolence, by which we can in a faint and humble measure imitate, in our conduct, that which he exemplifies in the whole of his wondrous doings. Beyond this, mental science does not carry us in support of religion: the rest depends on evidence of a different kind. But it is surely much that we thus discover in nature a provision for things so important. The existence of faculties having regard for such things is a good evidence that such things exist. The face of God is reflected in the organization of man, as a little pool reflects the glorious sun.'

When we have arrived at that stage of the inquiry by which we discover that there is a general adaptation of the mental constitution of man to the circumstances in which he lives, as close as between all the parts of nature to each other: when we find that for our physical constitution, the Almighty Author of all things has destined it, like everything else, to be developed from inherent qualities, and to have a mode of operation dependent solely upon its own organization; the inquiry seems complete. We have seen the masses of space formed by Law, and in due time made theatres of existence for plants and animals: we have seen in like manner developed and sustained in action by Law, sensation, disposition and intellect; and we have observed that in the case of inorganic nature, the Law is Gravitation, and in organic, Development. But the question so inexpressibly interesting remains, of man's final condition on the earth in his relation to Supra-Mundane things.

It is the subject of the last chapter of the book. Its views may in important points seem too material, but let them not be hastily judged. We might again resort to the Greek philosophy for resemblances unheeded by the author. The Socratic idea of science is, that nothing can be known except together with the rest and along with its relation to all things beside. And it would be hazardous to say that a nobler definition of philosophy has been or could be given, than that which declares it to consist not in a partial cultivation either of morals or physics, but in the co-existence and intercommunion of both.

We take a passage of most benignant wisdom from this concluding chapter.

Appendix

G

'To secure the immediate means of happiness it would seem to be necessary for men first to study with all care the constitution of nature, and, secondly, to accommodate themselves to that constitution, so as to obtain all the realizable advantages from acting conformably to it, and to avoid all likely evils from disregarding it. It will be of no use to sit down and expect that things are to operate of their own accord, or through the direction of a partial deity, for our benefit; equally so were it to expose ourselves to palpable dangers, under the notion that we shall, for some reason, have a dispensation or exemption from them; we must endeavour *so to place ourselves, and so to act, that the arrangements which Providence has made impartially for all may be in our favour and not against us*; such are the only means by which we can obtain good and avoid evil here below. And in doing this, it is especially necessary that care be taken to avoid interfering with the like efforts of other men, beyond what may have been agreed upon by the mass as necessary for the general good. Such interferences, tending to injure the body, property or peace of a neighbour, or to the injury of society in general, tend very much to reflect evil upon ourselves, through the reaction which they produce in the feelings of our neighbour and of society, and also the offence which they give to our own conscientiousness and benevolence. On the other hand, when we endeavour to promote the efforts of our fellow-creatures to attain happiness, we produce a reaction of the contrary kind, the tendency of which is towards our own benefit. The one course of action tends to the injury, the other to the benefit of ourselves and others. By the one course the general design of the Creator towards his creatures is thwarted: by the other it is favoured. And thus we can most readily see the most substantial grounds for regarding all moral emotions and doings as divine in their nature, and as a means of rising to and communing with God. Obedience is not selfishness, which it otherwise would be—it is worship. The merest barbarians have a glimmering sense of this philosophy, and it continuously shines out more and more in the public mind, as a nation increases in intelligence. Nor are individuals alone concerned here. The same rule applies between one great body and class of men and another, and also between nations. Thus if one set of men keep others in the condition of slaves—this being a gross injustice to the subjected party, the mental manifestations of that party to the masters will be such as to mar the comfort of their lives: the minds of the masters themselves will be degraded by the association with beings

so degraded: and thus with some immediate or apparent benefit from keeping slaves, there will be in a far greater degree an experience of evil. So also, if one portion of a nation, engaged in one particular department of industry, grasp at some advantages injurious to the other sections of the people, the first effect will be an injury to those other portions of the nation, and the second, a reactive injury to the injurers, making their guilt their punishment. And so when one nation commits an aggression on the property or rights of another, or even pursues toward it a sordid or ungracious policy, the effects are sure to be re-doubled evil from the offended party. All of these things are under laws which make the effects, on a large range, absolutely certain; and *an individual, a party, a people, can no more act unjustly with safety, than I could with safety place my leg in the track of a coming wain, or attempt to fast thirty days. We have been constituted on the principle of only being able to realise happiness for ourselves when our fellow-creatures are also happy: we must therefore both do to others only as we would have others do to us, and endeavour to promote their happiness as well as our own, in order to find ourselves truly comfortable in this field of existence. These are words which God speaks to us as truly through his works, as if we heard them uttered in his own voice from heaven.*'
Again:

H

'It may be that, while we are committed to take our chance in a natural system of undeviating operation, and are left with apparent ruthlessness to endure the consequences of every collision into which we knowingly or unknowingly come with each law of the system, *there is a system of Mercy and Grace behind the screen of nature, which is to make up for all casualties endured here, and the very largeness of which is what makes these casualties a matter of indifference to God.* For the existence of such a system, the actual constitution of nature is itself an argument. The reasoning may proceed thus: The system of nature assures us that benevolence is a leading principle in the divine mind. But this system is at the same time deficient in a means of making this benevolence of invariable operation. To reconcile this to the supposed character of the Deity, it is necessary to suppose that the present system is but a part of a whole, a stage in a Great Progress, and that the Redress is in reserve. Another argument here occurs—the economy of nature, beautifully arranged and vast in its extent as it is, does not satisfy even man's idea of what might be: he feels that, if this multiplicity of theatres for the exemplification of such phenomena as we see on earth were for ever to go unchanged, it would not be worthy of the Being capable of creating it. *An endless monotony of human generations, with their humble thinkings and doings, seems an object beneath that august Being. But the mundane economy might be very well as a portion of some greater phenomenon, the rest of which was yet to be evolved.* It therefore appears that our system, though it may at first appear at issue with other doctrines in esteem amongst mankind, tends to come into harmony with them, and even to give them support. I would say, in conclusion, that, even where the two above arguments may fail of effect, there may yet be a faith derived from this view of nature sufficient to sustain us under all sense of the imperfect happiness, the calamities, the woes, and pains of this sphere of being. For let us but fully and truly consider what a system is here laid open to view, and we cannot well doubt that we are in the hands of One who is both able and willing to do us the most entire justice. And in this faith we may well rest at ease, even though life should have been to us but a protracted disease, or though every hope we had built on the secular materials within our reach were felt to be melting from our grasp. Thinking of all the contingencies of this world as in time to be melted into or lost in the greater system, to which the present is only subsidiary, let us wait the end with patience, and be of good cheer.'

What are these, but, in another and simpler shape, the noblest thoughts and the loftiest aspirations that have consoled and elevated the hopes of humanity in this world? What is it that hath sustained the Martyrs of our race in all their great extremities, if not a like sublime persuasion that the Good and Beautiful in the world were not ordained for the beginning, but only as in fullness of time to be brought about, by the development of the Divine Essence, and the entire completion of the Divine Will. What is the comfortable faith and trust to which the mere unassisted truths of natural science have led this ardent and sincere investigator, if it is not that which the Religion of Christ has assured to its humble and undoubting followers—that this Present Existence is the preparation for a Better, and that the road leading thither is the love of God and Man, the practising every virtue, the living reasonably and justly while we are here, the proportioning of our esteem to the value of things, and the so using the world as not to abuse it.

Let the writer of this book, then, take his own lesson and himself 'be of good cheer'. He doubts the reception of his labours, and intimates that, for reasons connected with them, his name will in all probability never be generally known. For this last he cares little, we will dare to say. The writing of such a book implies the power of waiting its due appreciation, however long deferred. But it is possible that he underrates the aptness of the time for an inquiry conducted with so much modesty and so much knowledge. With a firm persuasion that the Truth can never be unseasonably urged, we believe that there is now abroad in the world a certain rare disposition to hear it patiently, when a beneficent spirit accompanies it, and when its actuating principle would seem to be, as in the case before us, establishment of just principles among men and a reverent admission of the Goodness and Mercy of God.

INDEX

Index

Index

Index